Samuel G. Drake, Increase Mather

Early History of New England

Samuel G. Drake, Increase Mather

Early History of New England

ISBN/EAN: 9783744661577

Printed in Europe, USA, Canada, Australia, Japan

Cover: Foto ©ninafisch / pixelio.de

More available books at **www.hansebooks.com**

Early History of New England.

In 1862 I republished Dr. Increase Mather's "Brief History of King Philip's War," with an Introduction and Notes. I now propose to republish his other work, (which covers the most interesting period of the History of New England,) entitled—"A Relation of the Troubles which have happened in New England, by reason of the Indians there, from the year 1614, to the year 1675." It was printed in Boston in 1677, in a small quarto volume.

This work, abounding in important facts, has never been republished.

I propose to issue it in the small 4to form, printed with antique type, uniform with the Brief History, with an Introduction and Annotations. It will comprise about 300 pages. Price for copies in paper, $3 00; full bound in cloth, gilt tops, $3 50. Ten copies will be printed on large paper, at $10 00 per copy, in paper covers.

Subscribers names will be printed in the work.

Those desirous of the work will please give early notice to

SAMUEL G. DRAKE,

13 *Bromfield St.*

Boston, June, 1863.

EARLY HISTORY

OF

NEW ENGLAND;

BEING A RELATION OF

HOSTILE PASSAGES BETWEEN THE INDIANS AND EUROPEAN VOYAGERS AND FIRST SETTLERS:

AND A

FULL NARRATIVE OF HOSTILITIES, TO THE CLOSE OF THE WAR WITH THE PEQUOTS, IN THE YEAR 1637;

ALSO A

DETAILED ACCOUNT OF THE ORIGIN OF THE WAR WITH KING PHILIP.

BY INCREASE MATHER.

With an Introduction and Notes,

BY SAMUEL G. DRAKE.

BOSTON:
PRINTED FOR THE EDITOR,
AND SOLD BY HIM AT NO. 13 BROMFIELD-STREET.
ALSO BY J. MUNSELL, ALBANY, N. Y.

1864.

TO HIS EARLY AND CONSTANT FRIEND,

JOHN CARTER BROWN, Esquire,

OF PROVIDENCE, RHODE ISLAND,

Whoſe extenſive and invaluable Collection of Works on the whole Range of American Hiſtory and Antiquities is a Monument to his fine Taſte, Judgment and perſevering Induſtry, of which not only himſelf and his State ſhould be proud, but New England likewiſe; inaſmuch, as through his Kindneſs and Liberality his moſt uſeful Collection is not a ſealed one, but is aiding in various Ways the Bibliographer and Hiſtorian: To him, therefore, this Volume is, by permiſſion, reſpectfully Dedicated, by

THE EDITOR.

INTRODUCTORY BY THE EDITOR

FOR many Years I had contemplated publiſhing Editions of the two Works of Dr. Increaſe Mather on Indian Hiſtory; they having been for a long Time rarely to be met with. The firſt of theſe Works, in point of Time of Publication, was the *Brief Hiſtory of Philip's War*, an Edition of which I iſſued laſt Year (1862). As ſoon as that was publiſhed I commenced preparing this to follow it. Various Demands upon my Time have prevented its earlier Appearance. Chronologically this ſhould have appeared before the other Work; but ſo the Author wrote and ſo he publiſhed them; thus as it were writing Hiſtory backwards. But ſome great Hiſtorians have ſince either followed Mr. Mather's

Plan, or employed one ſimilar; for it was in this Way Mr. Hume wrote and publiſhed his celebrated Hiſtory of England.

In reſpect to theſe two Works of Dr. Mather, while the Firſt may be thought to be more important to Hiſtorians, the Latter is the more difficult to be found. The former is a contemporaneous Hiſtory, while the latter is a Hiſtory of a previous Age; chiefly drawn from Works ſince as well known as in the Time of this Author. This may account in ſome Degree for its having met with but a ſingle Impreſſion in one hundred and eighty-ſix Years.

Being poſſeſſed of nearly all of Mr. Mather's Authorities, I have been able to ſupply numerous and important Deficiencies in his Narrative. He doubtleſs felt himſelf obliged to compreſs his Materials as much as poſſible, ſo as not to make a large Book; for in his Time there were but few Buyers of even ſmall Books.

There may be thoſe diſpoſed to berate and undervalue the Works of all the early Mathers, and to conſider them of little or no Account. To ſuch the Editor would ſay, that with full Conſideration of the Condition of Society in New England when the Mathers wrote, he thinks they would change their

Opinion. We can have but a vague and indifferent View of the State which our Anceſtors paſſed through, except by their Works. By beſtowing a little Attention upon theſe we have in our Minds a very good Picture of the Steps by which we have arrived at our partially civilized Exiſtence. To the Mathers then we owe a great deal, and we can acknowledge it without endorſing their peculiar Tenets or ſubjecting ourſelves to the Charge of ſharing in the Superſtitions and Bigotry of their Age.

But a faint and imperfect Opinion can be formed of the Condition of New England from the brief Chronicles of the Period of the Pequot War. The Author is a good deal more Minute reſpecting that War than any of the early Writers upon it; but even from him we have a very incoherent Narrative. He did not poſſeſs all of the printed Accounts—neither Underhill's nor Vincent's; yet they are indiſpenſable — being both by Eye-witneſſes of the principal military Operations. Gardiner's Hiſtory was not publiſhed, and its Exiſtence does not appear to have been known to Mr. Mather. In ſome Reſpects it is the moſt valuable of the contemporary Records of the War. It gives us a political View, and with an "old ſoldier's" Honeſty. Maſon's Hiſtory the Author poſſeſſed, though under another Name. It came into Mr. Mather's Hands from Mr. John Allyn, then "Secretary of "Connecticut Colony," who appears to have transcribed it with various Alterations and Additions, and allowed it to pass for his own Work. Mr. Mather says he prints it "without the least Alteration as to "Sense, and very little as to the Words." As Mason's Work was afterwards printed as Mason left it; a comparison will show what Liberties Mr. Allyn took with it. Some of these Liberties will be pointed out in the Notes.

We are told by the Author of a very important manuscript Account of the Pequot War which he found in the Library of a brother Minister, but he was not able to learn the Name of the Author; and as if to prevent Others from learning, he does not tell us in whose Library he found it. He seems to have given us the Substance of it, and that confirms what he says of its Importance. But had he been at the Pains to collect Everything he could, manuscript and printed, and composed a faithful History from Materials so collected, we might have had a much better History of the Pequot War than we now possess. He does not seem to have profited at all by Correspondence, and not much from Conversation with those living in the Time of the War, or their Descendants. In his Detail of Transactions he is provokingly ſilent reſpecting thoſe who performed them. This was a ſerious Fault of nearly all Writers of Hiſtory of that as well as a previous Age. Often no Name is mentioned but that of the Leader of the Expedition; and thus Oblivion hangs over the Memory of thoſe who expoſed their Lives to all the Dangers of a moſt dangerous Service, for the Benefit of us who come after them; thus denying their Poſterity the Gratification of honouring their Names.

Perhaps we ought not to complain of Deficiencies in our early Authors, but rather to be thankful they have given us ſo much as they have. But the Reader of this Hiſtory will not fail to obſerve, without our calling his Attention to ſuch Facts as the following:—That he hears Nothing of the Agency of Roger Williams in preventing a Union between the Pequots and Narraganſets for the avowed Deſtruction of the Engliſh; Nothing about the Efforts of Lieut. Gardiner in ſecuring the Friendſhip of the Long Iſland Indians; Nothing about the Diſſatisfaction of Plymouth in regard to the War; Nothing about the Complaints of Connecticut that Maſſachuſetts had unneceſſarily brought on the War; and Nothing about the relative Strength of the Colonies. And yet theſe Subjects are as Pillars to a Superſtructure.

It is true that Writers near the Time of an Event are neceſſarily deficient in documentary Vouchers. But few Letters were written at the Period of the Pequot War, and of that few but a Moiety ever come to Light. Important Letters paſſed between Governor Vane and Lieut. Gardiner, but none of them have been preſerved; at leaſt none have been diſcovered. Maſon perhaps never wrote one while upon his Expeditions, nor was it neceſſary, as he returned Home about as ſoon as a Meſſenger could have performed the Service of Bearer of Diſpatches. Captain Stoughton[1] from the Army ſent Home Letters. Officials at Home wrote Letters about the War. Winthrop on the Part of Maſſachuſetts. Winſlow[2] on that of Plymouth. Roger Williams wrote many. We have one, and but one, from the benevolent Mr. John Humfrey.[3] Among them all, ſaving thoſe of Humfrey and Williams,[4] we find no Expreſſions counſelling Mildneſs, Forbearance or Mercy towards the Indians.

[1] See Appendix A.

[2] See Appendix B.

[3] See Appendix C.

[4] Since the above was written, a Letter of Roger Williams has appeared, in which he ſays, in reference to the captive Pequots—"I much rejoice [to learn by Captain Patrick] that ſome of the Chiefe [Men] at Quonihticut (Mr. Heynes and Mr. Ludlow), are almoſt averſe from killing Women and Children." —*Maſs. Hiſt. Colls.* 36, 196.

Nor is this ſo much to be wondered at, taking the actual Condition of the Country into View—the very few white People then in New England, and thoſe ſcattered along a vaſt Extent of Sea-coaſt for two or three hundred Miles, with an unknown Number of Indians on every Hand—all jealous of thoſe Intruders. Knowing that the Indians might at any time combine and deſtroy them while in their Weakneſs, they thought it neceſſary for their own Preſervation to divide this jealous People as much as poſſible. And here it is fitting to remark that Jealouſies always grow up, ſpontaneouſly, as it were, between Races or Sections, where one is ſuperior to the other in any Reſpect. The more ignorant Race or Section always foſters this Jealouſy into Envy, and from Envy into deadly Hoſtility. It was thus aroſe the preſent moſt iniquitous Southern Rebellion. The Indians were perfect Seceſſioniſts. Their Philoſophy of Liberty taught nothing higher in the Scale of Government. Hence they were conſtantly breaking up into diſtinct Communities or Clans. Several of theſe Clans or Communities were uſually called a Tribe; and a Tribe held together no longer than it ſuited the Convenience of its individual Members. Seceſſion was at all times imminent, and although the Parties were conſtantly reaping the bitter Fruits of Seceſſion, they had "no Power to prevent it," as was averred by a recent Preſident of the United States, in reſpect to the American Union: thus virtually acknowledging that the Government of the Union was not in Advance of that of the Indians!

All barbarous Nations are natural Seceders. Incapable of binding themſelves together by any written Compact, the remedy for every Grievance, real or imaginary, was Deſertion or Seceſſion of the Party ſo aggrieved. Thus, continually weakened, a Tribe became nearly powerleſs to every foreign Foe. No Confederacy could hold together any Length of Time, becauſe private Ends were ſuperiour to publick Good. The Pequots ſeceded from an inland Tribe, and no ſooner were they permanently ſeated upon the Borders of the River bearing their Name, but a diſaffected Party broke from them, and became known as the Mohegans.

Precedents were never wanting for Seceſſion among a barbarous People. They acknowledged no Law but that of the ſtrongeſt. Their Exiſtence depended upon their Ability to keep forcible Poſſeſſion of whatever Place they found themſelves poſſeſſed of, or in their ability to diſpoſſeſs a neighbouring Community. From Time immemorial this had been their State of Exiſtence, and they had no other Traditions for their Guidance. Hence they lived in continual Fear; always in Expectation of an Attack from one diſpoſſeſſed Clan or another, as their Progenitors, near and remote, had been. This was the State of the Indians in New England when the firſt white People became acquainted with them. When the Pilgrims came to Plymouth, the Narraganſets were threatening the Wampanoags, and this was found to be the Secret of the ready Compliance of the Latter to the Wiſhes of their white Viſitors; and when theſe travelled to the Bottom of the Bay they found the Country had been deſolated by a barbarous War between the Maſſachuſetts and Tarratines. The Mohegans had broken from the Pequots, and War exiſted between them. Other Wars doubtleſs exiſted between other Tribes. None of theſe Wars could be attributed to the evil Influences of white Men. At the ſame Time it is clear that in ſuch a State of Exiſtence Seceſſion was continually going on, and conſequently Wars muſt be perpetual. Yet ſome modern Writers have aſſerted that Indians were peaceful and not given to Treachery before they had been learned to be ſo through their Intercouſe with Europeans. This Aſſertion is pretty fully diſpoſed of by what has been ſhown to have been the real Condition of the Country at and immediately after its Diſcovery and Settlement by the Engliſh. That the Wars among the Indians generally originated in bad Faith is ſcarcely to be doubted, it being conceded that Indians are much like other Races of Men, and that they are made up of good and bad Elements.

Roger Williams (and no man ever knew the Indians better), relates this remarkable Caſe of Treachery among them in his Vicinity in 1637: "The laſt Day of the Weeke [Saturday July 10th ?] "Wequaſh the Pequt Guide neere Hand, ſlue his "Countryman Saſſawwaw, a Pequt, alſo Miantun-"nomues ſpecial Darling, and a kind of Generall of "his Forces. There was Yeſterday ſome Tumult "about it becauſe Wequaſh liues with Canounicus, "and Miantunnomu purſues the Revenge and Juſ-"tice, &c." That is to ſay, the Narraganſets required Vengeance to be taken on that Pequot in Juſtice for Wrongs done them. Mr. Williams ſpeaks of the Juſtneſs of the Execution thus:—"Although We-"quaſh it may be haue treacherouſly allmoſt, ſlain "him, yet I ſee the righteous Hand of the moſt "High Judge, thus: Saſſawwaw turned to [joined] "the Nanhiggonſicks and againe pretends a Returne "to the Pequts, gets them forth the laſt Yeare "againſt the Nanhiggonſicks and ſpying Advantage, "ſlue the chiefe Pequt Captain and whips off his "Head, and ſo againe [returns] to the Nanhiggon-"ſick: their Treacheries exceede Machiavills," &c.

In another Letter to the ſame Party he recommends dealing with them wiſely and juſtly, as with Wolves endowed with men's Brains.

That Civilization is not compatible with the Indian Character has been clearly eſtabliſhed by Experiments oft repeated. The Exceptions in favor of ſome Tribes diſappear with thoſe Tribes. Some two hundred years Experience has pretty concluſively proved, that whenever a white or European Colony locates itſelf near an Indian Community, that Community melts away; ſlowly perhaps, but ſteadily and ſurely. Well has Dryden ſomewhere expreſſed the Indian Lamentation:—

"Old Prophecies foretell our Fall at Hand
"When bearded Men in floating Caſtles land."

Indians were always ready to "drive a Trade" with any People who viſited them. Moſt Europeans took what Advantages they could of their Simplicity. The firſt Settlers of Plymouth generally dealt honourably and liberally with them. Perhaps rather more ſo than the other Coloniſts of

New England. But it ſhould not be pretended that Trade was not an Object with them; and yet it is entirely true that it was not a paramount One originally.

Indeed, with the Exception of Plymouth and one or two others, Settlements were made with a View to the Benefits ariſing from Traffick with the Natives. Perhaps it was more notoriouſly ſo with the Spaniſh Settlers. At all Events the Author of Hudibras has in his inimitable Way ſettled the Matter as far as Song can ſettle Anything. The following Lines were intended for his Hudibras, but for ſome Reaſon were left out. The Paſſage was preſerved by the celebrated John Aubrey, F. R. S., and is as follows:—

"No Jeſuit e'er took in Hand
"To plant a Church in barren Land;
"Nor ever thought it worth the While
"A Swede or Ruſs to reconcile.
"For where there is no Store of Wealth,
"Souls are not worth the Charge of Health;
"Spain in America had two Deſigns,
"To ſell their Goſpel for their Mines.[1]
"For, had the Mexicans been poor,
"No Spaniard twice had landed on their Shore."

At the Time the *Relation* was written, there were but Few remaining who were cotemporary

[1] *Wines* in Aubrey's *Miſcels.* ii, 264.

with the Events of which the Author treats. In a few Inſtances he ſeems to have profited by Information obtained from ſome of the Actors in the Scenes of that Day: But I do not remember above two or three Inſtances. It is to be regretted that he did not profit more by ſuch Information. Perhaps he thought there might be Danger of drawing too freely from ſuch Sources, not imagining that that Kind of Information would be more valued than moſt other by ſucceeding Hiſtorians. But when we take a near View of a Writer of his own Times, and compare what he has done with what is being done in our own, it may be we ſhall be found quite as delinquent as thoſe who have gone before us. For who of us does not have Reaſon to regret his Remiſſneſs under ſimilar Circumſtances? Who has not neglected to inquire of aged Relatives and other Predeceſſors concerning family and other Memorials while they were able to give Information? In conſidering this Matter no one will fail to recur to our Want of Knowledge reſpecting our Progenitors in the Land whence they came. Becauſe the almoſt entire Lack of this Kind of Information is quite remarkable; inſomuch that ſcarcely one Family in fifty of the preſent Day has any Knowledge whence, or when its Anceſtors emigrated. In the Memorials they have left us, ſo ſeldom is Anceſtry referred to that we are led to doubt if it were not deſignedly ſo. We indeed ſometimes find in Documents of a buſineſs Nature the Country mentioned, as, "my Kindred in Old England," and ſimilar vague Expreſſions.

Notwithſtanding Dr. Mather's Works are moſtly theological, and the greater Part of them were produced ſolely to enforce theological Views, there is nevertheleſs ſcarcely any of them into which he does not bring ſome valuable hiſtorical Facts; either by Preface or Note. And although theſe are ſometimes very few, they are almoſt the only Parts of ſuch Works of the leaſt Value or Intereſt at this Day; and but for theſe incidental Items many of them would hardly have reached our Times. And although Dr. Mather was a man poſſeſſed of highly reſpectable Talents, there is indeed a wonderful Contraſt between his political Sagacity and Wiſdom, and his Details of certain Affairs requiring the moſt ſtupid Credulity. Compare his Acts in bringing about the Revolution of 1688 with the following Details: "A poor Man "being ſuſpected to have ſtolen a Sheep was queſ-"tioned for it; he foreſwore the Thing, and wiſhed,

" that if he had ſtolen it, God would cauſe the " Horns of the Sheep to grow upon him. This " Man was ſeen within theſe few dayes by a Min- " iſter of great Repute for Piety, who ſaith that " the Man hath an Horn growing out of one " Corner of his Mouth, juſt like that of a Sheep; " from which he hath cut ſeventeen inches, and is " forced to keep it tyed by a String to his Ear, " to prevent its growing up to his Eye. This " Miniſter not only ſaw but felt this Horn."

This Circumſtance is ſaid to have happened in 1658, in Liſmore in Ireland; and though it came ſecond hand to our Author he believed the Story implicitly, and publiſhed it in his *Remarkable Providences.* One other will ſuffice for preſent Illuſtration. In the ſame curious Work, ſpeaking of remarkable Caſes of Thunder and Lightning, this is recorded: " It is not Hereſie to believe that Satan has ſome- " times a great Operation in cauſing Thunder " Storms. I know this is vehemently denied by " ſome: the late Witch Advocates [thoſe who de- " fended the ſo called Witches] call it Blaſphemy; " and an old Council did anathmatize the Men that " are thus perſwaded; but by their Favour an ortho- " dox and rational Man may be of the Opinion " that when the Devil has before him the Vapours

" and Materials out of which the Thunder and " Lightning are generated, his Art is ſuch as that " he can bring them into Form. If Chymiſts can " make their *aurum fulminous*, what ſtrange Things " may this infernal Chymiſt effect? The Holy " Scriptures intimate as much as this cometh to. " In the ſacred Story concerning Job, we find that " Satan did raiſe a great Wind which blew down " the Houſe where Job's Children were faſting. " And it is ſaid that the Fire of God fell from " Heaven and burnt up the Sheep and the Servants. " This was no doubt Thunder and Lightning, and " ſuch as was extraordinary, and is therefore ex- " preſſed with the name of God, as is uſual amongſt " the Hebrews. Satan had a deep Policy in going " that way to work, thereby hoping to make Job " believe God was his Enemy."

There ſeems to have been no Teſt by which it could be ſatisfactorily determined to which Power an apparently miſchievous Phenomenon was to be attributed. Hence there was Danger of charging an Event to the wrong Party. But our Fathers do not ſeem to have entertained many conſcientious Scruples about overcharging the Devil, and appear willing to make him the Scape-goat in all dubious Caſes, not giving him even the benefit of a Doubt.

Among the Signers to a Commendation of our Author's *Cafes of Confcience concerning Witchcraft*, publifhed in 1693, is that of the venerable William Hubbard. How far he endorfed all the Views expreffed in that Work cannot be certainly known; but the Fact of his Signature being there is prefumptive Evidence of his general Affent to its Principles. Including Mr. Hubbard, there were fourteen Signers, and thefe were the principal Minifters in this Part of New England.

Thefe Minifters fay, "That there are Devils "and Witches; the Scripture afferts, and Experi-"ence confirms that they are common Enemies of "Mankind, and fet upon Mifchief, is not to be "doubted: That the Devil can (by Divine Per-"miffion) and often doth vex Men, in Body and "Eftate, without the Inftrumentality of Witches, "is undeniable." If the Commendators had left the Matter here, their Credit would ftand much better in this Age, but they go on: "That he "often hath and delights to have the Concurrence "of Witches, and their Confent in harming Men, "is confonant to his native Malice to Man, and "too lamentably exemplified: That Witches, "when detected and convicted, ought to be exter-"minated and cut off, we have God's Warrant for."

It will be ſeen that theſe Obſervations are pretty carefully worded, and that although the Exiſtence of Devil and Witches could not be denied, a grand Queſtion, very difficult to be diſpoſed of, naturally preſents itſelf—ſuch as, if the Devil can act without the Agency of a Witch, how is it to be determined when he employs their Agency?

Nevertheleſs theſe fourteen Miniſters ſay in Concluſion, "All that we are concerned in, is to aſſert "our hearty Conſent to, and Concurrence with "the Subſtance of what is contained in the follow- "ing Diſcourſe."

In the Poſtſcript to the *Caſes of Conſcience*, the Author ſeems as far gone as his Son in the Witch Deluſion. Perhaps the Fourteen[1] did not include the Poſtſcript in their Commendation. Indeed it is quite probable they knew Nothing of it until

[1] Their Names as ſigned to the original Commendation are very differently arranged in the printed Book; and as they are partly Autographs, I inſert them here as they originally ſtood:

Charles Morton
Michael Wiggleſworth
John Bayly
Samuel Whiting
Jabez Fox
Samuel Angier
Nehemiah Walter
[*Thus far in Dr. Mather's hand. The reſt are Autographs.*]
James Allen
Sam^ll^ Willard
William Hubbard
Samuel Phillips
Joſeph Gerriſh
Jno Wiſe
Joſeph Capen.

after the Book was printed. In that Addenda Mr. Mather ſays, if he had been one of the Judges at the Trial of Mr. Burroughs, he could not have acquitted him. And in the ſame Poſtſcript he ſays, "Some I hear have taken up a Notion that "the Book newly publiſhed by my Son [*Wonders* "*of the Inviſible World*] is contradictory to this of "mine: 'Tis ſtrange that ſuch Imaginations ſhould "enter into the Minds of Men: I peruſed and "approved of that Book before it was printed." Hence it is apparent that the elder Mather was at heart as much inclined to puniſh Witches as the younger. The only Difference being in their Temperaments: the elder was ſlow and cautious, while the younger was ſanguine and impetuous.

This Poſtſcript, in which theſe ſtrong Convictions are found, did not probably appear in the original Edition of the *Caſes of Conſcience.* I have a manuſcript Copy of it (chiefly in the Autograph of the Author) to which there is no Poſtſcript.

As has been elſewhere obſerved, that although Dr. Mather's Works are chiefly Theological, almoſt all of them contain ſome valuable Facts. He is treated rather cruelly by Mr. Oldmixon in his account of the *Britiſh Dominions in North America*, which is duly noticed by his Biographer, and ſcarcely requires to be alluded to here. All that need be ſaid reſpecting the ſevere Attack of Oldmixon is, that it principally relates to his preaching. This Conſideration alone renders his Criticiſms of no Value at this Day.

There is no Biography ſo valuable and intereſting as Autobiography. Under this Conviction I have made the following Extracts from Dr. Mather's Preface to a ſmall Volume of Sermons, entitled *Awakening Truths*, &c., publiſhed by him in Boſton in an 18mo Volume, 1710. He ſays:

"I was by my Parents devoted to the Service of "God in the Goſpel of *Jeſus Chriſt*. What "my Father was in *Lancaſhire* in *England*, all "*New England* knows. And many will bleſs "God to Eternity, that ever they did *know* him. "God has moreover been ſo gracious as to give me "to be born of a ſingularly pious, praying, holy "Mother. On her Death-bed, ſhe deſired to "ſpeak with me her youngeſt Son: All that ſhe "ſaid to me, was, *For the Lords ſake do thou devote* "*thyſelf to the Work of the Miniſtry; and remember* "*that Scripture, They that turn many to Righteouſ-* "*neſs, ſhall ſhine as the Stars forever and ever.* "From that Day I reſolved if the Lord would ſpare "my life, to obey that laſt Advice of my Parent. I

" was then a Youth, but ſixteen Years old, having " been in the Colledge but four Years. It is im- " poſſible for me to declare what Impreſſion thoſe " laſt Words of my dying Mother had upon my " Spirit. God has been ſo favourable to me, as to " uphold me (the moſt unworthy) in His Work, as " a publick Preacher of His Word, for the Space " of more than fifty Years; and this occaſionally " in very many Congregations, and in four ſeveral " Lands. In many places in *England*, in *Glouceſter*, " and in many Aſſemblies in *Devon*, and in *Dorſet* ; " but eſpecially in and near the City of *London*, in " *Ireland*, in *Guernſey*; in *New England*, very often " to the young Students in *Cambridge*, when for " many Years I preſided over them, but moſtly in " *Boſton*. It being now upwards of 48 years ſince " I began my publick Miniſtry in this great Town, " where I have ever ſince been conſtantly *Labour-* " *ing*, excepting thoſe 4 Years, when I was em- " ployed in *England* in Service for the *Churches* in " *New England*."

This Preface is dated—" Boſton Nov. 9, 1709."

" *The preſent Generation in New England is* " *lamentably degenerate.* As ſometimes Moſes ſpake " to the Children of Iſrael, Numb. 32. 14. Behold " ye are riſen up in your Father's ſtead an increaſe

" of ſinful Men. So may we ſay, the firſt Genera-
" tion of Chriſtians in New England, is in a Man-
" ner gone off the Stage, and there is another and
" more ſinful Generation riſen up in their ſtead.
" We have in former Years enjoyed a Sun-ſhine of
" Proſperity, and that hath been attended (as uſeth
" to be) with great Apoſtaſy. It is an apt Simili-
" tude which ſome uſe, that as the Heat of the Sun
" in Summer breeds a multitude of Inſects, ſo doth
" the warmth of Proſperity a Multitude of Apoſ-
" tates. Men are loth to hear on this Ear, but [64]
" if we ſhould deny it, the Lord doth teſtify againſt
" us that it is ſo, as Ioel. 1. 2. *Hear this ye old Men*
" *and give Ear all ye Inhabitants of the Land, hath*
" *this been in your Dayes, or even in the Dayes of your*
" *Fathers, ſaith the Lord.* Were there (ſaith the
" Prophet) ſuch Iudgements formerly as now there
" are, you may therefore conclude that you are de-
" parted from God, and by your Sins have provoked
" him ſo to puniſh you. Thus may it be ſpoken
" with reference to our State and Caſe, and the Diſ-
" penſations of God towards us, you old Men that
" are here before the Lord this Day, what ſay you
" to this Queſtion, did you know ſuch Judgements
" upon New England formerly, as of late we have
" ſeen? was it ſo in the Dayes of our Fathers?

"were there ſuch general and killing Diſeaſes? ſuch "a long continuing Warr? ſo many hundreds cut "off by the Sword, yea, ſo many hundred Familyes "brought to Ruine? Candleſticks removed out of "their Places, and Plantations made deſolate! In "former Times we heard of little beſides Settle- "ment of Plantations, and gathering of Churches, "but of late Years, in ſtead of that, Ruins have been "multiplied, yea, Miſchief upon Miſchief. God "hath been ſpending his Arrows, and heaping "Miſchief upon this Generation. This Generation "is not like the firſt. How many ignorant Ones? "how many ſcandalous Ones? There is great "Rudeneſs amongſt young Ones in this Land; and "in that reſpect degeneracy from the good Man- "ners of the Chriſtian World. And ſuch Sins as "were not formerly known in *New England* are "now become common, ſuch as ſwearing, ſinful "gaming, &c. yea, the preſent Generation as to "the Body of it, is an unconverted Generation .... "We may ſee here and there one that hath much "of his bleſſed Father's Spirit and Principles, but "how rare are ſuch amongſt us? Nay, the Intereſt "of *New England* is now changed, from a reli- "gious to a worldly Intereſt; and in this Thing is "*the great* radical Apoſtaſy of *New England*. Is

" not this to chuſe a ſtrange God? Hence do we " ſee Warr in the Gates. And the Lord hath been " letting this Generation blood in the right Vein, " ſince he hath taken the World away from them. " Trade is almoſt ruined. Farmes, Oxen, Mer- " chandize, which Things have been ſought after " in the firſt Place, how have they failed? New " England is not like this twenty Years, to be in " that comfortable Eſtate it was in but two Years " agoe." P. 65.

The State of Families with reſpect to Government is thus laid open in the ſame Election Sermon in the before mentioned Volume:

"Families are the Nurceryes for Church and " Commonwealth, ruine Families, and ruine all. " Order them well and the publick State will fare " the better; the great Wound and Miſery of *New* " *England* is that Families are out of Order. As " to the generality of Houſeholders, Family Govern- " ment is loſt and gone; Servants do not fear their " Maſters, Children do not honour their Parents, " in that reſpect the *Engliſh* are become like unto " the *Indians*." P. 91.

The Author was quite as hopeleſs of Old England as New ſeveral Years later, and in his Preface to *Ichabod* thus diſcourſes: " *England* (in whoſe

" Peace we ſhall have Peace) ſeems to be ripe for " Judgment. The grievous National Sins com- " mitted in the late Reigns have not yet been ac- " counted [atoned] for. Never was there a Nation " in the World (the Jewiſh excepted) that ſinned " againſt the Light of the Goſpel ſo as the Engliſh " Nation has." P. 8. This Train of Thought was ſuggeſted to the Author's Mind in View of his Apprehenſions that Popery had taken, or was about to take Poſſeſſion of the Engliſh Government. His Fears were not only for England, as the following Paſſage ſhows: " Things at this Day, look " with a Diſmal Aſpect, on all Proteſtant Churches " throughout the World."

The Millenium had been confidently looked for " about theſe Times," but rather deſpairingly at the Beginning of the laſt Century, owing to the believed Increaſe of Popery. Mr. Mather ſays: " So " as that ſome who not long ſince hoped that the " happy Dayes promiſed to the Church on Earth, " were at the Door, begin now to fear that *the laſt* " *Slaughter of the Witneſſes* is yet to come."

About 1710 our Author publiſhed " A Diſcourſe " concerning Faith and Fervency in Prayer, and " the Glorious Kingdom of our Lord Jeſus Chriſt, " on Earth, now approaching. Delivered in ſeve-

" ral Sermons; in which the Signs of the present " Times are considered," &c. In this Work the learned Author argued very much as the Followers of the late William Miller argued respecting the End of the World. I have not seen a Copy of the original Edition, and am indebted to the Kindness of Mr. Thomas Waterman for the Use of a Copy of the Work printed at Newry, in Ireland, as late as 1820. It was republished " by Matthew Lank-" tree, Minister of the Gospel among the Method-" ists." Mr. Lanktree says in his Title-page, that he has " carefully revised and corrected it." For its Reproduction in that singular " Corner of the World," we can only account by a Presumption that a millenial Excitement then prevailed there, and that some Accident threw a Copy of the Original in the Way of Mr. Lanktree. Hence it appears that " End of-the-world" Excitements are no new Things, and are in a Manner periodical. That of the greatest Note in modern Times, probably, was about 1588, when the papal Powers attempted the Conquest of England, by the Armada.

In 1713 one of Dr. Mather's Sermons was reprinted in Edinburgh,[1] " by John Reid, in Liber-

[1] The only Copy of this Sermon which has ever come to my Knowledge, is owned by Mr. W. H. Whitmore, who remarks that it is not contained in the List of Dr. Mather's Works as published by his Son. There are also several others not found in the List.

ton's Wynd." Its Title is, "A Sermon ſhewing, "that the preſent Diſpenſations of Providence de-"clare That wonderful Revolutions in the World are "near at Hand; with an Appendix, ſhewing ſome "Scripture Grounds to hope, that within a few "Years, glorious Prophecies and Promiſes will be "fulfilled." The Scotch Publiſher prints the following on the reverſe of the Title-page: "To the "Reader. The Author of the following Sermon "and Appendix, tho' little known in this Country, "is much eſteemed in other Places of the World, "for his great Piety, Learning, and Solidity. For "many Years he has been a burning and ſhining "Light in the Church: Having publiſhed this "Piece laſt Year in Boſton, he ſent a Copy thereof "to his Correſpondent in Scotland, who, according "to his Deſire ſignified in a Letter, doth offer it "to Publick View, hoping it will not be unaccept-"able to his Country Men."

A leading Feature in Dr. Mather's Time was an almoſt univerſal Belief in "Special Providences;" and the recording of them was no new Idea in the Minds of the learned Men of that Day. There had been, in the Colonial Aſſembly of Plymouth, an Agitation of the Subject, to which Mr. Mather thus refers in his Election Sermon of 1677. After citing Pfalms lxxviii 5 and 6, and cii, 18, he continues: "I perceive that fome good Men are afraid "left our too great Neglect in this Matter, may be "one thing that God is offended at. And there "be two Confiderations, which may caufe fuch "Apprehenfions not to feem Groundlefs, one is in "that this Thing hath been formerly urged. That "faithful Shepard who fpake here in the Name of "the Lord upon the like Occafion, five years agoe,[1] "infifted upon this very Thing, and yet the Matter "remains unfinifhed to this Day. Moreover, whilft "the Body of the firft Generation, whom God "planted in this Wildernefs was alive, there were "Effays this Way, for it[2] was propounded to, and "concluded amongft the Commiffioners of the "United Colonies above thirty Years agoe, that "there fhould be a Collection of Special Providences of God towards his New England People. "And that Memorials being duly communicated, "an Hiftory fhould be compiled according to "Truth, for the Benefit of Pofterity, that they "might fee how God had been with their Fathers, "in laying the Foundation of the Churches, and "of the Common Wealth. Now that fuch Things

[1] Thomas Shepard preached an Election Sermon, 1672.

[2] Records of the Commiffioners, Sept. 9, 1646.

" ſhould be concluded, and yet never done, cannot " pleaſe God. P. 71.

A Belief in "Special Providences" is very near akin to a Belief in Witchcraft, which is noticed as a prominent Feature of that Age.

In 1718 Dr. Mather preached a Series of fifteen Sermons, " on the *Beatitudes*, as they are commonly " called," which was printed in Boſton in 1719. The ſame was reprinted in Dublin in 1721, in a handſome octavo Volume. The Preface is dated " Boſton, Auguſt 8, 1718." In the Cloſe of this Preface he ſays: " Now that I am entred on the " eightieth Year of my Age, tranſcribing is irk- " ſome to my trembling Hand," &c.

At this Time he ſpoke encouragingly of the Succeſs of Chriſtianity among the Indians: " It is " a great Thing," he remarks, " (although little " conſidered by the moſt among us) that there are " at this Day, not leſs than thirty Congregations " of Indians, who commonly aſſemble every Lord's " Day, to worſhip God. And there are above " thirty Indians who are Teachers and Preachers " of the Goſpel to their Countrymen, who awhile " ago were all Pagans. There are alſo Churches " among them gathered according to the Order of " the Goſpel, with Paſtors and Elders of their own

" ordaining with the Impoſition of Hands. And " ſome of the Indians are, as to Religion beyond " many of the Engliſh among whom they live."

About eighteen Years earlier,[1] he however ſpoke with great Deſpondency of the Indians and their Religion. " Alas," he exclaims, " What can we " think of, that has been the *Peculiar Glory* of " New England, but the blaſting Rebukes of " Heaven has been upon it! That Work of *Goſ-* " *pelizing the* INDIANS, has been one of the pe- " culiar Glories of *New England.* I have in an- " other Part of the World, heard great and noble " Perſonages, and thoſe too of ſeveral Nations, " ſpeaking honourably of *New England,* in that " *there* the whole Bible has been tranſlated into " the *Indian Language:* And in that there ſome " that a while ſince were *Pagans* are now become " *Preachers* of the Goſpel. I have received Letters " from Men in *Foreign Univerſities,* ſignifying the " Reſpect which their Divines had for *New Eng-* " *land* on this Account. But ſince the Death of " that Apoſtolical Man, Old Mr. *Eliot,* how has " that glorious Work been dwindling and dying? " What is the *Firſt Church* that was gathered

[1] In his Sermons entitled *Ichabod, or, the Glory of the Lord is Departing from N. England,* printed 1701, ſee Pages 66-7, Edition 1729.

"among the Natives come to?[1] There was of late "a Deſign to divert thoſe Supplies another Way, "whereby the Preaching of the Goſpel has been "ſupported among the *Indians* in this Province, "but thoſe unhappy Propoſals are at preſent hap-"pily prevented from taking Effect: But how "ſoon there may be new and fatal Attempts of "that Nature who can ſay? The greateſt Num-"ber of *Indians* who have given clear Evidences "of real Converſion to Chriſt, were in *Martha's* "*Vineyard*, where there was *of them* a conſiderable "Number of ſerious Chriſtians, but God has ſent "Sickneſs amongſt them which has ſwept away "moſt of thoſe in that Place who were of Reputa-"tion for Godlineſs and real Chriſtianity. As for "many of thoſe *Indians* who now make a Profeſ-"ſion of Chriſtianity, Men who paſs under the "Name of *Engliſh Proteſtants* have debauched "them with Drink, and ſo made them more "brutiſh, and *inglorious Creatures;* yea, more the "Children of Hell than they were before the Light "of the Goſpel came among them. So then *that* "*Glory* is dolefully departing."

[1] This Firſt Indian Church was at a Place called by the Indians, *Nonantum*. It was on the ſouth Side of Charles River, in what is ſince Newton. See Homer's *Hiſt. Newton*, p. 4.

And ſtill later, 1726, Dr. Cotton Mather wrote: “ It muſt be confeſſed and bewailed, that if our “ memorable Eliot, when he lay in his dying Lan- “ guiſhments about ſix and thirty Years ago, ſaw “ Cauſe to mourn in that Complaint, ‘There is a “ Cloud, a dark Cloud, upon the Work of the “ Goſpel among the poor *Indians*, the Lord revive “ and proſper that Work, and grant that it may “ live when I am dead:’ there has been a growing “ Occaſion ſince his Death for ſuch a Complaint.”[1] And the elder Mather thus[2] ſpeaks of his untiring Labours: “ It was our bleſſed Eliot, who has by a “ great Man[3] been called, The American Apoſtle.”

The foregoing Extracts from the Author's own Works not only ſhow the Mind of one high in publick Eſtimation, but they ſhow very clearly the governing Sentiments of the greater Number of the People of New England, at one of the moſt inter-eſting Periods of its Hiſtory.

It remains for the Editor to make his Acknow-ledgements to all thoſe enough intereſted in the

[1] Atteſtation to Mayhew's Indian Converts by the United Miniſters of Boſton, p. xvii. This though ſigned by the eleven Boſton Miniſters, is pretty evidently the Work of Dr. Cotton Mather.

[2] Awakening Truths, p. 80.

[3] It does not appear how early Mr. Eliot received the Title of *Apoſtle*. Perhaps the *great man* referred to conferred it.

early Chronicles of New England, ſo much to Aid in their Republication as to become Subſcribers to thoſe he has undertaken, and to thank them for their generous Encouragement, as well in another, as in a pecuniary Way. To his Friend Mr. Charles Deane he is indebted for the Uſe of a fine and perfect Copy of the original Edition of the *Relation*, by which the proof Sheets of the preſent Edition have been corrected.

In the Introduction to the *Brief Hiſtory of King Philip's War*, conſiderable Uſe was made of a large Number of manuſcript Letters, written by Samuel Mather, D. D., to his unfortunate tory Son. Since that Work was publiſhed I have met with the following Notice of Dr. Mather, which as it illuſtrates the Character of that remarkable Man, is here introduced:

"Died [in Boſton, June 27th, 1785], Samuel "Mather, aged 79. He left poſitive Orders, that "his Interment ſhould be private, and without any "Ceremony—alſo ſignified his Deſire, that he "may not have any funeral Encomiums from any "Quarter."—*Columbian Cent.*, 29 June, 1785.

P. S. The ſame Rule has been obſerved in this Reprint as in that of the *Brief Hiſtory;* namely, in following the Orthography and in the Uſe of italic Letters. In reſpect to the Uſe of Capitals, there being no Uniformity in the original Edition, the Compoſitor has been allowed to follow his own Taſte in that Particular. The Punctuation has not been changed but very ſlightly.

The foot Notes are all chargeable to the Editor, and are therefore unſigned. The ſide References in the laſt Tract are the Author's.

A RELATION

Of the Troubles *which have hapned in*

New-England,

By reaſon of the Indians *there.*

From the Year 1614. to the Year 1675.

Wherein the frequent Conſpiracyes of the Indians to cutt off the Engliſh, and the wonderfull providence of God, in diſappointing their devices, is declared.

Together with an *Hiſtorical Diſcorſe* concerning the Prevalency of

P R A Y E R

Shewing that *New Englands* late delivrance from the Rage of the Heathen is an eminent Anſwer of Prayer.

By INCREASE MATHER

Teacher of a Church in Boſton *in* New-England.

Job. 8. 8. *Enquire I pray thee of the former age, and prepare thyſelf to the ſearch of their Fathers.*

Pſal. III. 2. *The works of the Lord are great, ſought out of all them that have pleaſure therein.*

Joel. I. 3. *Tell ye your Children of it, and let your Children tell their Children, and their Children another Generation.*

Hiſtoria eſt teſtis temporum, nuntia vetuſtatis, lux veritatis, vita memoriæ, magiſta vitæ. *Cic. de Orat.*

Alius alio plura invenire poteſt, nemo omnia.

B O S T O N;

Printed and ſold by *John Foſter*. 1677.

TO THE READER.

THE Occasion of my undertaking what is here presented, was a Letter which I received from a worthy Person, who upon the Perusal of that *Brief Historical Account* of the War with the Indians in *New England*, published the last Summer,[1] importuned me to write the Story of the *Pequot War;* taking his Motion into Consideration,[2] it came into my Thoughts, that it would be a Service and Benefit for Posterity, if all other general Troubles which have happened by the *Heathen* in this Land, were recorded and made known; and the rather, in that as to those *first Motions and Commotions* there are very few that know any thing of them.[3] Wherefore I set my

[1] This Work was republished with an Introduction and Notes by the present Editor. It is a small Tract in 4to, as it originally appeared, and contained but about sixty Pages. It was printed in Boston, by John Foster, and reprinted in London the same Year, for *Richard Chiswell*, 1676.

[2] The Writers of the Time of our Author are remarkable for beginning to tell Something and ending in telling Nothing, on Occasions like this.

[3] Forty Years had elapsed since the Pequot War had closed. The Author himself was not born till two Years after, and nearly all those who had been concerned in it had passed away.

ſelf to make Enquiry into thoſe Matters, and ſhall for the Satisfaction of the *Reader*, give him an Account where and from whence I obtained, what Light and Information touching theſe *Indian Troubles*, I have been any Wayes able to arrive unto.

Such Books as I had by me, that relate to any Thing of thoſe Affaires J have been willing to revolve. e. g. *Johannes de Laet* his *Deſcription of America*, written in Latin;[4] Alſo ſeveral of Capt. *Smith* his Books;[5] And *A Relation of the Diſcovery of New England*, publiſhed by the Preſident and Council of New England, Anno 1622.[6] And the *Relation or Journal of the firſt Planters in Plymouth*[7] together with ſeveral Letters which ſome of them wrote to *England*, ſoon after their firſt com-

[4] De Laet was a Man of Learning, a Director of the Dutch Eaſt India Company. His Work on America is uſually cited as *Novus Orbis*. It was publiſhed at Leyden in 1633, in Folio. He was the Author of ſeveral other Works, and had a Controverſy with Grotius upon the Origin of the Indians. Maſter Benjamin Tompſon did not forget him in his Lines upon Mr. Hubbard's *Hiſtory of the Indian Wars*:

"Purchaſe wrote much, Hacluyt traverſed far,
Smith and Dutch John de Laet famous are."

[5] Capt. Smith's Books are too well known to need any Account of them here. In ſome late Works an Attempt is made to caſt Suſpicion on Smith's Statements reſpecting his Diſcoveries in Virginia, but I would caution Writers and Readers not to be too anxious to impeach a Character ſo well eſtabliſhed for Veracity as is that of Capt. John Smith.

[6] A Tract of great Rarity. The only Copy I have ever ſeen is that in the Britiſh Muſeum. It is contained in Purchas, vol. iv, 1827-32.

[7] Uſually cited as *Mourt's Journal*, or *Mourt's Relation*. It is reprinted in Young's *Chronicles of the Pilgrims*. But that Compiler, becauſe he was not acquainted with the Name of the original Publiſher, ſet him down as a Myth; and a caſual Examiner of his *Chronicles* might almoſt affirm it was not contained in his Book. It has alſo been republiſhed by Mr. Cheever in New York ſeveral Years ago. He has, like Mr. Young, I am ſorry to be

ing into this Countrey; and Mr. *Winſlow* (then whom hardly any one that hath deſerved more eminently from New England) his *Good News from New England*,[8] [iv] publiſhed Anno 1624. which Relations are in the Hands of but few in this Countrey, and therefore I have been the larger in excerping Things out of them. They are epitomized in *Purchaſe* his *Pilgrims*[9] Lib. 10. who declares that he had by him a Deſcription of the Voiage made by Capt. *Hanham*[10] to *Sagadehock*, and the written Journals of Mr. *Raleigh Gilbert*,[11] and of Mr. *Harly* and Capt. *Hobſon*,[12] who were in this Land before any Engliſh Plantation was ſettled therein. I doubt not but in thoſe Scripts a more

obliged to ſtate, ſadly marred the Original; both having changed the Pilgrim Orthography to that of their own! Nothing can be more abſurd, in my Opinion, than to change the Orthography of an old Author, and not change his Style. Why change one and not the other? I proteſt againſt a Change in either Caſe.

8 This is alſo to be found reprinted in Young's *Chronicles of the Pilgrims.*

9 The Author might as well have ſtated that the Articles to which he refers are contained in the fourth Volume of Purchas. Purchas's Volumes were publiſhed at different Times and their Titles vary. The firſt was iſſued 1613, in a ſtately Folio of 752 Pages. The Title commences, *Purchas his Pilgrimage. Or Relations of the World.* At the Time this Volume was publiſhed the Author was "Miniſter at Eſtwood in Eſſex."

10 Different Writers give the Name of this Captain, *Hanam*, Haman and Hanham. He made a Voyage to New England, 1606, in company with Capt. Pring. His Chriſtian Name was Thomas.

11 Son of the renowned Sir Humphrey Gilbert, whoſe Pedigree and Family are pretty fully deſcribed in Prince's *Worthies of Devon*, and his Authorities.

12 Probably Edward Harley and Nicholas Hobſon. See Prince and his Authorities. In Dr. Drake's *Shakeſpeare and his Times*, is a curious Omiſſion of the Name of Hobſom, by which the baptiſmal Name ſtands for the Surname.

full and particular Account is given, of the *firſt Concerns* with the *Indians* here.[13] But I could not come by the Sight of them, nor do I know certainly whither thoſe things are extant.[14] I have alſo peruſed Sr. *Ferdinando Gorges Narration* of original Undertakings here.[15] Moreover J have read a large Manuſcript of Governour *Bradford's* (written with his own Hand;) being expreſſive of what the *firſt Planters* in this Countrey met with, whether from the Heathen or otherwiſe, from the Year 1620. to the Year 1647.[16] As for the *Pequot Troubles*, the

[13] The "Scripts" here referred to went probably with Purchas's Papers, but what became of his Collections is not ſatisfactorily known. It is ſaid that Purchas died "at his own Houſe in London in 1628," and that he died in debt, owing to his great Outlays in publiſhing his *Pilgrimes*. Beſides poſſeſſing the great Collection left by Hakluyt, he no doubt had a vaſt one of his own, for like Hakluyt he travelled into different Seaports to ſee thoſe Captains who had been on important Voyages. Thus he tells us that in 1618 he ſaw Capt. John Winter at Bath, and that Winter gave him important Facts concerning Sir Francis Drake's Voyage, &c. *Pilgrimes*, iv, 1187.

[14] If any at this Time are wiſer than our Author was then, ſuch are unknown to the Editor.

[15] The Title of the Work is *A Brief Narration of the Originall Undertakings of the Advancement of Plantations in the Parts of America. Eſpecially ſhewing the Beginning, Progreſs, and Continuance of that of New England.* London: 1656. A ſmall 4to.

[16] This MS., until recently, was ſuppoſed to have been irrecoverably loſt; and there was good Reaſon for ſuch a Suppoſition. It could be traced to Gov. Hutchinſon, and it was well known that many of his Papers were deſtroyed by a Mob in the turbulent Times of the Stamp Act. But Bradford's MS. was not deſtroyed, though it was doubtleſs taken to England with many other Papers and Documents in Hutchinſon's poſſeſſion which did not belong to him (ſee Mather's *Brief Hiſtory of King Philip's War*, p. 22-3). If any one had even a Shadow of Faith in its Exiſtence, it was too much of a Shadow to ſend him upon a Search in which a rational Being would about as ſoon expect to find the Philoſopher's Stone. But the long deſired MS. was diſcovered; not

World is beholding to the Induſtry of Mr. *John Allyn*[17] of Hartford (as is in the ſubſequent Relation acknowledged) for what is thus made publick, reſpecting the great Commotions which then happened. Only I have been willing to add ſome Particulars out of a *Manuſcript Narrative* of the *Pequot War*, which I lately met with in Reverend Mr. *Davenports* Library,[18] as alſo what Mr. *Johnſon*,[19] or Mr. *Morton*[20] (out of Mr. *Bradfords* Manu-

by an American, but by a Gentleman of the Manuſcript Department of the Britiſh Muſeum, Mr. N. E. S. A. Hamilton, as he himſelf informed me. He was rumaging in the Lambeth Library, among a Maſs of Manuſcripts, and when he detected this of Bradford he called the Attention of the Librarian to it, who allowed him to take it and to cauſe it to be repaired as it is now ſeen. Thus but for Mr. Hamilton's Intereſt in old MSS., and his calling the Attention of the Biſhop of Oxford to it, Bradford's MS. might have ſlumbered for an indefinite Period beyond the preſent Generation. The Biſhop having made Extracts from it and publiſhed them in his Eccleſiaſtical Work on the Church in the Colonies, the Exiſtence of the MS. became known in this Country, and in due Time a Copy was obtained, and we now have it in print, as a Volume of Hiſtorical Collections by the Maſſ. Hiſtorical Society, 1856. Why it was not put forth on its own Merits, independent of a Series of Hiſtorical Collections, thoſe who managed the Affair may explain.

17 Mr. Allyn was Secretary of the Colony of Connecticut. He was not the Author of the Paper which he ſent to Mr. Mather. He merely copied and ſent him Maſon's Account of the Pequot War. He probably varied his Copy ſome from the Original. Whether he intended to paſs it off as his own, it is difficult to ſay. At all events Mr. Mather appears to have been deceived.

18 We are quite in the Dark reſpecting the Authorſhip of this Manuſcript.

19 Capt. Edward Johnſon of Woburn, gives ſome Account of the Pequot War in his *Wonder-Working Providence*, &c., ſometimes cited as a *Hiſtiry of New England.* It was printed in 1654, anonymouſly. See Prince, *Introduction to his N. E. Chronology.*

20 *New England's Memorial*, originally publiſhed in 1669. It is very meager in all reſpects, nor have recent Editions been what they ſhould be.

ſcript) hath heretofore noted. Touching the Narraganſets; I have ſearched the publick Records of the Colonyes,[21] and from thence excerped the Subſtance of what as here related, as to former Troubles from them or by their Means procured. The *Relation* concerning Alexander and his Brother *Philip*, wherwith this *Narrative* is concluded, I received from the preſent Honourable Governour of *Plymouth* (who ſucceeds his bleſſed Father, as in Place, ſo in Spirit) and from the faithful *Secretary* of that Colony. I am ſenſible that there is a Reality in that which *Eraſmus* doth (after his Manner) wittily expreſs *Adeò nunc in omnes et omnia groſſatur comitata furiis* ʽη Διαβολὴ *ut non ſit tutum ullum emittere librum, niſi ſatellitio munitum*;[22] wherefore [v] I thought it neceſſary to give this particular Account of the Authors from whom I received my Information, reſpecting Paſſages inſiſted on. Nor ſhall I ſeek for any other *Guard* againſt thoſe, whoſe *Genius* is to calumniate Endeavours of this Kind.

I am not altogether ignorant of what is com-

21 The Records of the United Colonies are thoſe to which the Author probably refers. They were firſt printed in Hazard's *State Papers*. A vaſtly improved Edition of them has recently been iſſued at the Expenſe of the State of Maſſachuſetts, under the careful Superviſion of Mr. David Pulſifer.

22 Thoſe not familiar with Hebrew, Greek and Latin will regret that the Author's Conviction as expreſſed in the following Note had not happened before he wrote this Treatiſe: "The Reader will not "find in theſe Sermons [*Awakening* "*Truths*, printed 1710] any ſtudied "fine Phraſes, nor a Gingling with "Latin, Greek and Hebrew Sentences. I have long been of holy Mr. "Dod's mind, that ordinarily ſo "much Latin is ſo much Fleſh in a "Sermon."

monly and truly obſerved, viz. That thoſe *Hiſtories* which are partly *Chronological* are the moſt profitable; and that they that undertake a Work of this Nature, ſhould go by Preſcript of that ſo much celebrated Verſe,

Quis, Quid, Vbi, Quibus auxiliis, Cur, Quomodò Quandò.

which I have endeavoured to remember. Nor hath that Maxim been wholly forgotten, *Stylus Hiſtoricus quo ſimplicior eo melior*. And J may expect that *Ingenuous Readers* will act according to that which a learned Man in his *Hiſtorica* layeth down as a Theorem, *Hiſtorici legantur cum moderatione et venia*, h. e. *cogitetur fieri non poſſe ut in omnibus circumſtantiis ſint Lyncei.* J have done what I could to come at the Truth, and plainly to declare it, knowing that that is (as uſeth to be ſaid) *the Soul and Sun of Hiſtory*, whoſe Property is, Μ'ονη τῆ 'αληθεί'α θυείυ.

As for what concerns the Story of the late War with the Indians, there are who have propounded, that ſome meet Perſons might be improved in the ſeveral *Colonyes* to collect what of Moment hath happened in each *Colony* ſince this War broke forth.[23] When *Caſſiodorus* compiled an Hiſtory out of the Collections of *Socrates, Theodoret, Sozomen*, it was of great Uſe in after Ages, bearing the Name of *Hiſtoria Tripartita*; if ſuch a Courſe as hath been intimated ſhould be attended, and the Deſign finiſhed, a *Compleat Hiſtory* many (ἑαυπες ἐπιτ]ἐπὃθεφ) be compoſed out of thoſe Collections, which J know

[23] This was an early Hint for the Formation of a Hiſtorical Society.

not but that it may derve the Name of *Hiſtoria Tripartita*, and be no leſſe beneficial to Poſterity, then ſome others have been. In the mean Time, the Reader muſt be ſatisfied with what is already extant.

The following *Relation* was written neer upon a Year ago; ſince which a Reverend Author has emitted a Narrative of the [vi] Troubles which have happened by the Indians in New England, whoſe Pains and Induſtry doth (in my Judgement) deſerve an Acknowledgment.[24] Nevertheleſſe it hath been thought needful to publiſh this; conſidering that moſt of the Things here inſiſted on, are not ſo much as once taken Notice of in that *Narrative*.[25] And although the *Pequot War* be therein deſcribed (and that, as to the Subſtance of the Story, truely and impartially) it is not ſo fully done as is here to be ſeen. If this Endeavour ſhall contribute any Light or Help in writing an *Hiſtory of New England*,[26] I hope they whoſe Hearts are

[24] The Acknowledgment of an Author's "Pains and Induſtry," is indeed a very cheap Commendation, and in this Caſe appears only to have been recognized for Condemnation. The Reader does not require to be told that the Rev. William Hubbard of Ipſwich is referred to.

[25] The Title of Mr. Hubbard's Work is, *A Narrative of the Troubles with the Indians in New England, from the firſt Planting thereof in the Year* 1607, *to this preſent Year*, 1677. *But chiefly of the late Troubles in the two laſt Years*, 1675 *and* 1676. *To which is added a Diſcourſe about the Warrs with the Pequods in the Year* 1637. Boſton: printed by John Foſter, in the Year 1677. It is a cloſely printed Quarto of about 250 Pages. A much improved and corrected Edition appeared in London the ſame Year. The Title of the London Edition begins, *The Preſent State of New England. Being a Narrative*, &c., as in the other Edition.

[26] The Author takes occaſion in ſeveral of his Works to ſpeak of a

upon ſeeking out and declaring the Works of God in the Generation which he caſt them into, will accept of my Labour, however mean and inconſiderable. I ſhall do no more, but pray that the Bleſſing of Heaven may be upon Undertakings of this Nature.

Boſton N. E.
Sept. 14. 1677.

Increaſe Mather.

Hiſtory of New England. Not long after this his Son commenced what he intended as ſuch—his well known *Magnalia*.

[1]

A RELATION of the first Troubles in New-England,

by Reasons of the INDIANS there.

IT is now above seventy Years, since that Part of this Continent which is known by the Name of NEW ENGLAND, was discovered and Possession thereof taken by the English. No Man that made it his Concern to be acquainted with Things of this Nature can be ignorant, that the *Northern* (or to us Northeast) Parts of this Land were the first wherein were English Inhabitants; whence it was for some Years known by the Name of the *Northern Plantation*, until such Time as

King *Charles* the firſt (then Prince of Wales) gave it the Name of *New England.*[27]

For *in Anno* 1602. and in the Year following ſome of our Countrymen made notable Diſcoveryes in that Land which lyeth North and by Eaſt of Virginia, between the Degrees of 43 and 45 northern Latitude.

Four or five Years after this that noble Lord, *Sir John Popham* (then Lord Chief Juſtice) ſent out a Ship into theſe Parts to make further Diſcovery, who arriving at the Place deſigned, quickly returned, and made ſuch a Report of what they had ſeen, as did greatly animate the Adventurers to go on with their begun Undertaking; whereupon in Anno 1607. a Gentleman [2] whoſe Name was *Popham* was ſent into theſe Coaſts, with two Ships and one hundred Land-men and Ordnance, and other Things neceſſary for their Suſtentation and Defence, in order to the making Way for the Settlement of a Plantation. But that noble Lord being taken out of the World by ſudden Death, alſo the Planters here meeting with ſad Diſaſters (for in the Depth of Winter, their Lodgings and Stores were burnt, and Capt. *Popham* dyed amongſt them) when the next Year a Veſſel arrived bringing the

[27] The Author is not quite right in this Statement. Smith himſelf named the Country New England, as he found it to lie "oppoſite to Nova Albion in the South Sea, diſcovered by the moſt memorable Sir Francis Drake in his Voyage about the World, in regard whereof this is ſtiled New England." On ſhowing his Map to Prince Charles (afterwards Charles the Firſt), then a Boy of about fifteen, he, at Smith's Requeſt, ſubſtituted Engliſh Names for the Indian. This appears to be all the Agency Prince Charles had in naming New England; both whimſical and nonſenſical. See Smith's *Gen. Hiſtorie,* ii, 176, 179.

News of the Lord *Pophams* Death, the whole Company of the Englifh refolved upon a return home, which proved the Death of the Englifh Plantation, at that Time defigned in thefe Parts of the World. Only S^r^ *Fr. Popham* (Son to the Lord Chief Juftice) fent divers Times to thefe Coafts for Trade and Fifhing.[28]

As yet there was not (fo far as I can learn) any Difturbance from the *Indians*, then the only Natives of this Land.[29] But not long after this, an unworthy Ship-Mafter whofe Name was *Hunt*, being fent forth into thefe Coafts on the Account of the fifhing Trade, after he had made his Difpatch and was ready to fail, (under Pretence of trucking with them) enticed Indians into his Veffel, they in Confidence with his Honefty went aboard, to the Number of twenty from *Patuxet*, fince called *Plimouth*, and feven from Noffet (now known by the Name of Eftam) thefe did this *Hunt* feize upon, ftowed them under Hatches, and carried them to the Streights of *Gibraltar*, and there did he fell as many as he could of them for 20*l.* a Man, until it was known whence they came; for then the Friars in thofe Parts took away the reft of them, that fo they might nurture them in the Popifh Religion. The pernicious and avaritious Felony of this Ship-Mafter, in ftealing and felling the *Indians* to the

28 The Events glanced at in the preceding Paragraphs will be found minutely enough ftated by Hubbard, Prince, Holmes, and others.

29 It will be feen, however, that the Author relates fome *Troubles* between the Indians and Voyagers which muft have happened anterior to this Period. See Smith's *Defcript. N. Eng.*, 15, and his *Gen. Hift. N. Eng.*, ii, 194.

Spaniards, as hath been expreſſed, laid the Foundation to great *Troubles* which did, after that befall the Engliſh, eſpecially in the *North-eaſt* Parts of this Land. Yea that inhumane and barbarous Fact was the unhappy Occaſion of the Loſs of many a man's Eſtate and Life, which the Barbarians in thoſe beginning Times did from thence ſeek to deſtroy.[30]

For when the Gentlemen Adventurers[31] did again diſpatch a Veſſel hither commanded by Capt. *Hobſon*[32] in order to erecting a Plantation and ſet-

[30] Hunt was with Capt. Smith in his Voyage, and Smith gives us the Particulars of the Manner in which he kidnapped the Indians thus: "But one Thomas Hunt, when I "was gone, thinking to prevent that "Intent I had to make there a "Plantation, thereby to keepe this "abounding Countrey ſtill in Ob- "ſcurity, that onely he and ſome "few Merchants more might enjoy "wholly the Benefit of the Trade, "and Profit of this Countrey, be- "traied foure and twenty of thoſe "poore Saluages aboord his Ship, "and moſt diſhoneſtly and inhu- "manely for their kinde vſage of "me and all our Men, carried them "with him to Maligo and there for "a little priuate gaine ſold thoſe "ſilly Saluages for Rials of Eight; "but this vilde Act kept him euer after "from any more imploiment to thoſe "Parts." *Deſcript. of N Eng.* See more from Smith in Note 37. The Indians told the Pilgrims in March, 1621, that Hunt took the Indians "vnder colour of trucking with "them, twentie out of this very "Place [Plymouth] where we in- "habite, and ſeuen Men from the "Nauſites." *Mourt in Purchas*, 1849. Other Accounts ſay twenty-four was the Number of Indians kidnapped No doubt ſome were killed, and theſe were reckoned by the Indians, while the Engliſh reckoned only thoſe actually carried off.

[31] Sir Ferdinando Gorges ſeems to have been the chief Adventurer in this buſineſs.

[32] When Gorges had arranged to employ Capt. Hobſon, he ſays: "I knew the Captain had ſome re- "lation to Lord Southampton, and "I not willing in thoſe Days to un- "dertake any Matter extraordinary "without his Lordſhip's Advice; "who approved of it ſo well that he "adventured one hundred pounds "in that Employment, and his Lord- "ſhip being at that Time Com- "mander of the Iſle of Wight, "where the Captain had his abid-

tling a Trade with the Natives here, *Hunt's* forementioned Scandal, had caused the *Indians* to contract such a mortal Hatred against all Men of the English Nation, that it was no small Difficulty to settle any where within their Territoryes. And whereas there were two *Indians* called *Epenow* and *Manawet*, who having been carried out of these Parts of the World into *England* had learned to speak *English*, that were returned in *Hobsons* Vessel, as hoping they might be servicable toward the Design on foot, it [3] fell out otherwise; since being exasperated by what *Hunt* had done, they contrived with their Country-men how to be revenged upon the English. *Manawet* dyed within a short Time after the Ships Arrival. *Epenow* secretly plotted to free himself out of the English Hands, which he effected, though with great Hazard to himself and other *Salvages* that were his fellow *Conspirators*, which came to pass after this Manner.

Upon the Ships Arrival, many of the Indians (some of them being *Epenows* Kinsmen) came aboard and were kindly entertained by the Captain; at their Departure they promised to return the next Day, and bring some Trade with them. *Epenow* had not Liberty granted him to go on Shoar, only much Discourse (and probably a Contrivement for his Escape) was between him and the other *Indians*

" ing under his Lordship, out of " his Nobleness was pleased to fur- " nish me with some land Soldiers, " and to commend me to a grave " Gentleman, one Capt. Hobson, " who was willing to go that Voy- " age and to adventure one hundred " pounds himself." P. 15.

in the Veſſel, which nobody but themſelves could underſtand. The *Indians* returned at the Time appointed with twenty *Canoos*, but were ſhy of coming aboard. *Epenow* cunningly called to them as if he would have them come into the Veſſel, to Trade, and ſuddenly did himſelf leap overboard: He was no ſooner in the Water, but the *Indians* ſent a Shower of Arrows into the Veſſel, and came deſperately near to the Ship, and (in deſpite of all the Engliſh Muſketiers aboard) went away with their Country-man *Epenow*.[33]

Divers of the Indians were then ſlain by the

[33] It appears from Gorges own Account that Epanow had made great Pretenſions as to what the Country contained, and at the ſame Time pretended that if he revealed his Knowledge to the Engliſh, "he "was ſure to have his Brains knock-"ed out as ſoon as he came aſhore." But Gorges did not put implicit Faith in him: "For," ſays he, "I "gave the Captain ſtrict Charge to "endeavour by all Means to pre-"vent his Eſcape; and for the "more Surety, I gave Order to "have three Gentlemen of my own "Kindred (two Brothers of Stur-"ton's, and Maſter Matthews) to "be ever at hand with him, clothing "him with long Garments, fitly to "be laid hold on if Occaſion ſhould "require. Notwithſtanding all this, "his friends being all come at the "Time appointed, with twenty "Canoes, and lying at a certain "Diſtance with their Bows ready, "the Captain calls to them to come "aboard; but they not moving, he "ſpeaks to Epenow to come unto "him where he was, in the Fore-"caſtle of the Ship. He being then "in the Waiſt of the Ship between "two of the Gentlemen that had "him in guard, ſtarts ſuddenly from "them, and coming to the Captain, "calls to his Friends in Engliſh to "come aboard; in the interim ſlips "himſelf overboard; and although "he was taken hold of by one of "the Company, yet being a ſtrong "and heavy Man, could not be "ſtayed; and was no ſooner in the "Water but the Natives ſent ſuch a "Shower of Arrows, and came "withal deſperately ſo near the "Ship, that they carried him away "in deſpite of all the Muſketeers "aboard, who were for the Num-"ber as good as our Nation did "afford." P. 16. Conſult *Gorges* for other Particulars.

Engliſh, and the Maſter of the *Engliſh* Veſſel and ſeveral of the Company wounded by the *Indians*.[34]

Hereupon the Captain and the whole Company were diſcouraged, and returned to *England*, bringing nothing back with them but the News of their bad Succeſs, and that there was a War broke out between the *Engliſh*, and the *Indians*.[35] The Time when theſe Troubles hapned, is controverted more than the Things themſelves.[36] *Johannes de Laet* in his *Deſcriptio Indiæ Occidentalis*, writeth that it was between the Years 1608 and 1615. So doth *Purchaſe*. Sr. *Ferdinando Gorges* relates that he

[34] Gorges ſays nothing about any being killed or wounded. But Purchas ſays " they wounded the Maſ-" ter of our Ship, and diuers other " of our Company, yet was not " their Deſign without the Slaugh-" ter of ſome of their People, and " the Hurt of others, compaſſed, as " appeared afterwards." Vol. iv, p. 1829. Gorges complained that the Voyage was unneceſſarily abandoned, as he had given Orders for its Proſecution elſewhere if this firſt Attempt failed. But if the Captain and others were badly wounded it is a good Reaſon for the Return of the Ship to England. See alſo the *Brief Relation of the Preſident and Council of New England*, as reprinted in *Colls. Maſs. Hiſt. Soc.*, ix, 2d Ser., p. 6.

[35] Here our Author follows Purchas, but not with ſufficient Care, for the Reader is left in Doubt about " a War broke out," as to where and when; while Purchas is clear and explicit, and in theſe Words: " Hereupon Captaine Hobſon and " his Company, conceuing the End " of their Attempt to bee fruſtrate, " reſolued without more adoe to " returne, and ſo thoſe Hopes, that " Charge and Voyage was loſt alſo; " for they brought home Nothing " but the Newes of their euill Suc-" ceſſe of the vnfortunate Cauſe " thereof, and of a Warr now near " begun betweene the Inhabitants " of thoſe Parts and vs. A miſer-" able Comfort for ſo weak Meanes " as were now left, to purſue the " Concluſion of ſo tedious an En-" terpriſe." *Pilgrims*, iv, 1829. Prince, *Chronology*, 41.

[36] This Sentence ſeems to have been thrown in without Reflection, as by a careful Compariſon of his Authorities the Author would have ſeen that Dates were available, to an Extent ſufficient for his Purpoſe.

ſent Capt. *Hobſon* into theſe Parts in Anno 1614, and what *Hunt* did was before that, as being the grand procuring Cauſe of the Broyle between the Engliſh and the Indians, which firſt began in that Year.[37]

After theſe Things another Veſſel was ſent into theſe *Northern* Parts under the Command of Capt. *Rocraft*, he deſigned to winter there, but ſome of his own Ships Company conſpired againſt him, intending his Death, he having ſecret Intelligence of this Plot againſt his Life, held his Peace until the Day was come wherein the intended Miſchief was to be put in Execution, then unexpectedly apprehended the Conſpirators; he was loth himſelf to put any to Death, though they were worthy of it. But therefore he reſolved to leave them in the Wilderneſs, not knowing but they might haply diſcover ſomething which might be advantageous.[38]

[4] Accordingly he furniſhed them with Ammunition, and ſome Victuals for their preſent Subſiſtence, and turned them Aſhore to *Socodehock*,

[37] This is according to Smith's *Deſcription of New England* in his *General Hiſtory*, but in his *New England Trials*, 16 (Force's Edit.), he ſays the Place where Hunt kidnapped the Indians was ſo remote from that where Capt. Hobſon was attacked, that that Act of Hunt could not have been the Cauſe of the Hoſtility. "However it was "alleged for an Excuſe." Purchas calls Hunt's "Sauage hunting of "Sauages a new and Deuelliſh Pro-"ject." *Pilgrims*, 1828.

[38] The Author omits much important Matter reſpecting Capt. Edward Rocroft's Proceedings. On his Arrival on the eaſtern Coaſt, he captured a French Veſſel fiſhing and trading there. This Veſſel he went into himſelf, and ſent home the Men in his own Ship. After the Mutiny above recorded, Rocroft went to Virginia, and there getting into a Quarrel was killed. Pretty full Details may be read in Purchas, 1829-30. See alſo Belknap's *Amer. Biography*, i, 361.

himſelf with the reſt of his Company departing to *Virginia*. Thoſe Engliſh Mutineers got over to the Iſland of *Monhegin*, three Leagues from the Main, where they kept themſelves ſafe from the Fury of the exaſperated *Indians*, until the next Spring, when a Veſſel that came on the Coaſt on a fiſhing Voyage, found them all (except one Perſon that died of Sickneſs in this Interim) alive, and carried them away back for England.

Not many Years after this, *viz*. in Anno 1619. a Gentleman whoſe Name was *Darmer* was ſent to proſecute the Deſign of planting and ſettling a Trade in *New England*, and to endeavour that a right Underſtanding of Matters between the Indians and the Engliſh might be accompliſhed.

He therefore brought with him an *Indian* called *Squantum*, who was one of thoſe that *Hunt* had treacherouſly carried away from *Patuxet*, but was bought by an Engliſh Merchant, and lived ſome Time with Mr. *Slany*[39] a Gentleman in *Cornhil*, until he could ſpeak broken *Engliſh*, and after that at *New-found-land*, where Capt. *Maſon* was then Governour, who was willing that Mr. *Darmer* ſhould take *Squantum* with him to *New England*. Upon hs Arrival here, he told his Country-men very ſtrange Storyes, giving them to underſtand what Kind of Uſage he had met with among the Engliſh where he had been, and how much the wicked Fact of that covetous *Hunt* was condemned,

[39] Probably "Maſter John Slany," one of the Council of the Newfoundland Company. This will account for Squanto's being ſent to Newfoundland. See Stow's *Survey of London*, p. 591, Edition folio, 1633.

ſo that many of them began to converſe with, and become friendly toward the Engliſh, and Mr. *Darmer* conceited that he and *Squantum* had made a firm Peace between the Nations. But, *manet alta mente repoſtum—Indians* are not wont to forget Injuries, when once they have ſuſtained any: ſo did that Gentleman find it to his after Sorrow: For being near the Place where *Hunt* had formerly betrayed the *Indians* aboard his Veſſel, they treacherouſly ſet upon him, and gave him fourteen Wounds, ſo that he had much adoe to eſcape with his Life. And though he got to *Virginia* after this, ſome write that he never recovered of thoſe Wounds which he received of the *Nauſit Indians*.[40] And *Epenow* (before mentioned) was the Cauſe of Capt. *Darmers* being aſſaulted, whom he hapned to meet with at his firſt landing in that Place: The *Indian* being able to ſpeak *Engliſh*, reported to Capt. *Darmer* the Story of his Eſcape out of Capt. *Hobſons* Veſſel, laughing heartily at the Conceit of it. The Captain told him that Sr. *Ferdinando Gorges* was much troubled that he ſhould meet with ſuch ill Uſage as to put him upon a Temptation to ſteal away. This *Salvage* after ſome Enquiries about Sr. *Ferdinando* (and his Family) with whom he had ſometimes lived in England, belike ſuſpecting that Capt. *Darmer*

[40] There can be no Queſtion as to the Death of Capt. Dermer in Virginia, but not immediately from the Effect of his Wounds, as may be ſeen in Purchas. "He fell ſicke "of the Infirmities of that Place, "and thereof dyed." *Pilgrims*, iv, 1831. Dermer was well known to Purchas, who had received Letters from him while upon his Voyage. See his *Pilgrims*, iv, 1778-9, where a valuable one is inſerted.

had a Purpose to surprize [5] him, he conspired with some of his Fellows to take the Captain, and laid Hands on him, who did with his Sword manfully defend himself against those barbarous and treacherous Assailants.[41] What other particular Mischiefs were done by the *Northern Indians* (or others) about this Time, I cannot learn: Only Capt. *Smith* writeth that he met with many of their *silly Encounters* (as he calls them) but without any Hurt.[42] Also a little before the first Planters in *Plymouth* Colony arrived in this Land, three

41 Capt Smith makes this Summary of Capt. Dermer's Adventures: "Master Thomas Dirmire, an vnderstanding and industrious Gentleman, that was also with me "amongst the French-men, hauing "liued about a Yeere in New-"found-land, returning to Plimoth, "went for New England in this "Ship, so much approued of this "Countrey, that he staied there "with fiue or six Men in a little "Boat, finding two or three French "men amongst the Saluages who "had lost their Ship, augmented "his Company, with whom he "ranged the Coast to Virginia, "where he was kindly welcomed "and well refreshed, thence re-"turned to New England againe, "where hauing beene a Yeere, in "his backe returne to Virginia he "was so wounded by the Saluages, "he died upon it." Vol. II, 219. See also Gorge's *Narration*, p. 20. According to Mourt (Purchas, 1849) Dermer's Fight was about July, 1620.

42 The following is Smith's Account of some of his Skirmishes with the Indians. I suppose they happened while he was surveying the Coast of Massachusetts: "We found "the People in those Parts very "kinde, but in their fury no lesse "valiant, for vpon a Quarrell we "fought forty or fifty of them, till "they had spent all their Arrowes, "and then we tooke six or seuen of "their Canowes, which towards the "Euening they ransomed for Beuer "Skins, and at Quonahasit [Cohas-"set now] falling out there but "with one of them, he with three "others crossed the Harbour in a "Canow to certaine Rockes where-"by we must passe, and there let "flie their Arrowes for our Shot, "till we were out of Danger, yet "one of them was slaine, and an-"other shot through his Thigh. "At Accomack [Plymouth harbor] "we fought also with them, tho "some were hurt, some slaine, yet "within an houre after they be-"came Friends." It seems that

Engliſhmen belonging to Sr *Ferdinando Gorges*, were killed by theſe *Salvages*, and two more narrowly eſcaped with their Lives. And thus far wee have a *Cold* Account of the Deſign reſpecting the Advancement of a Plantation in the *Northern* Parts of *New England*.[43]

In Anno 1620. A Company of Chriſtians belonging to the *Northern Parts of England*, who propoſed not ſo much worldly as ſpiritual Ends in their Undertaking, ayming at the *Converſion* of the *Indians*, and the Eſtabliſhment of the Worſhip of God in purity, did therefore tranſport themſelves and Familyes into this howling Wilderneſs. The firſt Land they made was that of *Cape Cod*, Novemb. 9. where they came to an Anchor, and went on Shore, Novemb. 11. Perceiving the Incommodiouſneſs of that Place for planting, they reſolved to ſeek out for another that might be more accommodate. But their Shallop not being in trimm to be ſent out upon Diſcovery, ſome were deſirous to improve the Time, in making what Searches they could upon the Land thereabout.[44]

theſe Affairs occurred but a ſhort Time before Capt. Hunt ſeized the Indians at and near Plymouth.

43 The Author took little Pains about his Chronology. When the three of Gorge's Men were killed does not appear from any of the Accounts; but in a Conference with the Indians held by the Pilgrims on the 17th of March, 1621, thoſe Indians told the Pilgrims that "about "eight moneths agoe [the Nauſites] "ſlew three Engliſhmen, and two "more hardly eſcaped by Flight "to Monhiggon." See Mourt in Purchas, iv, 1849, who adds, "they "were Sir Ferdinando Gorge his "Men." *Ibid.*

44 The Author in this and what follows relating to the Settlement of Plymouth, takes his Narrative from Mourt's and Bradford's Relations as

Novemb. 5. Sixteen Men well armed were ſet on Shore under the Conduct of Capt. *Miles Standiſh.* After they had gone about a Mile near the Shoar, they deſcryed five or ſix Indians, who like wild Creatures ran away from them at the firſt Sight, they followed them, by the Trace of their Footings, about ten Miles, til Night came on, but could not come to any Speech with them.[45]

At laſt they met with a Kettle wherein was Indian Corn, which after much Conſultation they ſeized upon, reſolving that if they could come to ſpeak with *Indians*, they would return them their Kettle, and give them full Satisfaction for their Corn, which they intended for planting, not knowing how elſe to be ſupplyed. So did they return the next Day, but loſt themſelves awhile in the Woods, and as they were wandering up and down, they hapned to eſpy a ſmall Tree that was blown down, and ſome Acorns ſtrewed underneath, whilſt they were viewing of it, and wondering what it ſhould mean, it gave a ſudden Jerk, whereby one

abſtracted in Purchas's *Pilgrims.* As thoſe Works are acceſſible entire, in tolerable Reprints, few Notes will be needed ſo far as thoſe are followed.

[45] This Paragraph is very much abridged. When "they had marched about the Space of a Mile by "the Sea, they eſpied fiue or ſix "People with a Dogge, comming "towards them, who were Sauages, "who when they ſaw them, ran "into the Woods and whiſtled the "Dogge after them. At firſt they "ſuppoſed them to be Maſter Jones, "the Maſter and ſome of his Men, "for they were a Shoare, and knew "of their comming; but after they "knew them to be Indians they "marched after them into the "Wood, leaſt other of the Indians "ſhould lye in Ambuſh: but when "the Indians ſaw our Men following them, they ran away with "Might and Maine." *Mourt in Purchas*, 1843-4. See alſo Belknap's *Amer. Biog.*, ii, 194-5.

of the Company was caught up by the Leg, it being an Indian Deer Trap;[46] the reſt looſed him, and at laſt they found their Way to the Ship again.

After this their Shallop being fitted for the Purpoſe, they went a coaſting [6] upon Diſcovery, but of ſome Dayes could meet with no *Indians*. Albeit they found old deſerted Indian Forts, and more of their Corn and Baſkets, and a Bottle of Oyle which doubtleſs ſome how was brought out of Europe.[47]

About the tenth of December, they diſcerned the Track of Indians Feet upon the Sand, and followed it, till they perceived where it ſtruck up into the Woods, at laſt they light upon an Indian Path, which led them a great Way up into the Woods, and ſaw where there had been Corn planted, and found Indian Graves &c. but no Man appeared.[48]

So they returned to their Shallop, and ſome watching, others betook themſelves to their Reſt. But in the Night they were alarmed by the Senti-

46 " Stephen Hopkins ſaid it had " beene to catch ſome Deere; ſo as " we were looking at it, William " Bradford, being in the Reare, " when he came looking alſo vpon " it, and as he went about, it gave " a ſodaine Ierke vp, and he was " immediately caught by the Legge." *Ibid.*, 1845.

47 " We marched to the Place " where we had the Corne formerly, " which Place we called *Corne-hill*, " and digged and found the reſt, of " which we were very glad: we " alſo digged in a Place a little far- " ther off, and found a Bottle of " Oyle. We went to another Place " which we had ſeen before and " digged and found more Corn, viz. " two or three Baſkets full of Indian " Wheat, and a Bag of Beans, with " a good many of faire Wheateares. " Whilſt ſome of vs were digging " vp this, ſome others found another " Heape of Corne, which they dig- " ged vp alſo, ſo we had in all " about ten Buſhels." *Mourt in* " *Purchas*, 1845.

48 The " Indian Graves " are minutely deſcribed by Mourt, in *Purchas*, 1845, 1847. See alſo Belknap's *Amer. Biog.*, ii, 197.

nels crying *Arm*, *Arm*, ſuppoſing *Indians* to be near them. They heard a moſt hideous Howling, but one in the Company perſwaded the reſt, that it was the Noyſe of Wolves and Foxes, which uſed (as he ſaid) to make ſuch a Noiſe in *New-found-Land* where he had been, too Gunns were ſhot off, at which the Noiſe ceaſed.

But betimes in the Morning,[49] on a ſudden, they heard the ſame Voices again, and one of the Company cryed *Indians*, *Indians*, and immediately Arrowes came pouring in upon them. This barbarous Salutation was amazing to the Engliſh, but that which did moſt of all terrife was the horrid Cry of thoſe Salvages, whoſe Note was after this Manner, *Woach woach ha hahoac woach*. A ſtout Indian who was thought to be their Captain, ſtanding behind a Tree let fly his Arrows apace, and ſtood three Shotts of a Muſket, until one took full Aim at him, and (as 'tis ſuppoſed) ſorely wounded him, upon which he gave an extraordinary Shriek and went away, and all the other Indians fled with him. Providence ſo ordered as that none of the Engliſh received any Hurt, though they gathered up eighteen Arrows[50] (and many more were ſhot at them) ſome whereof were headed with Braſs, others

[49] " About fiue a Clocke in the " Morning we began to be ſtirring, " vpon a ſudden wee heard a great " and ſtrange Cry, which we knew " to be the ſame Voices, though " they varied their Notes; one of " the Company being abroad came " running in, and cried, *They are* " *Men, Indians, Indians;* and withal " their Arrowes came flying amongſt " vs."

[50] " Wee tooke vp eighteene of " their Arrowes, which wee had " ſent to England by Maſter Jones," &c.

with Harts-horn, others with Eagles Claws, and ſundry of the Engliſh had their Coats ſhot through and through.[51]

December 19. The Engliſh landed and reſolved to endeavor the ſetling of a Plantation, at that Place which is now called *Plymouth*. No Indians then as yet appeared to give them any Diſturbance: yea though ſome were ſent to ſeek after them, they could find none.

There were not many Dayes[52] after this, two Engliſhmen[53] who being by the Side of a Pond hapned to ſee a Deer, and having Dogs with them, they purſued the Deer until ſuch Time as they loſt themſelves in the Woods, where they were forced to lodge that Night, and were terrified with the Yelling (as it ſeemed to them) of two *Lions*, who

[51] I do not find this mentioned in Mourt or any other earlier Writer than our Author. But Mourt does ſay, "thoſe Arrowes wee found "were almoſt couered with leaues; "yet by the ſpeciall Prouidence of "God, none of them either hit or "hurt vs." *Purchas*, 1847. Yet in the ſeparate Work of Mourt we read, "though many [Arrows] "came cloſe by vs and on euery "Side of vs, and ſome Coates which "hung vp in our Barricado were "ſhot through and through."

It is not ſtrange that there ſhould be found ſome Variation in the different Narratives. Purchas is ſaid to haue abridged Mourt's *Relation*. We know there is more in the *Relation* as originally printed than in Purchas. But he may have been furniſhed with a Copy containing Eraſures and verbal Alterations. Capt. Edward Johnſon, who came over ten Years after the firſt Plymouth Settlers, was doubtleſs intimate with ſome of the firſt that came there, and heard from their own Lips ſome of the Circumſtances of their Settlement. See his *Wonder-Working Providence*, Pages 17, 18, Ed. 4° London, 1654. See alſo *Bradford's Hiſtory*, 85 and 86, who agrees exactly with Mourt, though in ſome Inſtances he is more particular, and in others leſs ſo.

[52] January 12th, 1621.

[53] "Iohn Goodman and Peter "Browne." *Mourt*. Goodman died ſoon after *Bradford*.

roared exceedingly, and [7] a third that they thought very neer them: they betook themſelves to a Tree purpoſing if the Lions ſhould come to climb that for their Security; but they ſaw none.[54] The next Day they perceived that Indians had made Fires thereabouts, but it was wel they met not with any until they came home, being then unarmed and not fit for Encounter with ſuch Enemies.

Now it was that a ſpecial Providence of another Nature hapned: For the Engliſh having built an Houſe in *Plymouth*, a Spark of Fire flying into the Thatch, it was inſtantly burnt down. Mr. *Carver* and Mr. *Bradford* were then ſick, yet if they had not riſen with good ſpeed, they had been blown up with Powder. The Houſe was full of Beds as they could lye one by another, and their Muſkets charged, yet (through the good Providence of God) no hurt done.[55]

[54] Several of the early Writers imagined that Lions were found in New England. Thoſe Writers do not ſeem to have known that the Lion could not exiſt ſo far north. Wood, Joſſelyn, Johnſon, Vanderdonk, and it may be others, write of the Exiſtence of Lions in New England. The firſt named Author ſays: "I will not ſay that ever I " ſaw any myſelf; but ſome have " heard ſuch terrible roarings, as " have made them much aghaſt; " which muſt be either Devils or " Lions." But Morton, the Maligner, was probably more of a Naturaliſt than any of the Writers above named. He ſays there are no Lions in New England. "It is " contrary to the Nature of the " Beaſt to frequent Places accuſ- " tomed to Snow; being like the " Catt, that will hazard the burn- " ing of her Tayle rather than abide " from the Fire." *New Engliſh Canaan*, Pt. ii, Chap. v.

[55] This Calamity befel them on the 14th of January, 1621. "The " Houſe was fired occaſionally [ac- " cidentally] by a Sparke that flew " into the Thatch, which inſtantly " burnt it all vp, but the Roof ſtood " and little hurt; the moſt loſſe was

Febr. 16. An Englifh-man that had gone forth upon a fowling Difign, efpied twelve Indians marching towards the Englifh Plantation and heard the Noife of many more not far off, he lay clofe until they were gone by, and then with all Speed returned home and gave the Alarm, but no Indians followed, only they took away the Tools of the Englifh that had been at work in the Woods.

The next Day two Indians prefented themfelves at the Top of an Hill,[56] two Englifh went out to parly with them,[57] but they ran away, and the Noife of a Multitude of them was heard on the other Side of the Hill.

In the Beginning of *March*, an Indian called *Samofet* came boldly along the Houfes which they had built in Plymouth, and to their great Amazement fpake to them in Englifh, faying *Welcome Englifhmen*: This Indian was a *Sagamore* belonging to the *Northern Parts* about *Monhiggen*,[58] where he had often converfed with Englifh Fifhermen, and he had learned to fpeak broken Englifh; Hee was the firft Indian that they of Plymouth had opportunity to difcourfe with. Hee could tel them of the *Huggery* (as he called it) i. e. *Fight*, which the Englifh had with the *Nauffet*[59] Indians; and that

" Mafter Caruer's and [Mr.] William Bradford's, who then lay " ficke in Bed, and if they had not " rifen with good Speed, had been " blowne vp with Powder." *Mourt* " *in Purchafe*, iv. 1848.

56 Since called Watfon's Hill. Its Indian Name was Cantaugcanteeft.

57 Capt. Standifh and Stephen Hopkins. *Mourt.*

58 Monhegan, an important and well known Ifland on the Coaft of Maine. It was varioufly written, which has confufed fome Authors.

59 The Affair with the lamented

the Name of that Place was called *Patuxet* where a Multitude of Indians had formerly lived, but they were all dead of the Plague which had been there a few Years before the English came.[60] This

Dermer. A Letter written by him within a Month of his Disaster is preserved by Gov. Bradford in his History. Bradford says it was given him by a Friend. No doubt by Sir Ferdinando Gorges.

60 It happened in 1617, or perhaps 1616-17. The most authentic Account of it is given by Capt. Dermer, in a Letter dated at Virginia, 27 Dec. 1619, "to his Wor-"shipful Friend, M. Samvel Pvr-"chas." He says he sailed from Monhegan May 19th. "I passed "alongst the Coast where I found "some ancient Plantations, not long "since populous now vtterly void; "in other Places a Remnant re-"maines, but not free of Sicknesse. "Their Disease the Plague, for we "might perceiue the Sores of some "that had escaped, who described "the Spots of such as vsually die. "When I arrived at my Sauages "native Country [afterwards Ply-"mouth] (finding all dead) I tra-"uelled alongst a daies Iourney west-"ward, to a Place called Nummas-"taquyt [since Middleborough] "where finding Inhabitants," &c. *Purchas*, 1778. Gov. Bradford says under Date of 1621, the Indians about Plymouth "not many, "being dead and abundantly wasted "in the late great Mortalitie which "fell in all these Parts about three "Years before the coming of the "English; wherein thousands of "them dyed, they not being able "to bury one another. Their "Sculls and Bones were found in "many Places lying still above "Ground, where their Houses and "Dwellings had been. A very sad "Spectacle to behould. But they "[the Indians] brought Word "that the Narighansets lived but "on the other side of that great "Bay, and were a strong People, "and many in Number, living "compacte together, and had not "been at all touched with this "wasting Plague." Bradford's *Hist. Plymouth*, 102. Thomas Morton thinks the Disease was the Plague, and intimates that it was his Belief that "the Hand of God fell heavily "upon them" for their Cruelty to the Crews of the Ships they had taken; and relates, that when one of their Captives told them God would destroy them for their Wickedness, boastingly replied that they were too strong for him; in other Words, "they were so many God "could not kill them." But says that Author, "the Hand of God "fell heavily upon them, with such "a mortal Stroake, that they died "on Heapes, as they lay in their "Houses; and the Living that were "able to shift for themselves would "run away and let them dy, and "let there Carkases ly above Ground "without buriall. And the Bones

Samoſet within a few Dayes after his Departure returned again, and brought *Squantum* (whom that wicked *Hunt* had ſtolen away and ſold for a Slave) along with him: which *Squantum* was born in that Place. *Samoſet* and *Squantum* made it their Buſineſs to bring the Engliſh into Acquaintance with the next neighboring *Indians*:[61] wherefore they undertook to bring *Maſſaſoit* (Father to that *Philip* who began the War with the *Engliſh* Iun. 24. 1675.) to treat with the *Engliſh* at Plymouth.

[8] Accordingly, March 22. *Maſſaſoit* with his Brother *Quadequina* came accompanied with about ſixty of his Men; and an Agreement of Peace between the *Engliſh* and *Indians* was then concluded

" and Skulls upon the ſeverall " Places of their Habitations, made " ſuch a Spectacle after my coming " into thoſe Parts, that as I travailed " in that Forreſt, nere the Maſſa- " chuſetts, it ſeemed to me a new " found Golgotha." *New Engliſh Canaan*, iii.

[61] The firſt friendly Interview between the Pilgrims and the Indians is graphically and quaintly related in Mourt's Journal. It was omitted by Mr. Mather, becauſe the Preſence of Indians at the Time he wrote was too common a Thing to be of any Intereſt to his New England Readers. But no valid Excuſe could be given for its Omiſſion in theſe Times.

" On this Day [Sunday, March " 18] came againe the Sauage, and " brought with him fiue other tall " proper Men, they had euery Man " a Deeres Skin on him, and the " Principall of them had a wild " Cat's Skin, or ſuch like, on the " one Arme: they had moſt of them " long Hoſen vp to their Groynes, " cloſe made; and aboue their " Groynes to their Waſt another " Leather, they were altogether " like the *Iriſh*-trouſes; they are of " complexion like our Engliſh Gip- " ſeys, no Haire or very little on " their Faces, on their Heads long " Haire to the Shoulders, onely cut " before; ſome truſſed vp before " with a Feather, broadwiſe, like a " Fan, another a Fox Taile hang- " ing out: thoſe left (according to " our Charge giuen him [Samoſet] " before) their Bowes and Arrowes " a Quarter of a Mile from our " Towne." *Mourt in Purchaſe*, iv, 1849.

on. This Peace was in more Refpects then one fingularly advantagious to the *Englifh*, whilft they were thus but few in Number, and Strangers in this Land.[62]

And as for the Reafons inducing *Maffafoit* to this Accord with the *Englifh*, there were feveral Things that prevailed with him thereunto; For *Squantum*[63] had told him what a great Prince *King James* was, and how well he would take it if his Subjects were kindly entertained, and how ill if

62 Maffaffoit's Vifit to Plymouth, and the Treaty then entered into between the Englifh and Indians, forms one of the moft interefting Chapters in the Hiftory of New England. As Juftice to the Subject can hardly be done in a Note, and as many Works are acceffible containing the full Details, a Reference to them muft here fuffice. See Bradford's *Hiftory*, Morton's *Memorial*, Hubbard's *Narrative*, Prince's *Annals*, Holmes's *Annals*, Cheever, and Young's Edition of Mourt's *Journal*, &c., &c.

63 His Name is given in the early Accounts *Tiffquantum;* in fome of the later ones *Squando*, and *Squanto*. He was one of the five Natives carried from New England by Capt. Weymouth in 1605. He had been fo much with the Englifh that he was a very tolerable Interpreter to the Pilgrims in their early Intercourfe with the Indians. But he was a mifchievous Fellow and caufed much Trouble between the Englifh and his Countrymen, by circulating falfe Reports. So much were they incenfed againft him for his evil Practices, that Maffaffoit directed that he fhould be put to Death. But the Pilgrims knew not how to fpare him he had made himfelf fo ufeful to them as well in other refpects as an Interpreter. They managed however to appeafe his Wrath, and Squantum efcaped Death at that Time. He was born in or near Plymouth, and was the only one belonging to that Place who efcaped the Plague before fpoken of. In Nov. 1612, he accompanied the Englifh to the foutherly Part of Cape Cod to procure Corn, of which they ftood in great need. Through Tifquantum's Intervention eight Hogfheads were obtained. This Tranfaction was at a Place called by the Indians *Manamoycke*, fince by the Englifh *Monamoy*, now Chatham. Here Tifquantum was taken fick of Fever and in a few Days died. Bradford fays he died of "an In-"dean Feavor, bleeding much at "the Nofe (which the Indeans take "for a Simptome of Death)." *Hift. Plymouth*, 128.

otherwiſe, and how eaſy it was for him to ſend over Ships and Men enough to deſtroy *Maſſaſoit* and all his People. At that Time alſo there was Enmity between *Maſſaſoit* and the *Narraganſets*, ſo that he hoped the *Engliſh* might be a Defence to him againſt them. Thus did the Feud which was kindled amongſt the *Indians*, one againſt another, advantage the poor Church in Plymouth. *Sic Canes lingunt ulcera Lazari.*

Moreover the Conſideration of the Guns, and other warlike Weapons which ours brought with them was terrible to the *Indians*, yea, they had more formidable Apprehenſions thereof, than there was real Cauſe for: They imagined that the *Engliſh* could by their great Guns cauſe the Trees to fall down and kill the *Indians*. Furthermore *Sqantum* did wickedly poſſeſs them with one Deluſion about the Engliſh, which had diſmal Impreſſions upon the Minds of theſe ignorant Barbarians; For whereas the Plague (a Diſeaſe which was never known in this Land before or ſince) had newly been raging amonſt them, whereby many of their Towns were totally depopulated, and deſolated: he made them believe that the Engliſh kept the Plague in a Place under Ground, and that they could let it looſe upon the Indians when they would. An Indian called *Hobbomock* one of *Maſſaſoits* Counſellors, obſerving in one of the Engliſh Houſes a kind of Cellar, where ſome Barrels of Powder were beſtowed, enquired of *Squantum* what that was. To whom he replyed, that there the Engliſh kept the Plague that he told them of, which they could let loofe upon Indians at Pleafure. When this *Hobbomock* become acquainted with the Englifh, he ferioufly afked them whether they had any fuch Power, they anfwered him truly that they had not, but withall added that the God whom they ferved had Power to fend that or any other Difeafe upon thofe that fhould doe any Wrong to his People. The Confideration of that alfo, was fome Terror to the Indians.

In the Month of *June* 1621. The Englifh fent Meffengers[64] with a Prefent to *Maffafoit* at *Pocanoket*,[65] By the Way they were accofted, with feveral of the Indians, who having them at an Advantage as they paffed [9] through a River,[66] were ready to fhoot at them: Only having Indian Guides Interpreters in their Company, who gave them to underftand that they were Friends, no hurt was done.[67] Being come to *Maffafoit*, they

[64] Stephen Hopkins and Edward Winflow. They fet out June 10th.

[65] "Partly to know where to find "them, if Occafion ferued, as alfo "to fee their Strength, difcouer the "Countrey, preuent Abufes in their "diforderly coming vnto vs, make "Satisfaction for fome conceiued "Iniuries to be done on our Parts, "and to continue the League of "Peace and Friendfhip betweene "them and vs. And hauing a fit "Opportunitie by Reafon of a "Sauage called *Tifquantum* (that "could fpeak Englifh) coming vnto "vs: with all Expedition prouided "a Horfeman's Coat of red Cotton, "and laced with a flight Lace for "a Prefent, that both they and their "Meffage might bee more acceptable amongft them." *Mourt in Purchafe*, 1851. Bradford's *Hift.*, p. 102.

[66] Probably Tehticut River. "Being willing to haften our Iourney we went, and came thither "at Sunne fetting, where we found "many of the Namafcheucks (they "fo calling the Men of Namafkchet) fifhing vpon a Ware which "they had made on a Riuer which "belonged to them, where they "caught abundance of Baffe." *Purchafe, ib.*

[67] Our Author has given us fuch a miferable Abftract of his Authorities at this Point, that I fhould feel

presented him with a red Cotton Coat, whereon was some Lace, this he accepted with great Thankfulness, *and having put it on* (saith my Author) *He was not a little proud to behold himself, and his Men also to behold their King so bravely attired.* He then promised to continue in Amity with the English, and to take Care that his Men should not be injurious.[68]

that I had done Injustice were I to omit the following remarkably interesting Passage:

" The next Morning [June 11th] " wee brake our Fast, tooke our " leaue and departed, being then " accompanied with some sixe Sau- " ages, hauing gone about sixe Miles " by the Riuer side, at a knowne " shoale Place, it being low Water, " they spake to vs to put off our " Breeches, for wee must wade " thorow. Here let mee not for- " get the Valour and Courage of " some of the Sauages, on the op- " posite Side of the Riuer, for there " were remainining aliue onely two " Men, both aged, especially the one " being aboue threescore: These " two espying a Company of Men " entring the Riuer, ran very swiftly " and low in the Grasse to meet vs " at the Banke, where with shrill " Voyces and great Courage, stand- " ing charged vpon vs with their " Bowes, they demanded what " wee were, supposing vs to be Ene- " mies, and thinking to take Ad- " uantage of vs in the Water: but " seeing wee were Friends, they " welcomed vs with such Food as " they had, and we bestowed a " small Bracelet of Beads on them. " Thus far we are sure the Tide " ebbes and flowes." Mourt *in Purchase*, iv, 1851-2. The Point at which they crossed is not clearly ascertained.

68 When Hopkins and Winslow arrived at Massasoit's town, the Chief was not at home. He was immediately sent for, "and being " come we discharged our Peeces, " and saluted him, who after their " Manner kindly welcomed vs, and " tooke vs into his House, and set " vs downe by him, where hauing " delivered our Message and Pre- " sents, and having put the Coat on " his Backe, and the Chaine about " his Necke, he was not a little " proud to behold himselfe, and his " Men also to see their King so " brauely attired." Among other Things he said his Men should no more annoy the English at Plymouth by their ill timed Intrusions. He then deliuered "a " great Speech" to his Men, setting forth his Importance, naming "at " least thirtie Places" as belonging to him, to which they assented. The Speech appeared to delight

About this Time it was that an Engliſh Lad (one Iohn Billington) loſt himſelf in the Woods, living five Days upon Berries untill he fel into the Hands of the Indians. Some were (upon Maſſaſoits Information) ſent to Noſſet to ſeek after him,[69] when they came thither the Indians flocked together, many not having ſeen Engliſhmen before: Amongſt others there was an old Woman, judged to be an hundred Years old, who when ſhe ſaw the Engliſh fel into an extream Paſſion of bitter weeping, the

the Indians, but very tedious to the Engliſhmen. He then "light-" ed tobacco for them and fell to " diſcourſing of England, and of the " King's Maieſtie, maruelling that " he would liue without a Wife." *Mourt in Purchaſe*, iv, 1852. Theſe Engliſh Meſſengers had a moſt uncomfortable Sojourn with Maſſaſoit: " For what with bad lodging, " the Sauages barbarous Singing (for " they uſe to ſing themſelves aſleepe), " Lice and Fleas within Doores, " and Muſkeetoes without, wee " could hardly ſleepe all the Time " of our being there." *Ibid.*

69 The Author as in numerous other Caſes throughout his *Relation*, does great Injuſtice to his Authorities; often rendering it difficult to ſupply his Defects in the compaſs of a Note. The Engliſh firſt hear of their loſt Boy at Cummaquid, and with ten of their Number proceed thither with their two Indian Friends, Tiſquantum and Tokamahamon. Here they learned "that " the Boy was well, but that he " was at Nauſet; yet ſince we were " there they of [Cummaquid] de-" ſired vs to come aſhore and eat " with them: which as ſoone as " our Boate floated we did: and " went ſixe aſhoare, hauing foure " Pledges for them in the Boate. " They brought vs to their Sachem " or Governour, whom they call " Iyanough, a Man not exceeding " twenty ſix Years of Age, but very " perſonable, gentle, courteous, and " faire conditioned, indeede not like " a Sauage, ſaue for his Attyre: his " Entertainment was anſwerable to " his Parts, and his Cheare plenti-" ful and various." *Purchas*, 1853. Cummaquid was at the Bottom of Barnſtable Bay, ſometimes called Cummaquid Bay.

Reſpecting *Iyanough*, Amos Otis, Eſq., the Antiquary and Hiſtorian of Barnſtable, remarks that it is his Opinion, that from Iyanough comes *Hyannis;* that Iyanough's Town was that Part of Barnſtable called Hyannis. *Hyanna* is early found on the Records. *MS. Letter*, 9 March, 1863. See APPENDIX, D.

Reaſon whereof being demanded, Anſwer was made, that ſhe had three Sons once living in that Place, but they were all ſtolen away by that *Hunt* (before mentioned) and now ſhe had no more left to releeve her in her old Age: The Engliſh were much greived to ſee the poor Creature in ſuch a Paſſion but telling her that it was only one wicked Man who did that Fact, and that they abhorred it, and withal giving her ſome Trifles ſhe was ſatisfied. In fine the Engliſh Lad was brought al bedecked with *Peag*, and the *Sachim* of that Place (called Aſpinét) made Peace with the Engliſh.[70]

Now it was that an Indian called *Coubatant*[71]

[70] " After Dinner we tooke Boate " for Nauſet [ſince Eaſtham], Iyanough and two of his Men accompanying vs. Ere we came " to Nauſet, the Day and Tide " were almoſt ſpent, in ſo much as " we could not go in with our " Shallop; but the Sachim or Governour of Cummaquid went aſhore " and his Men with him, we alſo " ſent Tiſquantum to tell Aſpinet, " the Sachem of Nauſet, wherefore " we came. After Sunſet Aſpinet " came with a great Traine, and " brought the Boy with him, one " bearing him through the Water: " he had not leſſe then an hundred " with him, the Half whereof came " to the Shallop ſide vnarmed with " him, the other ſtood aloofe with " their Bowe and Arrowes. There " he delivered vs the Boy behung " with Beades, and made Peace with " vs, we beſtowing a Knife on him, " and likewiſe on another that firſt entertained the Boy." *Purchaſe, ib.*

[71] Coubatant. Winſlow calls him *Combitant*. Purchas, iv, 1861; and Bradford *Corbitant*. The Affair about to to be related took place in Auguſt, 1621. The Machinations of Corbitant were diſcovered on the Return of the Expedition to Nauſet. Winſlow ſays, " Word was brought " unto us that Coubatant, whom " they ever feared to be too converſant with the Narrohigganſets, " was at Namaſchet, ſpeaking diſdainfully of us, ſtorming at the " Peace between Nauſet, Cummaquid and us, and at Tiſquantum, " the Worker of it; alſo at Tokamahamon and one Hobbamock, " two Indians our Allies, one of " which he would treacherouſly " have murdered a litttle before, " being a ſpecial and truſty Man of " Maſſaſoyts." *Mourt in Young*, 219.

Tiſquantum and Hobbamock were ſent to Namaſket to learn Corbitant's Intentions. Tiſquan-

(who, though a petty Sachem under Maſſaſoit, ſecretly conſpired with the Narraganſets againſt his Maſter) occaſioned ſome Diſturbance, ſeeking to deſtroy thoſe Indians that were Friends to the Engliſh, eſpecially *Hobbomock* and *Squantum*, ſaying if theſe were dead the Engliſh had loſt their Tongue, watching his Advantage at a Time when thoſe Indians were at *Namaſket*, *Coubatant* took *Squantum* Priſoner, and held a Knife at *Hobbomocks* Breaſt, who broke from him, and gave the Engliſh at *Plymouth* to underſtand what had hapned; whereupon 14.[72] Men were ſent armed to *Namaſket*, in order to revenge *Squantum's* ſuppoſed Death. They ſurprized the Houſe where *Coubatant* was thought to be, declaring the End of their coming, and that they would hurt no Man but him, charging all others not to ſtir at their Peril til they had ſearched for their Enemy; Conſternation and Trembling ſeyzed on the Indians: yet ſome of them violently brake away, whence they were wounded (and afterwards [10] healed) by the Engliſh.[73] *Coubatant* was not there, but fled to another Place, but within a while *Squantum* was brought forth alive and ſet

tum was taken Priſoner, and was ſuppoſed to be killed, for Corbitant had ſaid "if Tiſquantum was dead, "the Engliſh had loſt their Tongue." But Hobbamock made his Eſcape and arriving at Plymouth gave the Alarm.

[72] Ten Men, ſays Winſlow, under the Command of Capt. Standiſh.

[73] "As for thoſe that were wounded, we were ſorry for it, though "themſelues procured it in not ſtaying in the Houſe at our Command; yet if they would return "home with vs our Svergeons ſhould "heal them. At this Offer one "Man and a Woman that were "wounded went home with vs." *Winſlow.*

at Liberty. After this divers other *Sachims* ſent gratulations to the Engliſh; yea thoſe of the Iſles of *Capawack* entreated their Friendſhip. *Coubatant* uſed the Mediation of *Maſſaſoit* to make his Peace.

Things being brought to this peaceable State, ſo did they continue for a little Space, the *Church* in Plymouth being preſerved by a Miracle of Providence, like a Flock of Sheep amidſt a thouſand *Wolves;* much what as *Luther* ſaith the *Church* ſhould be pictured. Their next Neighbours amongſt the Heathen did (as hath been expreſſed) of Enemyes become their Friends, not ſhewing any Acts of Hoſtility.

Only in the latter End of the next Year, *Canonicus* the *Narraganſet* Sachim, ſent an Indian to them, who enquired for *Squantum,* at that Time gone ſomewhither elſe, whereupon the *Indian* left a Bundle of Arrows, wrapped in a Rattle Snakes Skin, and departed. When *Squantum* was returned, he informed the Governour that the Rattle Snakes Skin ſignfied *Enmity,* and that the Deſign of this bruitiſh Salutation was to intimate a Challenge, wherefore the Governour filled the Snakes Skin with Powder and Shot, and ſent it back again, withal giving *Canonicus* to underſtand, that if he had Shipping at hand, he would endeavour to beat him out of his Countrey.[74] The Indians durſt not let the Powder and Shot continue in their Houſes, but every one was afraid to meddle with it, and at

74 " This Meſſage was ſent by an " Indian, and delivered in ſuch Sort, " as it was no ſmall Terror to the " Savage King." *Ibid.*

laſt it came back again to Plymouth.[75] And there was an End of that Matter. Only they at *Plymouth* were by this *Bruit* awakened to impale their Town, and fortify, leſt there ſhould be an Onſet from the Enemy.[76]

In the meanwhile *Hobomock* (who reſided with the Engliſh) informed that there was Reaſon to ſuſpect that the *Maſſachuſet* Indians were Confederate with the *Narraganſets* in their bloody Deſigns; and *Squantum* in wicked Subtilty, laboured to make the *Engliſh* believe that *Maſſaſoit* was falſe to them. Capt. *Standiſh* with ten Men[77] was ſent to *Maſſachuſets*: they had no ſooner turned the Point of the Harbour[78] but there came an *Indian* running to ſome of the *Engliſh* that were from home, having his Face wounded, and the Blood freſh on the ſame (Zopirus[79]-like) calling to them to repair home, and of looking behind him, as if he had been purſued by Enemyes, ſaying that at *Namaſket* there were many of the *Narraganſets*, and *Coubi-*

[75] Canonicus "would not once "touch the Powder and Shot, or "ſuffer it to ſtay in his Houſe or "Country. Whereupon the Meſ-"ſenger refuſing it, another took it "up; and having been poſted from "Place to Place a long Time, at "length came whole back again." *Ib.*

[76] The fortifying the Town occupied all of the Month of February, 1622 "and ſome few Days; taking "in the Top of the Hill under "which our Town is ſituated." *Ib.*

[77] "With ten Men, accompanied "with Tiſquantum and Hobba-"mock." Winſlow was doubtleſs one of the Party, as he writes of the Affair in the firſt Perſon. The Time is the Beginning of April, 1622. We thus make up the Number nearly as in the Text.

[78] Called the Gurnet's Noſe, but wherefore does not appear. Perhaps from *Gurnard's* in the Iſle of Wight.

[79] Zopiro?

tant, and that *Maſſaſoit* was Confederate with them, purpoſing to aſſault the Town in the Captains Abſence, profeſſing that he had received that Wound in his Face, becauſe he had ſpoken on the Engliſh their Behalfe. [11] Whenas all this was a Piece of artificial and miſchievous Diſſimulation, whereby the Engliſh were put into a ſad Fright, and the Great Guns were diſcharged to remand the Captain back again, who immediately returned. *Hobbomock* was confident that that *Indian* diſſembled, for he was aſſured of *Maſſaſoit's* Fidelity; however that he would not engage in a Thing of that Nature, without conſulting him who was one of his *Panies's*,[80] i. e. Champions and Counſellors, and it was againſt the Indian Cuſtom for a *Sachim* to involve himſelf in War without them. Wherefore *Hobbomock* privately, upon the Governour's Advice ſent his *Squaw* to *Maſſaſoit* at *Pocanoket*, who ſeemed to be much troubled that the *Engliſh*, and he himſelf ſhould be ſo abuſed. And upon Enquiry it was found to be *Sqantum's* Knavery, who ſought his own Ends and plaid his own Game; for he would in a clandeſtine Way, make the *Indians* believe that the *Engliſh* were reſolved to cut them off, only he could prevent it, and ſo would obtain Gifts from his Countryemen to prevent their Deſtruction by the *Engliſh*, inſomuch that the blind *Salvages* began to have him in greater Veneration then their *Sachim;* taking him for their *Protector*. And he would deal with

80 "One of his chiefeſt Champions or Men of Valour." Winſlow, *ib.* The Word was extenſively uſed by the Indians.

no leſſe Falſneſs towards the *Engliſh* then towards thoſe of his own Nation.

When *Maſſaſoit* underſtood theſe Things he repaired to the *Engliſh* Plantation, endeavoring to clear his Innocency, deſiring the Governour that *Squantum*, who had thus abuſed both *Engliſh* and Indians, might be put to Death for his Treaſon. The Governour pacified him as much as he could for the preſent, and though he deſerved to dy, both in reſpect of *Engliſh* and *Indians*, yet deſired he might be ſpared, becauſe they ſhould want an Interpreter.[81]

But not long after this, *Maſſaſoit* ſent divers *Indians*, who brought to the Governour, their Sachim's own Knife (according to the *Indian* Mode) that his Enemyes Head and Hands might be cut off therewith.

At that Inſtant when the Governour was about to deliver *Squantum* into the Hands of his Executioners, a Boat was ſeen at Sea, and there being even in thoſe Days Jealouſies, that the *French* would join with the Indians to Miſchief the *Engliſh*; and ſome ſuppoſing it might be a *French* Veſſel, he told the Indians he would ſee what that was before he delivered *Squantum* up to them. So did they go away diſpleaſed.[82]

81 " For theſe and like Abuſes, " the Governour ſharply reproved " him; yet was he ſo neceſſary and " profitable an Inſtrument, as at " that Time we could not miſs " him." *Winſlow.*

82 Winſlow ſays theſe Meſſengers were " mad with Rage and departed in great Heat." Indeed it muſt be owned they had good Reaſon for their Anger. It was a Breach of good Faith his not being given up,

But this wrought well for the *Engliſh;* for it made *Squantum* be honeſt whether he would or no; inaſmuch as his own Countreymen ſought his Life; he ſaw it was his Intereſt to adhere to the *Engliſh.*

As for the Boat mentioned it proved to be one that belonged to a Ship that was fiſhing about *Monhiggen.*

Theſe [12] Things hapned in May, 1622. in which Year it was that Mr. [*Thomas*] *Weſton* (a Merchant of good Note in *London*) attempted the advancing a Plantation in this *Maſſachuſets Bay.*[83] He ſent over two Ships, and about ſixty Men to make a Beginning. The moſt of them were for the preſent refreſhed at *Plymouth,* whilſt ſome few Caſters went out to ſeek a convenient Place to ſit down in. They pitched upon a Place within *Maſſachuſets Bay,* then called by the *Indians Weſſeguſquaſet,*[84] at this Day known by the Name of *Weymouth.*

Mr. *Winſlow* (who was afterwards Governour of *Plymouth Colony*) reports that the *Weſtonians,* inſtead of proving an Help to the other *Engliſh* Colony, had like, within a few Months, to have brought Ruine, not only upon themſelves, but upon

as by the Treaty between Maſſaſſoit and the Engliſh ſhows. But it was a ſingular Caſe, and the great Neceſſity of the Engliſh muſt be their Juſtification.

83 The preciſe Time of the Arrival of Weſton's Colony is not ſtated by the early Writers. Winſlow ſays it was in the End of June or Beginning of July, 1622.

84 This Indian Name finally ſettled down into *Weſſaguſſet.* It is capable of great Variation, as will readily be perceived.

their Friends alſo: For Complaints were quickly brought to *Plymouth*, that the *Engliſh* at *Weſſeguſquaſet* did abuſe the Indians by ſtealing their Corn from them, yea and one of them was ſo brutiſh as to turn *Indian*.[85]

Others of them were of ſuch ſervile and ſlaviſh Diſpoſitions, as that they became Servants to the *Indians*, who would hire them to work with them in making Canoos, which Canoos were intended for the Surprizal of the *Engliſh* Ship, in the Day when they would execute their deſigned Maſſacre. Some of the Theeves were ſtockt and whipt, yea, one of them was at laſt put to Death to ſatiſie the *Indians*, but it was then too late.[86]

By the End of *February*, they had ſpent all their Bread and Corn, not leaving any for Seed, nor would the *Indians* be induced to lend or ſel them any, upon any Terms, hoping they would be ſtarved to Death.

Wherefore, they purpoſed to take away the *Indians* Store from them by Violence, and therefore made Preparations accordingly. Only ſome of the Company (at leaſtwiſe one of them who is yet alive)

85 "We heard many Complaints "both by the Indians and ſome "others of beſt Deſert amongſt "Maſter Weſton's Colony, how "exceedingly their Company abaſed "themſelves by vndirect Meanes, "to get Victuals from the Indians, "who dwell not far from them, "fetching them Wood and Water, "&c., and all for a meales Meate, "whereas in the meane Time they "might with Diligence haue gotten "enough to haue ſerued them three "or four Times." *Winſlow in Purchaſe*, iv, 1863. This was about the End of February, 1622-3.

86 This Execution furniſhed Butler with the Hint out of which he made his ſcurrilous Rhymes in Hudibras, too well known to be here quoted.

being more honeſtly minded then others were, adviſed *John Saunders* their Overſeer to write to *Plymouth* before they did actually attempt anything, which being done, they received Letters from the Governour there, ſignifying great Diſapprobation of their intended Proceedings; whereupon they deſiſted.

Theſe Motions muſt needs cauſe ill Blood between the Nations: ſo that the *Indians* grew very inſolent in their Carriage, and there were ſecret Conſpiracyes to cut of the *Engliſh*. And inaſmuch as they thought, that if they ſhould deſtroy the *Weſtonians*, and leave the *Plymoutheans* (who had not wronged them) alive, theſe would take an Opportunity to be revenged for thoſe: wherefore they concluded to kill all before them, as was afterwards revealed by *Maſſaſoit*, and by another Sachim
[13] called *Waſſapinawet*,[87] brother to *Obtakieſt*, the then Sachim of *Maſſachuſets*.

The *Engliſh* of *Plymouth* as yet being ignorant of the bloody Miſchief which the treacherous Hearts of the *Indians* had concluded againſt them, attended their Occaſions as formerly.

Upon a Time Capt. *Standiſh* going with ſome Men in a Shallop, to buy Corn of the *Indians* at *Noſſet*, one of them ſtole certain Trifles out of the Shallop; whereupon the Captain repaired to the *Sachim*, and told him, that if he did not immediately reſtore thoſe Things, he would revenge it

87 "Who had formerly ſmarted "for partaking with Coubitant." Winſlow, *ibid.* His Reſidence is not known.

before his Departure, and ſo took Leave for that Night.

The next Morning the *Sachim* came accompanied with his Train of *Salvages*, ſaluting the Captain in ſuch a Manner as was hugely ridiculous to the Engliſh; for he put out his Tongue that one might ſee the Root of it, and ſo licked the Captain's Hands, al his Men doing the like, and endeavouring (according to the rude Information they had received from *Squantum*) to make him a Leg, he did peform his Ceremony after ſuch an odd Manner, as the *Engliſh* were hard put to it to refrain from open Laughter.

Spectatum admiſſirifum teneatis Amici?

After theſe Complements were over, he reſtored the Things that were loſt; withal declaring, that he had much beaten the *Indian* that did *Commooten* (i. e. ſteal) the Trifles mentioned.

But not long after this, the Captain was in no ſmall hazard of his Life in another Place; for going to *Manomet* (now called *Sandwich*) and being entertained in the Houſe of *Kunacum*,[88] the *Sachim* there, the *Indians* deſigned tut off him and his Men.

There was with him at this Time a *Cape-Indian* called *Paomet*, who pretended Friendſhip to the *Engliſh*, but was ſecretly joined in the bloody Confederacy. That he might not be ſuſpected he profeſſed ſpecial Affection towards the Captain, and

88 The Author's Authorities all ſpell the Name of this Chief beginning with a C. Why he departed from them we ſee no Reaſon. Winſlow writes *Canacum* (in *Purchas*, iv, 1866.)

would, as a Gift beſtow ſome Corn upon him, and help him to carry the Corn to his Boat, and would lodge in the *Wigwam* with Capt. *Standiſh*, to manifeſt what Love and Honour he did bear towards him, having in the mean Time promiſed the Indians to kil him that Night, and when he was killed the reſt were to diſpatch his Men.

Alſo whilſt he was entertained in the *Sachims* Houſe, there came in two *Maſſachuſet Indians*, being deſperate bloody Villains. The Name of the Chief of them was *Wittawamat*, who took a Dagger from about his Neck, and preſented it to the *Sachim*, and made a Speech to him (which the Captain could not underſtand) boaſting of his own Valour, [14] and how he had been the Death of Chriſtians both *French* and *Engliſh* and what pittifull weak Creatures they were, that when they were killing, they died crying, and made ſower Faces, more like Children then Men, and that whereas they were determined to kil the *Engliſh* (who had injured them) of Mr. *Weſtons* Plantation, the beſt way for their own Security was to kill them of *Plymouth* too, now their Captain being in their Hands, having but ſix Men with him, two or three in the *Wigwam*, and no more in the Shallop, it was a good Opportunity to begin.

The murderous Counſel of this audacious Bloudſucker was highly applauded; and the *Indians* waited when Capt. *Standiſh* would fall aſleep, that they might attempt the bloudy Tragedy. But God ſo ordered that he could not ſleep that Night. Alſo an *Indian* ſecretly ſtole ſome Beads from him;

which when the Captain perceived, he immediately called his ſix Men together, and they beſet the *Sachims* Houſe profeſſing to him that as they would not doe Wrong to him, ſo neither would they receive any, and therefore, as they valued their Lives, they ſhould forthwith reſtore the ſtolen Goods. Hereupon the *Sachim* beſtirred himſelf to find out the Thief; and having done ſo, he cometh to the Captain deſiring him to look into his Boat, if the Beads that he had miſſed were not there, who looking found them lying openly on the Cuddy, the *Indians* having ſlily conveyed them thither. However, this did ſo daunt the Courage of the treacherous and cowardly *Indians*, that they attempted not their deſigned Miſchief.

All this while, they of *Plimouth* Colony had no certain knowledge of the Evil that was intended againſt them by the Heathen, albeit the Conſpiracy was very ſtrong, for the *Indians* at *Noſſet*, *Paomet*, *Saconet*, *Manomet*, *Matachieſt*, *Agawam*, were all in this Confederacy to cut off the *Engliſh*. But God who hath a ſpecial Eye of Providence over his People, did at that Time ſo order, that *Maſſaſoit* fell ſick; whereupon the Governour that then was, deſired Mr. *Winſlow* and another Gentleman to give the ſick Sachim a Viſit, and adminiſter ſome Phyſic to him. As they were upon their Journey toward *Pocanoket*, the Place of *Maſſaſoits* Reſidence, the *Indians* by the Way told that he was dead and buried; which cauſed *Hobbomock* (their Guide through the Woods) to break forth into bitter Lamentations, crying out "*Neen womaſu Sagimus!*

"O my loving Sachim, O my loving Sachim, thou "waſt no Lyar, not cruel like other *Indians*, thy "Paſſion was ſoon over, thou wouldſt hearken to "Reaſon from the meaneſt Subject, thou didſt love "*Engliſhmen*; among *Indians* I ſhall never know "the like to thee."

[15] So that it would have made the hardeſt Heart to have relented to hear him. Yet they proceeded in their Journey, being come ſo far as *Metapoiſet*, they underſtood that *Maſſaſoit* was not quite dead, but little Hopes of his Life.

When they came to *Pokanoket*, they found the *Indians Powawing* about *Maſſaſoit*, making ſuch a helliſh Noiſe as was enough to make a wel Man ſick, and was therefore very unlikely to make him that was ſick wel.[89]

Hobbomock told him that the Governour of Plymouth had ſent ſome Friends to viſit him in his Sickneſs, and that they had brought ſome *Maſkiet*, i. e. *Phyſick*, for him. Upon the receipt of which, he ſuddenly and ſtrangely revived, and before their Departure gave them great Thanks for their Love, ſaying, that now he ſaw that the *Engliſh* at *Plymouth* were his real Friends.

As they were ready to return home, he privately told *Hobbomock* of the Plot among the *Maſſachuſets*

[89] As Mr. Winſlow's Account ſuffers ſomewhat in the Text, I give it here in his own Words: "When "we came thither, we found the "Houſe ſo full of Men, as we could "ſcarce get in, though they uſed "their beſt Dilligence to make Way "for vs. There were they in the "middeſt of their Charmes for him, "making ſuch a helliſh Noiſe, as it "diſtempered vs that were well, "and therefore vnlike to eaſe him "that was ſicke." *Purchaſe*, 1861. Leſs particular in *Bradford*, 131.

and other *Indians* to deſtroy the *Engliſh*,[90] and how they had ſollicited him to join with them, but he ſaid that neither he, nor any of his Men were in that Combination. He adviſed that the Governour of *Plymouth* would, without delay, ſend and take off the *Principal Actors* in this wicked Deſigne, and then the reſt would be afraid. And whereas the Governour had ſometimes ſaid they would not begin with the *Indians*, until the *Indians* began with them, he earneſtly counſelled him not to ſtay for that leſt it ſhould be too late.[91]

The firſt Day whilſt on their Journey back again, they were accompanyed with *Coubitant* the Sachim of *Metapoyſet* (before mentioned) who was a politick and jocoſe *Indian*, and ſtil ſuſpected to be falſe to the *Engliſh*. He aſked Mr. *Winſlow*, how they, being but two, dared to truſt themſelves amongſt ſo many *Indians?* Anſwer was made that Love was without Fear, and they wiſhed wel to the *Indians*, and therefore did not fear Evil from them.

90 "At our coming away, he "called Hobbamocke to him, and "priuately (none hearing ſaue two "or three other of his Pueeſes, "who are of his Counſell) reuealed "the Plot of the Maſſacheuſeucks "before ſpoken of, againſt Maſter "Weſton's Colony, and ſo againſt "vs, ſaying that the People of Nauſet [Eaſtham], Paomet [about "Truro], Succouet [perhaps Falmouth], Mattachieſt [Barnſtable], "Manomet [Sandwich], Agowaywam [Wareham], and the Iſle of "Capawack [Martha's Vineyard]. Winſlow in *Purchas*, 1862.

91 This ſavage Advice of the Indians, was as will be ſeen, adopted, though with reluctance, well knowing it could be juſtified only upon the Grounds of Neceſſity. It is hard to ſay at this Day that the Deciſion was wrong, in View of all the Circumſtances; it was this Affair that much grieved Mr. Robinſon.

But then, ſaid the *Indian*, what is the Reaſon, that when we came to *Patuxet* you held the Mouthes of your Guns againſt us; he was told, that was the *Engliſh*, Manner of entertaining their Friends. At which the Sachim ſhaked his Head, withal declaring that he did not like ſuch Salutations.[92] The next Day *Hobbomock* acquainted the *Engliſh* with what *Maſſaſoit* had revealed to him.

So then being returned to *Plymouth* it was March 23.[93] reſolved, to hearken to *Maſſaſoits* Advice: many other Things at that Juncture appearing, which confirmed the Truth of what was by him diſcovered. [16] And conſidering that there was no dealing with Indians (as other Nations do with another) above board, it was thought moſt expedient by Policy, to catch them at unawares, as they are wont to do by others.[94] Wherefore Capt. *Standiſh* made Choice of eight Men to go with him to *Weſeguſquaſet*, pretending to Trade with

92 " By the way," ſays Winſlow, " I had much Conference with him, " ſo likewiſe at his Houſe, he being " a notable Politician, yet full of " merry Ieſts and Squibs, and neuer " better pleaſed then when the like " are returned againe upon him." *Purchas*, iv, 1862.

93 March 23d, 1622-3. " The " three and twentieth of March be- " ing now come, which is a yearly " Court Day, the Governour hauing " a double Teſtimony, and many " Circumſtances agreeing with the " Truth thereof, not being to vnder- " take Warre without the Conſent " of the Body of the Company, " made knowne the ſame in pub- " lique Court." Winſlow in *Purchas, ib.* 1863. This was probably the firſt Declaration of War by the white People in New England.

94 " Becauſe (as all Men know that " haue had to doe in that Kinde) it " is impoſſible to deale with them " vpon open Defiance, but to take " them in ſuch Traps as they lay for " others; therefore he [Capt. Standiſh] ſhould pretend Trade as at " other Times." *Ibid.*

them, and then to take his Opportunity to ſeyze upon the *Ringleaders* amongſt the Conſpirators.[95]

Being arrived at the Maſſachuſets Bay, two principal Conſpirators behaved themſelves very inſolently. One of them called *Pickſuot,* who was a *Panees* or Counſellour, jeered at Capt. Standiſh becauſe he was a Man of little Stature, and yet a Captain. Another, called *Wittawamat* (before mentioned) caſt out bloody Expreſſions, ſhewing a ſharp Knife, which had a Womans Face pictured on the Handle, ſaying that he had killed Frenchmen, and Engliſh too with that Knife, and that he had another Knife which had a Mans Face pictured on it, and his two Knives ſhould marry ſhortly, *and that by and by it ſhould eat though not ſpeak.* Likewiſe another *Indian,* and *Wittawamats* Brother,

[95] The Author here makes an important Omiſſion. Capt. Standiſh was inſtructed to repair firſt to Weſton's Men at Wiſſaguſſet, "acquaint them with the Plot, and "the End of his owne coming, that "comparing it with their [the Indians] Carriages towards them "[of Weſſaguſett] he might better "iudge of the Certainty of it, and "more fitly take Opportunity to "reuenge the ſame: but ſhould "forbare, if it were poſſible till ſuch "Time as he could make ſure of "Wituwamat, that bloudy and bold "Villain, whoſe Head he had Order to bring with him, that hee "might be a Warning and Terrour "to all of that Diſpoſition." *Ibid.* Standiſh was allowed to take as many Men as he deſired. He "made "Choice of eight, and would not "take more becauſe he would preuent Iealouſi." That is, he took a ſmall Number, that his Deſign might not be ſuſpected, "knowing "their guilty Conſciences would "ſoone be prouoked thereunto." *Ibid.*

But on the next Day, March 24th, before Standiſh began his March, "came one [Phinehas Pratt] of "Maſter Weſton's Company by "Land vnto vs, with his Packe at his "Backe, who made a pittifull Narration of their lamentable and "weake Eſtate, and of the Indians "Carriages, whoſe Boldneſſe increaſed abundantly, inſomuch as "the Victuals they got, they would "take it out of their Pots and eat "before their Faces; yea, if in any-who in Bloodinefs was like unto him, being prefent; Capt. *Standifh* fnatched *Pickuots* Knife from about his Neck, and killed him with his own Knife. At the fame Time his Men fell upon *Wittawamat* and the other *Indian*, and flew them, and took *Wittawamats* Brother, and hanged him.

After this they fet upon another Company of *Indians* and killed two or three of them, feeking ftil after more. At length they efpied a File of *Indians* making towards them, but as the *Englifh* came to the Encounter, they (i. e. the *Indians*) ran behind the Trees, and Shot at Capt. *Standifh*, until one, as he was fhooting, had his Arm broke by a bullet from one of Capt. *Standifh* his Soldiers; whereupon he and the reft fled into a *Swamp*.

" thing they gaine-faid them, they " were ready to hold a Knife at their " Breafts; but to giue them Con- " tent they had hanged one of them " that ftole their Corne, and yet " they regarded it not: that another " of their Company was turned " Sauage, that their People had moft " forfaken the Towne, and made " their Rendeuous where they got " their Victuals, becaufe they would " not take Paines to bring it home: " that they had fold their Clothes " for Corne, and were ready to " ftarue both with Cold and Hun- " ger alfo, becaufe they could not " indure to get Victuals by Reafon " of their Nakedneffe; and that " they were defperfed into three " Companies, fcarce having any " Powder and Shot left. As this " Relation was grieuous to vs, fo it " gaue vs good Encouragement to " proceede in our Intendments." *Ibid*.

On Pratt's leaving Weffaguffet an Indian was fent after him to kill him on the Way; but Pratt loft his Path, and thus the Indian miffed him This intended Murderer went to Plymouth, " pretending Friend- " fhip and in Loue to fee vs, but as " formerly others, fo his End was " to fee whether wee continued ftill " in Health and Strength, or fell " into Weakeneffe like their Neigh- " bours, but here the Gouernour " ftaid him, and fending for him to " the Fort, there gave the Guard " charge of him; fo he was locked " in a Chaine to a Staple in the " Court of Guard, and there kept " till Capt. Standifh fhould return." *Ibid*, 1864.

The Captain dared the Sachim to come out and fight like a Man, but in vain.

At the Time of thefe Skirmifhes, there was an *Indian* Youth, who notwithftanding the Slaughter made amongft his Countreymen, came running to the *Englifh*, defiring that he might be with them. He confeffed that the *Indians* had refolved to cut off Mr. *Weftons* Men, and that they only ftayed for the finifhing of two Canoos more (which if Capt. *Standifh* had not fo unexpectedly come upon them had been finifhed) that were intended for the Surprifal of the *Englifh* Ship in the Harbour.

Alfo an *Indian* Spye,[96] who was taken Prifoner and detained at *Pilmouth*, when he faw Capt. *Standifh* return with *Wittawamats* Head, looked on it with a guilty gaftred Countenance, and then confeffed the Plot that was in Hand to deftroy the *Englifh*, and that *Pickfuot* and [17] *Wittawamat*, together with three Powaws, were the principal *Confpirators*.[97] He was releafed and fent to *Oktakieft*, the Sachim of the *Maffachufets*, to fignify what he muft look for, in cafe he fhould continue in Hoftility againft the *Englifh*. The Sachim being amazed and terrified with the *Englifh* Succeffes, humbly begged for Peace, pretending that he could

96 The Prifoner mentioned in the laft Note.

97 " Now was the Captain returned and receiued with Ioy, the " Head being brought to the Fort " and there fet vp, the Gouernours " and Captaines with diuers others " went vp the fame further to examine the Prifoner, who looked pit- " tioufly on the Head; being afked " whether he knew it, he anfwered " yea. Then he confeffed the Plot, " and all the People prouoked Obta- " kieft their Sachim thereunto." Winflow in *Purchafe*, iv, 1865.

not keep his Men in Order, and that it was againſt his Will that Evil had been done to, or deſigned againſt the *Engliſh*.

Furthermore, the Effect of theſe Things was, that the reſt of theſe *Indians* were ſtriken with ſuch Terror and Dread of the *Engliſh*, that they left their Houſes and betook themſelves to live in unhealthful *Swamps*, whereby they became ſubject to miſerable Diſeaſes that proved mortal to Multitudes of them. Particularly *Kunacum*, Sachim of *Manomet*; *Aſpinet*, Sachim of *Noſſet*; *Janowgh*, Sachim of *Mattachieſt*: Theſe all ſell ſick and died.

This laſt Sachim ſaid that *The God of the Engliſh was offended at the Indians, and would deſtroy them in his Anger*.

And theſe ſignal Appearances of God for his Church in *Plymouth*, muſt needs be a great Conviction to the Heathen. Howbeit theſe Motions ended in the Subverſion and Ruine of Mr. *Weſtons* Plantation; God who determines the Bounds of Men's Habitations, having appointed that another People out of *England* ſhould come afterwards and poſſeſs that Place, as at this Day.

And thus far is Mr. *Winſlows* Relation of theſe *firſt Troubles* by *Indians* in theſe Parts, which I take to be undoubted Verity: For he was one that had particular Knowledge of thoſe Things, and a Man of Truth and Conſcience, that would not for the World willingly falſify in any Particular.

There is an old *Planter*[98] yet living in this Coun-

[98] This old Planter was Phinehas Pratt, before mentioned.

trey, being one of thoſe that were employed by Mr. *Weſton*, who alſo hath given ſome Account of theſe Matters.[99]

He doth relate and affirm, that at his firſt coming into this Countrey the *Engliſh* were in a very diſtreſſed Condition by reaſon of Famine and Sickneſs which was amongſt them, whereof many were already dead; and that they buried them in the Night that the *Indians* might not perceive how low they were brought.

This *Relator* doth moreover declare, that an *Indian Panies*, who ſecretly purpoſed bloody Deſtruction againſt the *Engliſh* and made it his Deſign to learn the *Engliſh* Tongue to the End he might more readily accompliſh his helliſh Devices;[100] told him that there had been a *French* Veſſel caſt away upon theſe Coaſts, only they ſaved their Lives and their Goods, and that the *Indians* took their Goods from them, and made the *French men* their Servants, and that they wept very much, when [18] the *Indians* parted them from one another, that they made them eat ſuch Meat as they gave their Dogs. Only one of them having a good Maſter, he provided a Wife for him, by whom he had a Son, and

[99] The exceedingly crude Narrative of Pratt is ſtill in Exiſtence, but in a very imperfect and damaged State. It is in the Hands of David Pulſifer, Eſq., the well known Editor of the Colonial Records of Maſſachuſetts and Plymouth—probably the ſame uſed by Mr. Mather. There is another Paper extant by Pratt, called a *Petition*, in Poſſeſſion of the Editor. Theſe Mr. Richard Frothingham edited and they were printed in the 4th Volume of the 4th Series of *Cols. Maſs. Hiſtorical Society*.

[100] Pratt gives his Name as *Pexſouth*, and Winſlow Peckſuot. The ſame killed by Standiſh as juſt related.

lived longer then the reſt of the *French men* did; and that one of them was wont to read much in a Book (ſome ſay it was the New Teſtament) and that the *Indians* enquiring of him what his Book ſaid, he told them it did intimate, that there was a People like French men that would come into the Countrey and drive out the *Indians*, and that they were now afraid that the *Engliſh* were the People of whoſe coming the *French* man had foretold them.[101] And that another Ship from *France* came into the *Maſſachuſets Bay* with Goods to Truck, and that *Indian Panies* propounded to the Sachim, that if he would hearken to him, they would obtain all the *French mens* Goods for nothing; namely, by coming a Multitude of them aboard the Veſſel, with great Store of Beaver, making as if they would Truck, and that they ſhould come without Bows and Arrows, only ſhould have Knives hid in the Flappets which the Indians wear about their Loins; and when he ſhould give the *Watchword*, they

101 The following is Pratt's Account of Pekſuot's Narrative: "He " imployed himſelf to learn to ſpeak " Engliſh, obſerving all Things for " his bloody Ends. He told me he " loued Engliſhmen very well, but " he loued me beſt of all. You ſay " French men doe not loue you, " but I will tell you what wee haue " done to them. There was a Ship " broken by a Storm. They ſaued " moſt of their Goods and hid it in " the Ground. We maed them tell " vs whear it was. Then we made " them our Sarvants. Thay weept " much. When we parted them we " gave them ſuch Meat as our Dogs " eate. One of them had a Booke " he would often read in. We " aſked him what his Booke ſaid. " He anſwered it ſaith there will a " People like French-men come " into this Cuntry and drive you all " a way, and now we thincke you " are thay. We took away their " Clothes. They liued but little " while. One of them liued longer " than the reſt, for he had a good " Maſter and gave him a Wiff. " He is now dead but hath a Sonn " aliue."

ſhould run their Knives into the *French mens* Bellyes, which was accordingly executed by the *Indians*, and all the *French men* killed, only Monſier *Finch* the Maſter of the Veſſel being wounded, ran down into the Hold, whereupon they promiſed him that if he would come up, they would not kill him; notwithſtanding which, they brake their Word and murdered him alſo; and at laſt ſet the Ship on Fire.[102]

Some enquiring of him how long it was ſince the *Indians* firſt ſaw a Ship, he replied that he could not tel, but ſome old *Indians* reported that the firſt Ship ſeemed to them to be a floating Iſland, wrapped together with the Roots of Trees, and broken off from the Land, which with their *Canoos* they went to ſee, but when they found Men there and heard Gunns, they haſted to the Shore again, not a little amazed. (Some write that they ſhot Arrows at the firſt Ship they ſaw thinking to kill it.)

This Relator doth alſo affirm, that after Jealouſies began between the Engliſh of Mr. *Weſtons*

102 Peckſuot's Account as detailed by him to Pratt is thus: "An other "Ship came into the Bay with much "Goods to Trucke. Then I ſaid "to the Sacham, I will tell you how "you ſhall haue all for nothing. "Bring all our Canows and all our "Beauer and a great many Men, "but no Bow nor Arrow, Clubs, "nor Hatchits, but Knives vnder "the Scins [Skins] about your Lines "[Loins]. Throw vp much Beauer "vpon thayr Deck. Sell it very "cheep, and when I giue the Word, "thruſt your Knives in the French "mens Bellys. Thus we killed them "all. But Mounſear Finch, Maſter "of thayr Ship, being wounded, "leped into the Hold. Wo bid "him come vp, but he would not. "Then we cut their Cable and the "Ship went Aſhore and lay vpon "her Sid and ſlept there. Finch "came vp and we killed him. "Then our Sachem devided thayr "Goods and fiered theyr Ship and "it maed a very great fier."

Plantation and the *Indians*, they built divers of their *Wigwams* at the End of a great Swamp, near to the *Engliſh*, that they might the more ſuddenly and effectually doe what was ſecretly contrived in their Hearts: and an *Indian* Squaw ſaid to them, that ere long *Aberkieſt* would bring many *Indians* that would kill all the Engliſh there and at *Patuxet*. After which the Sachim with a Company of his Men came armed towards them, and bringing them within the Pale of the *Engliſh* Plantation, he made a Speech to the *Engliſh* with [19] great Gravity, ſaying, " When you firſt came into this " Land, I was your Friend. We gave Gifts to one " another. I let you have Land as much as we " agreed for, and now I would know of you, if I " or my Men have done you any Wrong." Unto whom the *Engliſh* replied, that they deſired, that he would firſt declare whether they had injured him.[103]

[103] The ſame as told by Pratt: " Som tim after this thayr Sachem " cam ſudingly upon us with a great " Number of armed Men; but " thayr Spys ſeeing us in a redineſs, " he and ſome of his chif Men " terned into one of thayr Howſes " a Quarter of an Our. Then we " met them without the Pale of our " Plantation and brought them in. " Then ſaid I to a young Man that " could beſt ſpeke thayr Langwig, " Aſke Pexworth whi they come " thus armed? He anſwered, our " Sacham is angry with you. I ſaid, " Tell him if he be angry with us, " wee be angry with him. Then " ſaid thayr Sachem, Engliſhmen, " when you com into the Country, " we gaue you Gifts and you gaue " vs Gifts, we bought and ſold with " you and we weare Friends; and " now tell me if I or any of my " Men haue don you Rong. We " anſwered, Firſt tell us if we haue " don you any Rong. He anſwer- " ed, Some of you Steele our Corne " and I have ſent you Word " Times without Number and yet " our Corne is ſtole. I come to " ſee what you will doe. We an- " ſwered, It is one Man wich hath " don it. Your Men have ſeen vs " whip him divers Times, beſides

The Sachem roundly rejoined, that either ſome or all of them had been abuſive to him; for they had ſtolen away his Corn, and though he had given them Notice of it Times without Number, yet there was no Satisfaction nor Reformation attained.

Hereupon the *Engliſh* took the principal *Thief* and bound him and delivered him to the Sachim, withall declaring, that he might do with him what he pleaſed. Nay (ſaid he) Sachim do Juſtice themſelves upon their own Men, and let their Neighbours do Juſtice upon theirs; otherwiſe we conclude that they are all agreed, and then fight.

Now the Indians, ſome of them, began to tremble, and beholding the Guns which were mounted on the *Engliſh* Fort, they ſaid one to another (in their Language) that little Guns would ſhoot through Houſes, and great Guns would break down Trees, and make them fall and kill *Indians* round about. So did they depart at that Time diſſatisfied and enraged.[104]

" other Manor of Puniſhments, and " now, here he is, bound. We " give him vnto you to doe with him " what you pleaſe. He anſwered, " That is not juſt Dealeing. If my " Men wrong my nabur Sacham, " or his Men, he ſends me Word, " and I beat or kill my Men ac- " cording to the Ofence. All Sa- " chams do Juſtis by thayr own Men. " If not we ſay they ar all agreed, " and then we fite; and now, I ſay, " you all ſteele my Corne."

[104] Pratt's Account: " At this " Time ſom of them ſeeing ſom of " our Men upon our Forte, begun " to ſtart, ſaying, Machit Peſconk, " that is nawty Guns. Then look- " ing round about them, went away " in a great Rage. At this Time " we ſtrenthened our Wach untell " we had no Food left. In thes " Times the Salvages oftentime did " crep upon the Snow, ſtarting " behind Bouſhes and Trees to ſee " whether we kepe Wach or not. " [Many] Times I have rounded " [gone the Rounds] our Planta- " tion, untell I had no longer

The *Engliſh* now perceiving that the *Indians* were fully purpoſed to be revenged on them, they reſolved to fight it out to the laſt Man.

As they were marching out of the Fort, ſeven or eight Men ſtood ſtill, ſaying this is the ſecond Time that the Salvages had demanded the Life of him that had wronged them, and therefore they would have him firſt put to Death, and if that would not ſatisfy, then to fight it out to the laſt, wherefore he was put to Death in the Sight of the Heathen; after which the Engliſh marched out towards them, but they diſperſed themſelves into the Woods.[105]

This *Relator* endeavored to give Notice to them in Plymouth, how that the Indians had contrived their Ruin, but he miſſed his Way between *Weymouth* and *Plymouth;* and it was wel he did ſo; for by that Means he eſcaped the ſavage Hands of thoſe *Indians*, who immediately purſued him, with a murderous Intention ere he could reach *Plymouth*, they were informed by *Maſſaſoit* (as hath

" [Stre]nth. Then in the Night, " goeing into our Corte of Gard, I " ſee one Man ded before me, an- " other at my writ Hand, and an- " other att my left, for Want of " Food. O, all the People in New " England that ſhall heare ot theſe " Times of our week Beginning, " conſider what was the Strenth " of the Arm of Fleſh or the Witt " of Man."

105 Pratt's Account: " The Of- " ender being bound, we lett him " louſe, becauſe we had no Food " to giue him, charging him to " gather Ground-nitts, Clams, and " Muſells, as other Men did, and " ſteel no more. One or two Days " after this the Salvages brot him, " leading him by the Armes, ſay- " ing, Heare is the Corne. Com " ſee the Plaſe where he ſtole it. " Then we kep him bound ſom few " Days."

been declared) concerning what was plotted amongſt the *Indians*.[106]

Finally there were (as this *Relator* teſtifieth) three ſeveral Skirmiſhes with the *Indians*. One at *Weſe-*

[106] The Eſcape of Phinehas Pratt, although before mentioned, is one of thoſe perilous Adventures calculated to excite in all Readers in all Times a Deſire to know every Particular concerning it. Our Author altogether failed to give it in a Manner which its Intereſt deſerves. I therefore give it in Pratt's own Words: The Men of Weſſaguſſet having diſcovered that the Deſign of the ſurrounding Indians was to deſtroy all the Engliſh, beginning with them firſt, " I would have ſent a " Man to Plimoth, but non weare " willing to goe. Then I ſaid if " Plimoth Men know not of this " treacherous Plot, they and we are " all ded Men. Therefore, if God " willing, tomorrow I will goe. " That Night a yong Man, want- " ing Witt, towld Pexworth yearly " in the Morning. Pexworth came " to me and ſaid in Eingliſh, Me " heare you go to Patuxit. You " will looſe your ſelf. The Bears " and the Wolfs will eate you. But " becauſe I love you I will ſend my " Boy Nahamit with you, and I " will give you Vicktualls to eat by " the Way, and to be mery with " your Friends when you come " there. I ſaid, Who towld you " ſoe great a lye that I may kill him? " He ſaid it is noe lye. You ſhall " not know. Then he went whom " to his Howſe. Then came fiue " Men, armed. We ſaid, Why " come you thus armed? They " ſaid, We are Friends. You cary " Guns wheare we dwell, and we " cary Bowe and Arows wheare " you dwell. Thes attended me " ſeven or eight Days and Nights. " Then thay ſupoſeing it was a lye, " weare carlis of thayr Wach near " two [h]ours on the Morning. " Then ſaid I to our Company, " Now is the Time to run to Pli- " moth, Is ther any Compas to be " found? Thay ſaid, None but " them that belong to the Ship. I " ſaid, Thay are to bigg. I have " borne no Armes of Defence this " ſeven or eight Days. Now if I " take my Armes they will miſtruſt " me. Then they ſaid, The Salvages " will pſhue after you and kill you, " and we ſhall never ſee you agayne. " Thus with other Words of great " Lamentation we parted. Then " I took a How and went to the " Long Swamp neare by thayr " Howſes, and diged on the Ege " thereof, as if I had bin looking " for ground Nutts. But ſeeing no " Man, I went in and run through it. " Then looking round about me, I " run ſouthward tell three of the " Clock; but the Snow being in " many Places, I was the more diſ- " treſſed, becauſe of my Foot ſteps. " The Sonn being beclouded, I " wandered not knowing my Way; " but att the goeing down of the " Sonn, it apeared red. Then

gusquaset, before mentioned; another at a Place where the Town of *Dorchester* is since planted; and lastly at the Bay of *Agawam* or *Ipswich;* in all which Engagements the *Indians* [20] were notably beaten, and the *English* received no considerable

" hearing a great Howling of Wolfs, " I came to a River; the Water " being depe and cold, and many " Rocks, I passed through with " much adoe. Then was I in great " Distress. Faint for want of Food, " weary with running, fearing to " make a Fier because of them that " pshued me. Then I came to a " depe Dell or Hole, ther being " much wood falen into it. Then " I said in my thoughts, This is " God's Providence, that heare I " may make a Fier. Then haveing " maed a Fier, the Stars began to " a pear, and I saw Ursa Magor " and the [north] Pole. The Day " I began to trafell . . . but being " unable, I went back to the Fier. " The Day fall[owing I set out again, " the] Sonn shined, and about three " of the Clock I came to that Part " of Plimoth Bay, wher ther is a " Town of later Time [called] " Duxbery. Then passing by the " Water on my left Hand, cam to " a Brook, and ther was a Path. " Having but a short Time to con- " sider, [went on] fearing to goe " beyond the Plantation, I kept " running in the Path. Then pass- " ing through James Ryuer, I said " in my Thoughts, Now am I as a " Deare chased [by] the Wolfs. If " I perish, what will be the Con- " disch[on] of distresed English men! " then finding a Peec of a [ ] I " took it up and caried it in my " Hand. Then finding a [Peec] " of a Jurkin I caried them under " my Arme. Then said I in my " [Thoughts] God hath giuen me " these two Tokens for my Com- " fort; that now he will giue me " my Live for a Pray. Then run- " ning down a Hill I [saw] an " English man coming in the Path " before me. Then I sat down on " a Tree, and rising up to Salute " him, said, Mr. Hamdin, I am " glad to see you aliue. He said, " I am glad and full of Wonder to " see you aliue. Let us sitt downe. " I see you are weary. I said, Let " [me] eate som parched Corne. " Then he said, I know the Cause " [of your] coming. Massasoit hath " sent Word to the Gouernor to let " him [know] that Aberdikees " [Aberkiest] and his Confederates " haue contrived a Plot hoping to " [cut off] all English People in " one Day." [*Owing to Mutilations nothing can be made of a few Lines which follow.*]

The News which Pratt brought to Plymouth fully confirmed the People there, that what Massasoit had communicated was true, and hence the immediate Action of Standish already related.

Damage; ſo that the Sachims entreated for Peace; nor were the *Engliſh* (provided it might be upon Terms ſafe and honorable) averſe thereunto, *Pacem te poſeimus omnes.*

Theſe dark Clouds being thus comfortably diſpelled and blown over, the firſt Planters in this Country received no conſiderable Diſturbance from the *Indians* a long Time. It is true, that ſoon upon theſe Motions (viz. in Auguſt, Anno 1623), a Gentleman arrived here out of *England* (namely, Capt. *Robert Gorges*) being attended with many Servants, as purpoſing the Settlement of an *Engliſh* Plantation in this Bay of *Maſſachuſets*, and although that Plantation was quickly deſerted and diſſolved, other Things, and not any Anoyance from the Natives here cauſed thoſe Deſigns to prove abortive.[107]

The like is to be affirmed concerning Mr. *Wollaſtons* Plantation: For whereas he with ſeveral others, being Perſons of Quality, did (in the Year 1625) with a Multitude of Servants come into this *Maſſachuſetts Bay*, as intending to ſettle a Plantation therein, they met with ſuch croſs Providences as did diſcourage them, and at laſt diſſipate them; yet nothing from the *Indians.*[108]

107 Pratt thus ſpeaks of Gorges' Colony: "Thus [our] Plantation "being deſerted, Capt. Robert Gore "[Gorges] cam [into] the Country "with ſix Gentlemen atending him, "and diuers Men to doe his Labor, "and other Men with thayer Fa- "milys. They took Poſſeſſion of "our Plantation, but thayr Ship "ſuply from Eingland came to late. "Thus was Famine thayr final over- "throw. Moſt of them that liued "returned for England."

108 Of the next Colony Pratt thus remarks: "The Oforſeers of the "third Plantation in the Bay was "Capt. Wooliſton and Mr. Roſdell. "Thes ſeeing the Ruing of the "former Plantation, ſaid, We will

I have been informed, that this Gentleman, confidering the unhappy Cataftrophe's attending Mr. *Wefton* and Mr. *Gorges*, their Plantings at *Wefegufquafet*, conceited that the *Indian* Powas had brought that Place under fome Fafcination, and that *Englifhmen* would never thrive upon *Enchanted Ground*, and therefore they would pitch down their Stakes in a Place nearer to Bofton; even where the Town of *Brantree* has fince flourifhed, but the Difficultyes of a Wildernefs were too hard for them, that Mr. *Wollafton* removed a great Part of his Servants to *Virginia*, not having (fo far as I can underftand) received any Moleftation from the *Indians* here.[109]

In Anno 1628. Mr. *Endecot* (who deferves to be honorably mentioned, as having been a Patriot in *New England*) arrived here with a *Patent*[110] for the Government of the *Maffachufets*.[111] He and others

" not pich our Tents heare, leaft " we fhould doe as thay have done. " Notwithftanding thefe Gentlemen " wear wifs Men, they feemed to " blame the Oforfeers of the formur " Companies, not confidering that " God plants and pull vp, bilds and " pull down, and terns the Wifdom " of wifs Men into Foolifhnefs. " Thefe caled the Name of thayr " Place Mount-woolifton. They " continued neare a Yeare as others " had don before them; but Famin " was thayr final aforthrow."

109 Nothing appears to be known of Capt. Wollallafton, or Wallafton further than is contained in this Paragraph. We have not even his Chriftian Name. And Mr. Adams remarks (in his Braintree Addrefs of 20 July, 1858) rather facetioufly: " What became of him nobody " knows; I am fure we do not care " to know." This the Editor is far from endorfing. The Place where he fettled was named Mount Wollafton. It was three Miles north of Weffaguffet. Wood, *N. Eng. Profpect*, 31, ed. 4°, 1635.

110 The Author fhould have faid *Commiffion*. The Patent remained with the Company in England.

111 And yet, with aftonifhing Perverfity it has been afferted that Endicott was not a Governour at this Time!—that he was nothing but a Captain! Serious Argument againft

with him ſat down at a Place called *Nahumkeik* (as in a Parentheſis let me here obſerve, that that *Indian* word is alſo *Hebrew* נחום *Nahum* ſignifieth *Conſolation*, and חיק *Keik* is *Hebrew*, for *Booſome*, or *Haven*, and it ſo fals out, that the *Engliſh* have hapned to call that Place by another Name which is alſo *Hebrew*, viz. *Salem*). There did they enjoy Peace. Howbeit there are Antient Planters, who teſtifie that the *Indians* being poſſeſſed with ſome Fears leſt the *Engliſh* ſhould in Time take their Countrey [21] from them, were conſpiring to de-ſtroy them. And the ſmall Handfull of Chriſtians then in *Salem*, were alarmed with the Report of no leſs than a thouſand barbarous Natives, coming to cut them off; and that upon a Lord's Day, whereupon they diſcharged ſeveral great Guns, the ſmall Shot wherein made ſuch a terrible Rattling among the Trees a far off, that the amazed *Indians* returned not a little affrighted.[112] And it was a wonderfull Providence of God, now to reſtrain the Heathen, ſince it ſo hapned, that about this Time there were ſome Tumults about the *Engliſh* them-ſelves.[113] For whereas Mr. *Wollaſton* and his Part-ners left ſome of their Servants here, and gave

ſuch abſurd Nonſenſe will hardly be expected. See *N. Eng. Hiſt.-Gen. Reg.* for Oct., 1853, and Jan. 1854. Or *Review* of Savage's *Winthrop's Journal*, 18-22.

112 This Affair happened in April and May, 1630. The Author no Doubt had his Information reſpect-ing it from ſome of the early Settlers, as it differs from the earlier writ-ten Accounts; perhaps from Roger Conant, as he was living when the Author wrote. See Dr. Felt's *Annals of Salem*, i, 154.

113 The Author has Reference, very probably, to the Troubles between Gov. Endicott and the Browns. See *Annals Salem*, i, 87, 136, &c. *Hiſtory and Antiquities of Boſton*, Pages 65, 73.

Order that a Man whoſe Name was *Filcher*, ſhould command and overſee them. There was another, whoſe Name was *Thomas Morton*. He would needs take upon him to be *Lord of Miſ-rule;* and having gained much by trading with the *Indians*, this *Morton* and his drunken Companions quickly waſted all in riotous Living.[114]

This was the Man that taught the *Indians* in theſe Parts *the Uſe of Gunns;* how they ſhould charge and diſcharge them, and imployed them in hunting for him: and when they were inſtructed in the Uſe of theſe Inſtruments of Death, they would purchaſe them at any Rates; whereby the Safety of the *Engliſh* was not a little hazzarded.

In Concluſion, the Engliſh at *Plymouth* and *Salem*, agreed to ſeyze upon this *Morton*, which was

[114] The Story of Thos. Morton and his *Merry-Mount* Companions has been too often told to be introduced here. Morton was a remarkable Character, poſſeſſed of Learning, and perhaps was about half as a bad a Fellow—which would leave him quite bad enough —as the People of Plymouth and Salem report him to be. He was a Churchman, and ſeemed determined "to have a good Time "generally," in ſpite of his auſtere Neighbours. It does not appear that he went out of his Way to annoy them, or that he interfered with them in any Way, unleſs indirectly by furniſhing the Indians with Firearms. He publiſhed a curious Book about New England, which is indeed a Curioſity among the curious Things of that Day. One not knowing quite as much as its Author about the Country then, would underſtand but little of his Meaning, he employs ſo many Enigmas and ſingular Alluſions. He entitled it *New Engliſh Canaan*, and it was printed in 1637, in 4to, in London. Some Copies have a Title purporting it to have been iſſued at Amſterdam the ſame Year. It is not probable there were two Editions at that Period. It is reprinted in Force's *Tracts*. The Original is of great Rarity. For many Years but one Copy was known in New England, and that belonged to John Quincy Adams. To that Gentleman I was indebted for an early Uſe of his Copy. Many other Copies are now in this Country.

done *vi et armis*, and he was ſent over to *England*, there to receive ſuch Puniſhment as by the *Honourable Council* for *New England* ſhould be thought meet.[115]

All theſe Tumults notwithſtanding, the overruling Providence of God kept the Indians quiet.

It is to be wondered at, that the Church in *Plymouth* ſhould be preſerved when other Engliſh Plantations could not ſubſiſt in this Countrey; but either the *Indians*, or the Lords own Hand brought them to a ſudden End from time to time. But God, who ſaw that they deſigned ſomething better than the World in their planting here, brought it to paſs by ſuch Wayes as theſe:

I. *Maſſaſoit* (as was hinted before) was perſwaded by *Squantums* Information, that if the *Engliſh* ſhould be his Friends, he need not fear any Enemies in the World: ſo did he become a Wall to the *Engliſh* at *Plymouth* againſt other *Indians*. The Earth helped the Woman that was fled into the Wilderneſs, whom the Dragon would have ſwallowed up.

2. The Lord made them very ſuccesfull in their Expeditions againſt thoſe Enemies that firſt ſought their Deſtruction.[116]

[115] He returned however, ſoon after, no Notice having been taken of the Complaints againſt him, but his Days for troubling the Puritans were pretty nearly ended. Although he went to his former Place of Reſidence at the Mount, his Maypole was cut down and deſtroyed, and there were not enough of his Followers left to get up a Dance about it if it had been ſtanding.

[116] Reference is here made to Standiſh's ſummary Campaign againſt the Maſſachuſetts with eight Men, already detailed.

[22] 3. They prevailed with God by Faſting and Prayer to look upon them and bleſs them with ſpecial Mercy when it was a Time of need, which did greatly affect and aſtoniſh the *Indians*. Some of them, therefore, conceiving high Thoughts concerning the *Engliſh-mans* God, and his Love to his People, that truly fear and ſerve him. That which Mr. *Winſlow* (and ſince him another) doth publickly teſtifie concerning this Matter, deſerveth Commemoration, namely, that whereas after the *Firſt Indian Troubles* were over, there was a ſore Drought on the Land continuing for the ſpace of ſix Weeks; inſomuch that it was judged by ſome that the Corn was withered and dead, paſt recovery, the Church in *Plymouth* ſet themſelves by Faſting and Prayer, to ſeek Mercy from the Lord in this Thing. And though in the Morning when they aſſembled themſelves, the Heavens were clear, and the Drought as likely to continue as ever, yet before their ſolemn ſervice was ended, the Heavens grew black with Clouds, and the next Morning theſe Clouds diſtilled Rain, and for the Space of fourteen Days together there were moderate Showers; ſo that the drooping Corn was revived to Admiration.[117]

A friendly *Indian* before mentioned, known by the Name of *Hobbomock*, living in the Town of *Plymouth*, enquired why the *Engliſh* met together in that Manner, it being but three Days after the

117 Beſides the Account in Winſlow's *Relation*, of this ſevere Drouth, other Particulars may be found in Smith's *New England Trials*, and Morton's *Memorial*. Drouths have not been uncommon in all Times.

Sabbath; and being informed of the true Caufe thereof, and obferving the gracious Effects that followed, he was greatly affected, and told other *Indians* of it, who were alfo fmitten with deep Conviction, and the more in that, albeit in Times of Drought the *Indians* are wont to *Powaw* and cry to their Gods, fometimes for many Dayes together; yet if Rain follow, it is wont to be accompanied with terrible Thundering and Lightning and Tempefts, which often do more hurt than the Rain doth good; whenas it was otherwife with refpect to the Showers which at this Time came from Heaven, in Anfwer to the Prayers of the Church in *Plymouth*.[118] fo that the Heathen confeffed that the *Englifh mans* God was better than theirs. And fome amongft the *Indians* became faithfull to the *Englifh*, though as yet but very few.

Apparent rari Nantes in Gurgite vafto.[119]

There having been (as was faid) a Patent for the *Maffachufets* Government by royal Grant obtained, many out of *England* flocked into this Country almoft every Year. And for the moft Part, not fo much on the Account of Trade, or to profecute any worldly Intereft, as on the Account of Religion. Thefe did God own, having wonderfully made Way for their Planting here by cafting out

[118] This ingenious Turn of the Author has doubtlefs caufed many a Smile upon the intelligent Reader's Face, and will without doubt caufe many more upon the Faces of others. Whatever Affinity or Similitude powwowing had to Thunder and Lightning, it is rather ridiculous to fuppofe, that it caufed them.

[119] This is from Virgil, but its Appofitenefs is not very apparent.

the Heathen before them, [23] with mortal Diſeaſes; eſpecially by the *Plague* amongſt the *Indians* in *Plymouth* Colony, and the *Small-pox* among the *Maſſachuſets.*[120]

In Anno 1631. new Jealouſies aroſe concerning the treacherous *Indians.* Capt. *Walker* one Evening had two Arrows ſhot through his Coat, which cauſed an Alarm at *Lyn,* then known by the Name of *Sawguſt:* but no Lives were loſt; nor is there any Certainty to this Day who ſhot thoſe Arrows, whereby the Captains Life was ſo eminently endangered.[121]

About the ſame Time the *Indians* began to be quarrelſome touching the Bounds of the Land which they had ſold to the *Engliſh;* but God ended the Controverſy by ſending the Small-pox amongſt the *Indians* at *Sauguſt,* who were before that Time

120 The Ravages of the Small-pox are pretty minutely deſcribed in Winthrop's *Journal, The Book of the Indians,* and Johnſon's *Wonderworking Providence.* The latter ſays: "The Mortality among them "was very great, inſomuch that the "poor Creatures, being very timor-"ous of Death, would faine have "fled from it, but could not tell "how, unleſſe they could haue gone "from themſelves. Relations were "little regarded among them at this "Time, ſo that many who were "ſmetten with the Diſeaſe died "helpleſſe, unleſſe they were neare "and known to the Engliſh. Their "Powwowes, Wizards, and Charm-"ers were poſſeſt with the greateſt "Feare of any." *Page* 51.

121 "Once, about Midnight, Enſign Richard Walker, who was on "the Guard, heard the Buſhes break "near him, and felt an Arrow paſs "through his Coate and buff Waiſt-"coat. As the Night was dark, "he could ſee no one, but he diſ-"charged his Gun, which being "heavily loaded, ſplit in Pieces. "He then called the Guard, and "returned to the Place, when he "had another Arrow ſhot through "his Clothes." Lewis's *Hiſt. Lynn,* p. 76. See alſo Johnſon, p. 50.

exceeding numerous.[122] Whole Towns of them were ſwept away, in ſome of them not ſo much as one Soul eſcaping the Deſtruction. There are ſome old Planters ſurviving to this Day, who helped to bury the dead *Indians*, even whole Familyes of them all dead at once. In one of the *Wigwams* they found a poor Infant ſucking at the Breaſt of the dead Mother; all the other *Indians* being dead alſo.[123]

Not long after this, when the Town of *Ipſwich* was firſt planted it was vehemently ſuſpected that the *Tarratines* (or Eaſtern *Indians*) had a Deſign to cut off the *Engliſh* there. For a friendly *Indian* called *Robin* came to an *Engliſhman* whoſe Name is *Perkens*[124] acquainting him that ſuch a Thurſday there would come four Indians to draw him to the Water ſide under Pretence of trucking with him, and that they had prepared forty *Canooes* which ſhould ly out of Sight under the Brow of an Hill, full of armed Indians to cut off the Engliſh. The four Indians came at the Time, and to the Perſon mentioned. He inſtead of going to the Water ſide to truck with them, ſpoke roughly to them, and cauſed an Alarm, ſo they immediately returned, perceiving their Plot was diſcovered, and preſently

[122] Lewis ſays the Engliſh bought the Town of the Indians, for which they paid them £16:10*s*, and lived harmoniouſly with them. *Hiſt. Lynn*, 76. This was before the Purchaſe was made. They took Land where they pleaſed and the Indians made no Objecton. It is evident from various Sources, that the Indians had but vague Notions of ſelling Land.

[123] This painful Part of his Notice of the Small-pox, the Author probably took from Johnſon. See *Wond. Providence*, 52.

[124] Sergeant John Perkins.

fourty ſuch Canooes as the friendly Indian had given Warning of, were diſcovered.[125]

Beſides the Particulars which have been inſiſted on, I cannot underſtand that there was any general Diſquietment raiſed by the Indians, untill the Year 1636. It is true that ſome particular Miſchiefs and private Murthers were committed before that, after the forementioned Troubles were allayed. For Mr. *Weſton*, who himſelf (under another Name and the Diſguiſe of a Black-Smith) arrived here not long after his Plantation was ruined, ſuffering Ship wrack near *Paſcataqua* hardly eſcaped with his Life, in reſpect of the Indians, who took his Goods from him, and ſtripped him of his very Cloathes to the Shirt on his Back.[126]

[24] About eleven Years after that, Capt. *Stone*, Capt. *Norton*, with all their Ships Company, were

[125] A Narrative of this Affair was drawn up by the Rev. Thomas Cobbett of Ipſwich and ſent to our Author. I made a Copy of the original Paper and printed it in the *N. Eng. Hiſt.-Gen. Reg.*, vii, 211-12. See alſo *Hiſt. and Antqs. Boſton*, 198.

[126] The Trials and Misfortunes of Capt. Thomas Weſton are minutely dwelt upon by Gov. Bradford in his *Hiſtory of Plymouth Colony*. He was a Man of conſiderable Credit and in good Standing when he undertook to make a Plantation in New England, but Fortune was againſt him. One Diſaſter after another overtook him, until at laſt he was ſhipwrecked and fell into the Hands of the Indians. This was in 1623. By what Means he eſcaped out of the Hands of the Barbarbarians is not mentioned. It is probable that when they had ſtripped him of everything they ſuffered him to eſcape, and he found his Way to the Engliſh at Paſcataqua. There he borrowed a Suit of Clothes and found Means to get to Plymouth. " A ſtrange Alteration there was in him," ſays Bradford, " to ſuch as had " known him in his former flouriſh- " ing Condition." P. 133. The ſame Author tells us that from Plymouth he " ſhaped his Courſe for " Virginia," and that " he dyed at " Briſtoll in the Time of the Warrs, " of Sickneſs." P. 154. We have yet no Weſton Family Hiſtory.

barbaroufly murdered by the *Pequot* Indians (as in the Sequel more fully related.)

And two Years after that, Mr. John *Oldham* was maſſacred by the Indians of *Muniſſes*, now called *Block-Iſland;* which Things made Way for the *Pequot War*, whereby the whole Engliſh Intereſt (yea the Intereſt of Chriſt, who had ere that taken Poſſeſſion of this Land, and glorioufly began to erect his own Kingdom here) was threatened and endangered.

Great Pitty it is, that although it be now fourty Years ſince thoſe Motions, and albeit the Works which God then wrought for his People were admirable, yet that no *Compleat Memorial* thereof hath been publiſhed to this Day.[127] It is then high Time that ſomething more ſhould be done therein, that ſo both we and our Children after us, may ſee what great Things, the Lord God of our Fathers hath done for them and for us.

And there is a Gentleman in this Countrey (namely Mr. *John Allyn*, who is *Secretary* to the *Council* at *Hartford*, and one of the worthy Magiſtrates of that Colony) who hath been induſtrious in gathering up the Truth of Things, about thoſe Troubles, being under peculiar Advantages thereunto, by Informations from him, who was principally inſtrumental in fighting the Lords Battels at that Time againſt the Heathen.

[127] The Author does not appear to have known anything of the Publications of Underhill and Vincent; both were printed in London in 1638. When the Text was written Mr. Hubbard's Hiſtory, including a very good Account of the Pequot War, was alſo publiſhed.

This *Narrative* of Mr. *Allyns* I ſhall here inſert and publiſh, as I received it, without making the leaſt Alterations as to the Sence, and very little as to the Words. It is that which followeth.[128]

Some Grounds of the War againſt the Pequots.

'In or about the Year 1633.[129] One Capt. *Stone* ' arrived in the *Maſſachuſetts*, in a Ship from Vir- ' ginia, who ſometime after was bound for Virginia ' again, in a ſmall Bark, with one Capt. *Norton*,[130] ' who ſailing up Connecticut River, about two ' Leagues from the Entrance, caſt Anchor; there ' coming to them ſeveral Indians belonging to that ' Place, whom the Pequots tyranized over, being a ' potent and a warlike People, they being accuſtomed

[128] The Writer was miſtaken about the Authorſhip of the Narrative ſent him by Mr. Allen. The Author of it was Capt. John Maſon. It is hardly poſſible but that Mr. Allen knew who the real Author was. Had he communicated the whole of it Mr. Mather would have known that it was Maſon's Work; but he omitted to ſend the prefatory Matter, and hence Mr. Mather's Miſtake. Capt. Maſon lived at Norwich, and in or before 1736, his Grand-ſon put the original Manuſcript into the Hands of the Rev. Mr. Thomas Prince, who edited and publiſhed it in the Year above named. Mr. Prince ſays, in his Introduction, "I have been more "than uſually careful in correcting "the Preſs according to the Ori- "ginal." It will be ſeen by comparing Mr. Prince's Edition with this in our Text, that Mr. Allen, in making his Copy took the Liberty to make many verbal Alterations; probably thinking them Improvements.

[129] "About the Year 1632." Prince's *Edition*.

[130] I have been led to ſtate the Chriſtian Name of Norton—Walter. *Hiſt. Boſton*, 166. Savage gives it *William*. The Editors of the late (36th) Vol. of *Maſs. Hiſt. Colls.* would not commit themſelves by giving Norton a Place in their Index.

'ſo to deal with their neighbouring Indians. Capt. 'Stone having ſome Occaſion with the Dutch, who 'lived at a Trading houſe, near twenty Leagues up 'the River, procured ſome of thoſe Indians to go 'as Pilots with two of his Men to the Dutch; but 'they being [25] benighted, before they could 'come to their deſired Port, put the Skiffe, in 'which they went, aſhore; where the two Engliſh-'men falling aſleep, were both murdered by their 'Indian Guides, there remaining with the Bark, 'about twelve of the aforeſaid Indians, who had in 'all probability, formerly plotted their bloody De-'ſigne, and waiting an Opportunity when ſome of 'the Engliſh were on Shore, and Capt. *Stone*[131] 'aſleep in his Cabbin, ſet upon them and cruelly 'murthered every one of them, and plundered 'what they pleaſed, and afterward ſunk the Bark.

'Theſe Indians were not native *Pequots*, but had

[131] Capt. John Stone. He was murdered in the Autumn of 1633, the News of which was brought to Plymouth 21 Jan., 1634. See *Hiſt. and Antiqs. Boſton*, 166. He is doubtleſs the ſame of whom we find this Record in the Proceedings of the General Court: Sept. 1633. "Capt. John Stone, for his Outrage "comitted in confronting aucthori-"ty, abuſeing Mr. Ludlowe, both "in Words and Behavour, aſſalting "him and calling him a *iuſt as*, &c., "is fined C£, and prohibited come-"ing within this Patent without "leaue from the Gourmt, vnder the "Penalty of Death." In conſequence of this Baniſhment Capt. Stone went to the Connecticut River and was there murdered. The Fine of £100 was remitted about five Years after his Death. The Circumſtances of the Murder are particularly detailed in Winthrop's *Journal*, i, 148. See alſo Bradford's *Hiſt. Plymouth*, 349-50. Much Intereſt for Capt. Stone ſeems to have grown up long after his Death, and every Effort was made to ferret out his Murderers. Among others the Narraganſets were employed. On the 31ſt of Auguſt, 1637, they ſent to Boſton the Hands of three Pequots, one was aſſerted to have been the chief Murderer of Capt. Stone. Winthrop's *Journal*, i, 237.

'frequent Recourſe to them, to whom they tendered ſome of thoſe Goods, which were accepted by the chief Sachim of the *Pequots*: and ſome of the Goods were tendered to the Sachim of *Niantick* who alſo received them.[132]

'The Honoured Council of the *Maſſachuſetts* hearing of theſe Proceedings of the *Pequots*, ſent to ſpeak with them, and had ſome Treatyes, but no Iſſue was made to Satisfaction.[133]

'After which, Capt. *John Endicot* was ſent forth Commander in Chief, with Capt. *Underhill*, Capt. *Turner* and about an hundred and twenty Men, who were firſtly deſigned againſt a People living on *Block Iſland*, who were Subjects to the *Naraganſet* Sachim, they having taken a Barke of Mr. *John Oldham*, murthering him and his Company. They were alſo to call the *Pequots* to an Account about the murthering of Capt. *Stone*: who arriving at *Pequod*[134] had ſome Conference with them, but little was effected, only one *Indian* ſlain, and ſome *Wigwams* burnt.

'After which the *Pequots* grew enraged againſt the Engliſh who inhabited Connecticut, being

[132] In Maſon's *Hiſtory* it is: "Other of ſaid Goods were tendered to Nynigrett Sachim of "Nayanticke," &c.

[133] Nothing further than this appears on the Colonial Records: Dec. 1636. "The Court did intreate the Govern^r^ and Counſell "to conſider about the Proſecution "of the Warrs againſt the Pecoits "and Block-Iland againſt the next "Seſſion of this Courte." But a Treaty was made. See *Book of the Indians*, B. ii, p. 166. Hubbard's *Narrative*, 117, where the Articles may be ſeen.

[134] New London. The River on which New London ſtands was called Pequot River. Probably from its Mouth to Norwich.

'but a ſmall Number, about two hundred and fifty 'who were there newly arrived, and alſo about 'twenty Men at *Seybrook* under the Command of 'Lieut. *Lion. Gardner*,[135] who was there placed by 'ſeveral Lords and Gentlemen in England.

'The *Pequots* obſerving Lieut. Gardner going to 'Fire the Meadows about Half a Mile off the Fort, 'with ten Men with him, was violently aſſaulted 'by the *Pequod Indians*, ſo that ſome were ſlain, the 'reſt were reſcued by the Souldiers iſſuing out of 'the Fort upon the ſaid *Pequots* who fled.[136] They

135 Gardiner wrote a Hiſtory of the War ſo far as he was perſonally concerned in it, which laid in MS. until 1833, when it was printed as a Paper in a Volume of the *Maſs. Hiſt. Colls., Vol. 3., Third Ser.* It was drawn up about twenty-three Years after the War, "having," he ſays, "rumaged and found ſome old "Papers then written, it was a great "help to my Memory." Mr. Robert Chapman, Thomas Hurlburt and Major Maſon having urged him to do it.

136 "In the 22d of February, I "went out with ten Men and three "Dogs, half a Mile from the Houſe, "to burn the Weeds, Leaves and "Reeds, upon the Neck of Land, "becauſe we had felled twenty "timber Trees, which we were to "roll to the Water ſide to bring "home, every Man carrying a "Length of Match with Brimſtone-"matches with him to kindle the "Fire withal. But when we came "to the ſmall of the Neck, the "Weeds burning, I having before "this ſet two Sentinels on the ſmall "of the Neck, I called to the Men "that were burning the Reeds to "come away, but they would not "until they had burnt up the reſt "of their Matches. Preſently there "ſtarts up four Indians out of the "fiery Reeds, but ran away, I call-"ing to the reſt of our Men to come "away out of the Marſh. Then "Robert Chapman and Thomas "Hurlbut, being Sentinels, called to "me, ſaying there came a Number "of Indians out of the other Side "of the Marſh. Then I went to "ſtop them, that they ſhould not "get [to] the Woodland; but "Thomas Hurlbut cried out to me "that ſome of the Men did not fol-"low me, for Thomas Rumble and "Arthur Branch threw down their "two Guns and ran away; then the "Indians ſhot two of them that were "in the Reeds, and ſought to get be-"tween us and home, but darſt not "come before us, but kept us in a "half Moon, we retreating and

'alſo ſeized ſome that were paſſing up *Connecticut* 'River, and tortured them in a moſt cruel Manner, 'with moſt barbarous and inhuman Crueltyes; 'roaſting of them alive, &c.[137]

'They alſo lay ſculking about the Fort almoſt 'conſtantly, that the Engliſh could not go out of 'the Fort, but they were aſſaulted by the *Pequods*, 'ſo that *Connecticut* out of their ſmall Numbers, 'conſtrained [26] themſelves to ſend Capt. *John* '*Maſon* with twenty Men[138] to ſecure the Place. 'But after his coming, there did not one *Pequod* 'appear in View for a Moneths Space about the 'Fort, which was the Time he there remained.

'In the Interim, many[139] of the *Pequods* went to 'a Place now called *Wethersfield* on *Connecticut*, 'and having confederated with the Indians of that 'Place (as it was generally thought) they lay in 'Ambuſh for the Engliſh People of that Place, 'and divers of them going to their Labour in a

"exchanging many Shot, ſo that "Thomas Hurlbut was ſhot almoſt "through the Thigh, John Spencer "in the Back, into his Kidneys, "myſelf into the Thigh, two more "ſhot dead. But in our Retreat I "kept Hurlbut and Spencer ſtill "before us, we defending ourſelves "with our naked Swords, or elſe "they had taken us alive."

Gardiner does not mention by what Numbers he was ſurrounded, but Underhill ſays there were "a "hundred or more."

137 This has Reference to the horrible Torture of "Maſter John Tilley." See Underhill's *Hiſtory*, p. 15, and Gardiner, 147 (of *Hiſt. Colls.*, iii, III Ser.)

138 "Out of their ſmall Num-"bers," ſays Maſon. It ſhould be remembered that Connecticut had been ſettled by the Engliſh ſcarcely two Years; that in the Emigration of 1635, but about ſixty Men, Women and Children compoſed the Colony. This Murder was about the Middle of October, 1636.

139 "Certain Pequots, about one "hundred." *Maſon.* The Numbers of the Enemy were uſually magnified.

'large Field adjoyning to the Town, were ſet upon 'by the Indians, nine of the Engliſh were ſlain 'upon the Place, and ſome Horſes, and two young 'Women were taken Captive.[140]

'The *Pequods* at their Return from Wethersfield, 'came down to the River of Connecticut, (Capt. '*Maſon* then being at Saybrook Fort,) in three or 'more Canooes, with about an hundred Men, the 'Engliſh eſpying of them, concluded they had 'been acting ſ:me Miſchief againſt us, and there-'fore prepared one of their great Gunns, and made 'a Shot at them, which Shot ſtroock off the Head 'of one of their Canooes, wherein the two Captives 'were, although the Shot was made at them at a 'great Diſtance, near three Miles:[141] but ſeing it 'was ſo placed, they haſtned to the Shore, and 'drew their Canooes with what Speed they could 'over a narrow Beach and ſo got away.

'The Engliſh of *Connecticut* being ſo alarmed 'by theſe Inſolencyes of the *Pequods*, ſaw meet to

140 Mitigating Circumſtances often come to Light in the Lapſe of Years, which render Actions leſs atrocious, than they ſeem by a partial Recital at the Time of their committal.

" Sequin, a head Man of the " River Indians, gave Lands on the " River to the Engliſh, that he might " ſit down by them and be pro-" tected. But when he came to " Wethersfield [then called Water-" town] and ſet up his Wigwam, " the People drove him away by " Force. Reſenting the Wrong, " but wanting Strength to revenge " it, he ſecretly drew in the Pequots, " who came up the River and killed " ſix Men." Lothrop's *Cent. Ser. at W. Springfield*, 1796, p. 23-4. Mr. Goodwin, *Geneal. Foote Fam. Int* p. xxi-ii, gives the Names of two of the Men killed—Abraham and John Finch. One of the Girls taken was a Daughter of William Swain. See Gardiner's *Hiſtory*, p. 147. The Name of the Indian who commenced the Murder of the Engliſh at Wethersfield was Wauphanck. *Williams.*

141 The " near three Miles " is not in Maſon.

'call a Court, which met in *Hartford* upon *Connecticut* the firſt Day of May, 1637, who ſeriouſly 'conſidering their Condition, which did look very 'ſad, ſince the *Pequods* were a great People, forti- 'fied, cruel, warlike, munitioned, &c. and the 'Engliſh but a Handful in Compariſon of them. 'But their outrageous Violence againſt the *Engliſh* '(having murthered about thirty of them) their 'great Pride and Inſolency, and their conſtant 'Purſuit in their malicious Courſes, with their 'Endeavours to ingage other Indians in their 'Quarrel againſt the *Engliſh*, who had not offered 'them the leaſt Wrong.

'Theſe Things being duly conſidered, with the 'eminent Hazard and great Perill the People of '*Connecticut* were in, it pleaſed God ſo to ſtir up 'the Hearts of all Men in general, and the Court 'of *Connecticut* in ſpecial, that they concluded it 'neceſſary that ſome Forces ſhould be ſent forth 'ſpeedily, againſt the Pequots, their Grounds being 'juſt, and Neceſſity enforcing them to engage in 'an offenſive and defenſive Warr, with the good 'Succeſs the Moſt High was pleaſed to crown his 'People withall, we are nextly to relate.

[27] A

BRIEF HISTORY

of the War with the Pequot Indians in New-England; Anno 1637.[142]

'In the Beginning of May, 1637. there were 'ſent out by *Connecticut* Colony ninety Men under 'the Command of Capt. *John Maſon* (afterwards 'Major *Maſon*, and Deputy Governor of *Connecti-'cut* Colony) againſt the *Pequots*, with whom 'went *Uncas*,[143] an *Indian* Sachem of *Moheag*, who 'was newly revolted from the *Pequots*.[144]

'This ſmall Army was ſhipped in one Pink, one 'Pinnace and one Shallop, ſome of which Veſſels 'in their Paſſage down *Connecticut* River, fell on 'Ground, by Reaſon of the lowneſs of the Water, 'and the unſkilfulneſs of the *Engliſh* in the Chan-

142 "An Epitome or brief Hiſtory "of the Pequot War." *Maſon.*

143 "Onkos." *Maſon.* Our Author made uſe of the Form which has prevailed, but his Place of Reſidence Maſon ſays was at *Mohegan.*

Uncas proved faithful during the Expedition. When the Army were marching on the Pequot ſtrong hold, and were near to it, Capt. Maſon inquired of him if the Narraganſets would fight the Pequots, as they had made great Speeches as to what they would do. Uncas ſaid he could not depend on them: "and ſo it proved. "For which Expreſſions and ſome "other Speeches of his, I ſhall never "forget him. Indeed he was a "great Friend and did great Ser-"vice."

144 The Indians and other barbarous Nations continually practiced Seceſſion. The more barbarous a People is, the greater their Propenſity to this Kind of Self-deſtruction. See *Introduction.*

'nel.[145] The *Indians* not being wonted to ſuch 'Things with their ſmall Canooes, and alſo being 'impatient of all Delayes, deſired they might 'be ſet on Shore, promiſing they would meet our 'Army at *Seybrook;* which Requeſt of theirs was 'granted: and they being ſet at Liberty haſtning to 'their Quarters at *Saybrook,* met with about thirty 'or fourty of the *Pequots* near *Seybrook,* and en-'gaged them, and ſlew ſeven of them upon the 'Place, and had only one of their own wounded, 'who was conveyed back to *Connecticut* in a Skiffe.

'Capt. *Vnderhill* hearing of the Approach of the 'Army, went and met them and informed them 'what was performed by *Vncus* and his Men, which 'News was welcome to them, and looked upon 'as a ſpecial Providence; for before they were 'ſomewhat doubtfull of the Fidelity of their Indian 'Volunteers.[146]

'Capt. *Vnderhill* hearing of the Deſign our 'Army was upon, very freely offered his Service 'with nineteen Men to go along with them, if 'Leiut. *Gardner* would allow of it (who was chief 'Commander at *Seybrook* Fort) which Motion was 'no ſooner propounded to Lieut. *Gardner,* but he 'readily approved of it,[147] and our Councill of War

145 " Capt. Maſon having ſent " down a Shallop to Seybrooke Fort, " and ſent the Indians over Land " to meet and rendezvoouſe at Sea-" brooke for, themſelves came down " in a great maſſy Veſſel, which was " ſlow in coming, and very long " detained by croſs Winds." *Gardiner,* 16.

146 It is not eaſy to account for Maſon's Want of Knowledge reſpecting Lieut. Gardiner's Agency in this Act of Uncas's Men. See *Gardiner,* 149.

147 Gardiner's Account does not agree very well with this. He ſays: " Soon after came down from Hart-

'accepted of it alſo; who in liew of thoſe twenty, 'immediately ſent back [28] twenty of theirs to '*Connecticut* to help guard the Women and Chil-'dren, &c.

'Upon a Wedneſday our Army arrived at *Sey-'brook*, where they lay Wind-bound till Friday, in 'which Time the Councill of War conſulted how 'and in what Manner they ſhould proceed in their 'Enterprize, which was accompanied with much 'Difficulty; their Commiſſion ordering them to 'land their Men in the *Pequot* River, againſt 'which were theſe Difficultyes.

'Firſt, The *Pequods* kept a continual Gaurd 'upon the River, Night and Dey in a conſtant 'Courſe.

'Secondly, Their Numbers far exceeded ours; 'they had alſo ſixteen Gunns with Powder and 'Shot, beſides their *Indian* Artillery, as our Councill 'of War was informed by the two-captive Maids '(mentioned where we declared the Grounds of 'this War) who were redeemed by the *Dutch*, and

"ford Major Maſon, Lieut Seely, "accompanied with Mr. Stone and "80 Engliſhmen, and 80 Indians, "with a Commiſſion from Mr "Ludlow and Mr. Steel, and ſome "others. Theſe came to go fight "with the Pequits. But when Capt. "Undrill and I had ſeen their Com-"miſſion, we both ſaid they were "not fitted for ſuch a Deſign." But the Major ſaying the Government could do no better: "then we ſaid "that none of our Men ſhould go "with them, neither ſhould they go "unleſs we, that were bred Sol-"diers from our youth, could ſee "ſome likelihood to do better than "the Bay-men with their ſtrong "Commiſſion laſt Year." He next doubted the Fidelity of Uncas and his 80 Mohegans, who were ſo lately Pequots; but, on actual Trial he found them faithful. "And "having ſtaid there five or ſix Days "before we could agree, at laſt we "old Soldiers agreed about the Way "and Act, and took 20 ſufficient "Men from the 80," &c.

'restored now to us at Seybrook,[148] which was a 'very friendly Office, and not to be forgotten.

'Thirdly, They were on Land, and being swift 'of Foot, might much impede the Landing of our 'Men, and dishearten them, they continually 'gaurding that River, and our Men not knowing 'where to land nearer then *Narraganset*.

'Fourthly, It was alledged that if our Army 'landed at Narraganset, they would come upon 'their Backs, and possibly might Surprize them 'unawares; at worst they should be on firm Land 'as well as the Enemy.

148 Gardiner says he redeemed the Maids at a Cost to himself of £10, for which he had never even Thanks. He employed some Dutch Traders to redeem them, "who brought "them away almost naked, putting "on them their own linen Jackets "to cover their nakedness." P. 147. Underhill has a much more circumstantial Account than any of the early Writers. See his *History*, p. 17-19. Winthrop in his *Journal*, i, 223, gives an Account leaving out the Agency of Capt. Gardiner entirely. It is likely, as Winthrop says, that the Dutch Governour sent a Sloop and Men with Orders to rescue the Captives "even at the "Price of a War with the Pequots." These Girls were captured on the 23 of April, and brought to Saybrook Fort to Capt. Gardner on May 15th. Gardiner's Account is doubtless perfectly correct. Mr. Goodwin, in his *Genealogy of the Foote Family* does not appear to have profited by Underhill's Narrative. See *Underhill*, 17, 18.

Capt. Johnson has some Facts not contained in the other Authors about the Captivity of these Maids: "Three Women kind they caught, "and carried away, but one of "them being more fearfull of their "cruell Usage afterward then the "Losse of her Life at present, be-"ing borne away to the thickest of "the Company, resisted so stoutly "with scratching and biting, that "the Indian exasperated therewith, "cast her down upone the Earth "and beate out her Braines with his "Hatchet" *Wonder Working Providences*, 115. "They did not offer to "abuse their Persons [of the Maids] "as was verily deemed they would, "questioned them with such broken "English as some of them could "speak, to know whether they could "make Gun-powder; which, when "they found they could not doe, "their Prize proved nothing so "pretious a Pearle in their Eyes as "before." *Ibid.*

'Notwithſtanding theſe Reaſons, the Councill 'of Warr, all of them except the Captain, were at 'a ſtand, and could not judge it meet to ſail to '*Narraganſet*. Capt. *Maſon* in this difficult Caſe, 'went to the Reverend Mr. *Sauuel Stone*, late 'Teacher to the Church of Chriſt at *Hartford*, 'who was ſent as Preacher to the Army, and de-'ſired him that he would that Night commend 'their Caſe and Difficultyes before the Lord, and 'ſeek Direction of him in the Matter, how and in 'what Manner they ſhould demean themſelves. 'He retired himſelf from them aboard the Pink 'the remaining Part of that Day, and the follow-'ing Night was not wanting in ſpreading the Caſe 'before the Lord, and ſeeking his Direction, in 'the Morning he came on Shore to the Captains 'Chamber, and told him he had done as he deſired 'him, and though formerly he had been againſt 'ſailing to *Narraganſet* and landing there, yet now 'he was fully ſatisfied to attend it.

'The Councel being again called, and the Mat-'ter debated, and Reaſons conſidered, they agreed 'all with one accord to ſail to *Narraganſet*, [29] 'which the next Morning they put in Execution, 'which proved very ſucceſsful, as the Sequel may 'evidently demonſtrate. What ſhall I ſay? God 'led his People through manifold difficultyes and 'Turnings, yet by more than an ordinary Hand of 'Providence, *He led them in a right Way*.

'On Friday Morning, they in purſuance of their 'Deſign ſet Sail for Narraganſet Bay, and on Sat-

'urday toward Evening they arrived at their de-'fired Port, where they kept the Sabbath.[149]

'On Munday the Wind blew fo hard at Norweft 'that they could not go on Shoar, as alfo on Tuef-'day till it was near Sunfet, but the Wind abating, 'they and their Defign being commended to God 'by Mr. *Stone*, Capt. *Mafon* and his Company 'landed, and marched up to the Place of the chief 'Sachims Refidence,[150] and told him, that they had 'not an Opportunity before, to acquaint him with 'their coming around into his Country, yet they 'hoped it would be wel accepted by him, there 'being Amity between us and them, and alfo that 'the *Pequots* and they were Enemies, and that he 'could not be unacquainted with thefe intolerable 'Wrongs and Injuries, thofe *Pequots* had lately done 'unto the Englifh, and that they were now come '(God affifting) to avenge ourfelves upon them, 'and that they did only defire free Paffage through 'his Countrey.

'The Sachim returned this Anfwer, that he did

[149] May 23, 1637. It was to the Arrival of the Maffachufetts Men under Patrick, that Roger Williams referred, doubtlefs, in his Letter to John Winthrop, dated, "New Providence, this 4th of the "Weeke, at early Dawn." See *Mafs. Hift. Colls.*, 36, 194. (They fhould have given their Volume a better Index, or none at all, as it is deceptive.) Mr. Williams fays: "John Gallop (bleffed be the Lord) "is fafely arrived at our Dores, and "hath brought from the Lord and "you a mercifull refrefhing to vs.... "He [Gallop] relates that there is "now riding below three Pinnaces "(the Names of the Mafters Quick, "Jiglies [Giggles?] and Robinfon), "and the two Shalops, as allfo that "the other, whereof —— Jackfon "of Salem is Mafter, was in com-"pany with them the Night be-"fore," &c.

[150] Miantonimo was then the "great Sachem of Narraganfet," and this was on May 24th.

'accept of their coming, and did alſo approve of 'their Deſigne, only he thought our Numbers were 'too Weak to deal with the Enemy, who were (as 'he ſaid) very great Captains, and Men ſkilful in 'War, thus he ſpake ſomewhat ſlightingly of our 'Men.

'On Wedneſday Morning they marched from 'there to a Place called *Niantick*, it being about 'eighteen or twenty Miles diſtant, where another 'of thoſe *Narraganſet* Sachims lived in a Fort, it 'being a Frontier to the *Pequots*. They carried it 'very proudly to our Men, not permitting any of 'them to come into their Fort.[151]

'Capt. *Maſon* beholding their Carriage, and 'knowing the Falſehood of the Indians, fearing 'leſt they might diſcover them to the Enemy, 'eſpecially the *Indians* having many Times ſome 'of their neer Relations amongſt their greateſt 'Foes, ſaw Cauſe to ſet a Guard about their Fort, 'that no *Indian* might paſs in or out, and charged 'the *Indians* not to paſs out upon the Peril of their 'Lives. And there they quartered that Night, the '*Indians* not offering to ſtir out all the while.

'In the Morning came to the Army ſeveral of '*Miantinomie* his Men, who told them they were 'come to aſſiſt them in the Expedition, which 'encouraged divers Indians of that Place to engage 'alſo, who drawing [30] into a Ring, one by one, 'made ſolemn Proteſtation how gallantly they 'would demean themſelves, and how many Men 'they would kill.

[151] Ninigret, then a young Man, was Sachem of that Tribe.

'On Thurſday, about eight of the Clock in the 'Morning, they marched thence towards *Pequot*, 'having about *five hundred Indians* with them. In 'which March, through the Heat of the Weather, 'and Want of Proviſion, ſome of our Men fainted; 'but when they had marched about twelve Miles, 'they came to *Pawquatuck*[152] River, to a Ford, 'where the Indians ſaid the *Pequots* did uſually 'fiſh. There they made a ſtand and ſtayed ſome 'ſmall Time; but the *Narraganſet Indians* mani-'feſted great Fear, and many of them returned, 'although they had deſpiſed our Men, and ſaid 'they durſt not look upon a *Pequot*, and vaunted 'what great Things they themſelves would do.

'Capt. *John Maſon* ſaw Reaſon then to acquaint 'the *Indians* that they were come on Purpoſe, and 'were reſolved (God aſſiſting) to ſee the *Pequots*, and 'to fight with them before they returned, although 'they periſhed; and then he enquired of *Uncas* 'what he thought the Indians would do; who ſaid 'the *Narraganſets* would all leave them, but as for 'himſelf, he would never leave them, and ſo it 'proved.

'After they had there refreſhed themſelves with 'their mean Commons, they marched about three 'Miles, and came to a Field which had been 'planted with Indian Corn, where they made an-'other Alt: and ſuppoſing that they drew near to 'the Enemy, who, as they were informed, had two

152 Pawcatuck, a Bay and River, in Weſterly, R. I. The River riſes partly in Conecticut, and makes part of the Boundary between it and R. I. Parſons, *Indian Names*, 21. This Name has many other ſpellings.

'Forts almoſt impregnable, which did no Ways 'diſcourage the Souldiers, rather animated them, 'inſomuch that they reſolved to aſſault both the 'Forts at once; but the Council of War having 'conſulted the Matter, underſtood that one of the 'Forts, in which the bloodieſt Sachim reſided, was 'ſo remote that they could not poſſibly come up 'with it in Seaſon, and ſeeing ſome of the Soul-'diers ſpent in the March with extream heat, and 'Want of Neceſſaries, concluded and reſolved to 'aſſault and ſtorm the neareſt Fort.[153]

'Then they *marched* on in a *ſilent Manner*; the 'Indians that remained, who in the March hith-'erto kept the Van, (being ſurprized with great 'Fear) fell all into the Rear.

'They continued their March till about an Hour 'in the Night, and then coming to a little Swamp 'between two Hils, there they pitched their little 'Camp, being much wearied with hard Tra-'vell; ſuppoſing (by the Relations of the *Indians*) 'they were near the Fort, which proved other-'wiſe.[154] The Rocks were their Pillows, yet Reſt 'was ſweet and pleaſant to them. They appointed

[153] Capt Underhill thus deſcribes the Pequot Fort: "This Fort, or "Paliſado, was well nigh an Acre "of Ground, which was ſurround-"ed with Trees and half Trees, ſet "into the Ground three feet deep, "and faſtened cloſe to one another." The Hill is now called Pequot Hill, and lies eight Miles northeaſt of New London. There is a Repreſentation of the Hill in Barber's *Hiſt. Colls. of Connecticut*, 312.

[154] The Officers, ſuppoſing that they were now near the Fort, pitched their little Camp between or near two large Rocks, in the preſent Town of Groton, ſince called Porter's Rocks. Trumbull's *Hiſt. Ct.*, i, 83. A View of the Rocks may be ſeen in Barber's *Hiſt. Colls. of Connecticut*, p. 313.

'their Guards, and placed their Sentinels at ſome 'Diſtance, who heard their [31] Enemies, ſinging 'in their Fort until Midnight, with great inſulting 'and rejoycing (as they were afterwards informed 'by *Wequaſh* a *Pequot* Captain, who was revolted 'from the Pequots, and was one of their Guides 'in this March) For they ſeeing our Pinnaces ſail 'by them a few Days before concluded they were 'afraid of them, and durſt not to come near them.

'Towards Morning Capt. *Maſon* being awakened, 'and ſeeing it very light, ſuppoſed it had been day, 'and ſo they might have loſt their Opportunity, 'haveing determined to make their Aſſault before 'Day and therefore immediately rouſed up his 'Souldiers, and briefly commended themſelves and 'Deſigne to the Guidance and Protection of the 'Lord, and went to the Aſſault.

'Their Indian Guide ſhowing them a Path, ſaid it 'led directly to the Fort; they took the Path, and 'marched on the beſt Part of two Miles wondering 'that they ſaw not the Fort; and fearing that their 'Indian Guide might delude them, but coming to 'a Place where Corn was newly planted at the Foot 'of a great Hill, ſuppoſed the Fort was not far off, 'a champion Country being round about them.

'There the Captain cauſed his Company to make 'a Stand and gave Order that the Indians ſhould 'come unto him; at length *Uncas* and *Wequaſh* 'come up, of whom he demanded where the Fort 'was; they anſwered on the Top of that Hill; He 'alſo enquired where the Reſt of the Indians were, 'they anſwered, behind exceedingly afraid;[155] he 'then deſired them to tel the Reſt of their Followers that they ſhould by no Means fly, but ſtand 'at what Diſtance they pleaſed, an ſee whether 'Engliſh Men would now fight or not. Then Capt. '*Underhill* come up into the Front, and after Capt. '*Maſon* had commended their Caſe to God there 'being two Entrences into the Fort, they divided 'their Men; and Capt. *Maſon* lead up to that en-'trance on the North-eaſt Side, who approaching 'within a Rod of the Entrence a Dog bark'd, and 'an Indian cried *Wanux wanux*.[156] He commanded 'his Souldiers to cloſe up to the Fort, and fire 'upon them through the Palizadoes, which they 'did, the Indians being in a dead and indeed their 'laſt Sleep. The Souldiers having fired wheeled 'off and came to the main Entrence, which was 'blocked up with Buſhes about Breaſt high, over 'which Capt. *Maſon* very couragiouſly leaped, and 'ſtood to make good the Entrance, and command-'ed his Souldiers to follow him, one of which[157] 'endeavouring, was entengled in the Buſhes, but 'getting back, pulled out the Buſhes and ſo the 'Souldiers followed their Captain into the Fort 'with their Swords drawn, for they had concluded

[155] "Of five or ſix hundred In-"dians, not above half were left; "and they had followed the reſt "had not Capt. Underhill upbraid-"ed them with Cowardice, and "promiſed them they ſhould not "fight or come within ſhot of the "Fort, but only ſurround it afar "off." P. Vincent's *Hiſt. of the Battell*, 37.

[156] "Owanux! Owanux! which "is Engliſhmen! Engliſhmen!" *Maſon*.

[157] "Lieutenant Seeley endavor-"ed to enter," &c. *Maſon*.

' to deſtroy them with the [32] Sword, and ſo to ' ſave the Plunder.[158]

' The Indians as yet kept their *Wigwams*; Capt. ' *Maſon* entered a Wigwam, and his Guard not ' ſeeing him, paſſed away from him, where he ' was ſtrongly aſſaulted by many Indians, but he ' bravely defended himſelf, and ſlew ſeveral of his ' Oppoſers; at laſt *William Heyden* perceiving the ' Place where the Captain went in, eſſayed to go ' in himſelf, but in his Entrance ſtumbled upon a ' dead Man, but ſoon recovering himſelf, he fel ' upon the Indians. The Indians ſome were ' ſlain, ſome fled, others crept under their Beds,

[158] The following is Capt. Underhill's Account of the Onſet: " Having our Swords in our right " Hand, our Carbines or Muſkets " in our left Hand, we approached " the Fort. Maſter Hedge being " ſhot through both Arms, and " more wounded. Though it be not " commendable for a Man to make " mention of anything that might " tend to his own Honour, yet " becauſe I would haue the Provi- " dence of God obſerved, and his " Name magnified, as well for my- " ſelf as others, I dare not omit, but " let the World know, the Deliv- " erance was given to us that com- " mand, as well as to private Sol- " diers. Capt Maſon and myſelf " entering into the Wigwams, he " was ſhot, and received many " Arrows againſt his Head-piece, " God preſerving him from many " Wounds. Myſelf received a Shot " in the left Hip, through a ſuffi- " cient buff Coat, that if I had not " been ſupplied with ſuch a Gar- " ment, the Arrow would have " pierced through me. Another I " received between my Neck and " Shoulders, hanging in the Linen " of my Head-piece. Others of " our Soldiers were ſhot, ſome " through the Shoulders, ſome in " the Face, ſome in the Head, ſome " in the Legs. Capt. Maſon and " myſelf loſing each of us a Man, " and had near twenty wounded. " Moſt courageouſly theſe Pequeats " behaued themſelves. But ſeeing " the Fort was too hot for us, we " deviſed a Way how we might " ſaue ourſelues and prejudice them. " Capt. Maſon entering into a Wig- " wam, brought out a Firebrand, " after he had wounded many in " the Houſe. Then he ſet Fire on " the weſt Side where he entered. " Myſelf ſet Fire on the ſouth End " with a Train of Powder. The " Fires of both meeting in the " Centre of the Fort, blazed moſt " terribly, and burnt all in the Space " Half an Hour. Many courage-

'where they ſlept their laſt; the Captain going 'out of the Wigwams met with many of them 'and put them to the Sword; in which Time of 'Fight ſeveral Engliſh were wounded. Capt. *Maſon* perceiving his Men wounded, and the Enemy 'not yet routed, ſaw Cauſe himſelf to go into a 'Wigwam, and fetch out a Firebrand, and putting 'it in one of the Mats with which the Wigwams 'were covered; commanded one of his Souldiers 'to throw ſome Powder upon it, which ſet the 'Mat on Fire, which the Wind taking, it was 'quickly thoroughly kindled, which made the Indians run as Men moſt dreadfully amazed.[159]

"ous Fellows were unwilling to "come out, and fought moſt deſperately through the Paliſadoes, "ſo as they were ſcorched and "burnt with the very Flame, and "were deprived of their Arms—in "regard the Fire burnt their very "Bowſtrings—and ſo periſhed valiantly. Mercy they did deſerve "for their Valour, could we have "had Opportunity to have beſtowed it. Many were burnt in the "Fort, both Men, Women and "Children. Others forced [their "Way] out, and came in Troops "to the Indians, twenty and thirty "at a Time, which our Soldiers "received and entertained with the "Point of the Sword. Down fell "Men, Women and Children; "thoſe that eſcaped us fell into the "Hands of the Indians that were "in the Rear of us. It is reported "by themſelves, that there were "about four hundred Souls in this "Fort, and not above five of them "eſcaped out of our Hands. Great "and doleful was the bloody Sight "to the View of young Soldiers "that never had been in War, to "ſee ſo many Souls lie gaſping on "the Ground, ſo thick in ſome "Places that you could hardly paſs "along." *Underhill.*

"But this is very remarkable, one "of them being wounded to Death, a "Thruſt thorow the Neck with a "Halbert, yet after all, lying groaning upon the Ground, he caught "the Halberts Speare [Blade] in "his Hand, and wound it quite "round." Johnſon, *W. Prov.*, 115.

159 Mr. Allen has taken great Liberties with the Original, and his Liberty with this important Part of the Narrative is intolerable. I therefore extract the Paragraph as Prince has given it in the Words of Maſon: "Whereupon Capt. Maſon, ſeeing "no Indians, entered a Wigwam, "where he was beſet with many "Indians, waiting all Opportunities "to lay Hands on him, but could

'And indeed such a dreadful Terror did the 'Almighty let fall upon their Spirits, that they 'would fly from the Sword, and cast themselves 'into the very Flames, where many of them per-'ished.[160]

" not prevail. At length William " Heydon espying the Breach in " the Wigwam, supposing some " English might be there entred; " but in his Entrance fell over a " dead Indian; but speedily recover-" ing himself, the Indians, some fled, " others crept under their Beds: " The Captain, going out of the " Wigwam, saw many Indians in " the Lane or Street; he making " towards them, they fled, were " pursued to the End of the Lane, " where they were met by Edward " Pattison, Thomas Barber, with " some others, where seven of them " were slain, as they said. The " Captain facing about, marched a " slow Pace up the Lane, he came " down, perceiving himself very " much out of Breath, and coming " to the other End near the Place " where he first entred, saw two " Soldiers standing close to the Pal-" lizado with their Swords pointed " to the Ground: The Captain " told them that we should never " kill them after that Manner: " The Captain also said 'We must " burn them;' and immediately " stepping into the Wigwam where ", he had been before, brought out " a Firebrand, and putting it into the " Matts with which they were cov-" ered, set the Wigwams on Fire. " Lieut. Thomas Bull and Nicholas " Omsted beholding, came up; and " when it was thoroughly kindled, " the Indians ran as Men most " dreadfully amazed."

160 The following is Vincent's Ac.ount of the taking of the Fort: " The English went resolutely up " to the Door of the Fort. What! " shall we enter? said Capt. Under-" hill [This is denied by Under-" hill with an honest Soldiers em-" phasis.] What came we for else? " answered one Hedge a young " Northamptonshire Gentleman, " who advancing before the rest, " plucked away some Bushes and " entered. A stout Pequot en-" counters him; shoots his Arrow, " down to the Head into his right " Arm where it stuck. He slashed " the Salvage betwixt the Arm and " Shoulder, who pressing towards " the Door, was killed by the Eng-" lish. Immediately Master Hedge " encountered another, who per-" ceiving him upon him before he " could deliver his Arrow, gave " back; but he struck up his Heels, " and run him through. After him " he killed two or three more. " Then about Half the English en-" tered, fell on with Courage, and " slew many. But being straitened " for Room because of the Wig-" wams, (which are the Salvage " Huts or Cabins,) they called for " Fire to burn them. An English-

'The Fort being fired, the Captain commanded 'that all ſhould march out of the Fort, and ſur-'round it; which was readily attended by all, only 'one *Arthur Smith* was ſo wounded that he could 'not move out of the Place, who was happily 'eſpyed by Lieut. *Tho. Bull*, and by him reſcued 'from the Flames, which otherwiſe had conſumed 'him.

'The Fire was kindled on the Northeaſt Side to 'Windward, which did ſwiftly overrun the whole 'Fort, to the extream Amazement of the Enemy, 'and great rejoycing of our Souldiers, ſome of the 'Enemy climbed to the Top of the Pallizadoes, 'where they were ſhot down, others gathered to 'the windward Side of the Fort, and lay pelting at 'our Men with their Arrows, who repaied them 'with their ſmall Shot, others of the ſtouteſt iſſued 'forth of the Fort, about fourty of them who fell 'by the Sword.

'Capt. *Underhill* and thoſe with him acted their 'Parts in this Tragedy, eſpecially one Mr. *Hedge*[161]

"man ſtepped into a Wigwam, and "ſtooping for a Firebrand, an In-"dian was ready to knock out his "Brains; but he whipt out his "Sword and run him into the Belly, "that his Bowels followed. Then "were the Wigwams ſet on fire," &c.

161 Nothing ſeems to be known of this "Maſter Hedge," further than is reported by Vincent and Maſon. He is ſuppoſed to be a Volunteer in the Expedition, as probably was Vincent alſo, though we hear nothing of any Feats of the latter. They were doubtleſs Sojourners in the Country for a ſhort Time only. Maſon ſays, "a val-"iant reſolute Gentleman, one Mr. "Hedge, ſtepping towards the Gate, "ſaid, 'If we may not enter, "wherefore came we here;'" thus not corroborating what Vincent attributed to Capt. Underhill. Maſon moreover ſays that the Indian which Hedge encountered at his Entrance was killed by him and Sergeant Davis.

'who was the firſt that entred that Gate to which 'Capt. *Underhill* led up; the Fire was no ſooner 'kindled but the Smoke and Flames were ſo 'violent, that they were conſtrained to deſert the 'Fort and keep them in.

[33] 'Thus were they now at their Wits end, 'who not many Hours before exalted themſelves 'in their great Pride, threatning and reſolving the 'utter Ruin and Deſtruction of all the Engliſh, 'exulting and rejoicing with Songs and Dances; 'but God was above them, who laughed his Ene-'myes, and the Enemyes of his People to Scorn, 'making them as a fiery Oven; thus were the 'ſtout hearted ſpoiled, having ſlept their laſt Sleep, 'and none of their Men could find their Hands; 'thus did the Lord judge among the Heathen, fill-'ing the Place with dead Bodyes.

'And here we may take Notice of God's Judge-'ment upon this bloody Generation, in ſending the 'Night before the Aſſault an hundred and fifty 'Men from their other Fort to join with this Fort, 'who were deſigning (as ſome of themſelves have 'related) to go forth againſt the Engliſh at that 'very Inſtant when this Stroke came upon them, 'where the moſt of them periſhed with their Fel-'lows, ſo that the Miſchief they intended againſt us 'came upon themſelves; they were taken in their 'own Snare and we through the Mercy of God 'eſcaped. And thus in little more than one Hours 'Space was their impregnable *Fort* with themſelves 'utterly deſtroyed, to the Number of *five* or *ſix* 'hundred, as hath been confeſſed by the *Pequots* 'who eſcaped. There were ſeven taken captive, 'and about *eight* eſcaped; and *of the Engliſh* there 'were *two ſlain*[162] outright and above *twenty wounded.* 'Some of our Souldiers fainted for Want of ſuch 'Comforts and Neceſſaries as were needful in ſuch 'a Caſe. The Chyrurgion[163] was much wanted, 'who was left with the Barks in Narraganſet Bay, 'with Order there to remain until the Night be-'fore they intended to Aſſault.

'And thereupon grew many Difficultyes amongſt 'the Army, their Proviſion and Ammunition being 'neer ſpent, and they in the Enemyes Country, 'who did far exceed them in Numbers, being 'much enraged, and moſt of our Indian Friends 'having left them, and our Pinacnes a great Diſ-'tince from them, and their coming uncertain.

'But as they were conſulting what Courſe to 'take, it pleaſed God to diſcover our Veſſels to 'them under a fair Gale of Wind ſailing into the '*Pequot* Harbour, to their great rejoicing.

'They had no ſooner diſcovered our Veſſels, 'but immediately came up the Enemy from the 'other Fort, about three hundred of them. Capt. '*Maſon* led forth a File or two of Men to ſkirmiſh

162 "One of them by our own "Muſkets, as is thought." *Vincent*, 38. "In little more than an Hour "betwixt three and four hundred "of them weree killed." *Ibid.* Maſon ſets the Number ſlain at "ſix "or ſeven hundred," while Gardiner rates the killed at three hundred.

163 This "Chyrurgion" was probably Thomas Pell, who came over in 1635, in the Hopewell; and went with Lt. Lyon Gardiner to Saybrook. "Our Chirurgeon," ſays Underhill, "not accuſtomed to "War, durſt not hazard himſelf "where we ventured our Lives, but "like a freſh water Soldier, kept "aboard." Farmer ſeems not to have found this Perſon.

'with them, which ſtopt their Carrier, and put 'them to a Stand, and then they prepared to march 'towards our Veſſels, but four or five of our Men 'were ſo wounded that they were fain to be car-'ried, with the Armes of about twenty more which 'took up ſo many of the Souldiers, that there was 'not above forty [34] Men free, but at length they 'hired ſeveral Indians to carry the wounded Men, 'who eaſed them of that Burthen, and carried their 'wounded Men for them.

'And when the Souldiers had marched about a 'Quarter of a Mile, the Enemy come to the Place 'where the Fort had ſtood, and when they beheld 'the Runies thereof, and the Carcaſes of their 'Friends lye ſome upon the Earth, others ſcorched 'and ſome almoſt conſumed with the Fire, they 'ſtamped and tore the Hair from their Heads, and 'ran mouting down the Hill in their full Carreer 'and the Loſs they met withal made them wary 'not to come near.

'The Souldiers then meeting with a ſmall Brook 'at the foot of the Hil being very dry, ſat down 'and refreſhed themſelves, the Enemy being grown 'by this Time ſo wary they durſt not come too 'neer, to diſturb them.

'Then they marched on towards *Pequot* Har-'bour, and meeting with ſeveral Wigwams in the 'Way they burnt them; the Enemy followed 'them, and ſome lay in Ambuſh behind Rocks and 'Trees, often ſhooting at them, yet God ſo covered 'them, that not one of them was hurt, and when 'they came to any Swamp or Thicket, they made

‘ ſome Shot, and cleared a Paſſage, and ſome of the ‘ Enemy fell, which our Indians ſeeing, would ‘ give a great Shout and then venture to fetch ‘ their Heads,[164] and thus they continued, till they ‘ came within two Miles of Pequot Harbour, ‘ where the Enemy gathered theemſelves together, ‘ and left our Army; they marched on to the Top ‘ of an Hill adjoining to the Harbour, with their ‘ Colours flying, (as for their Drum, it was loſt,[165] ‘ or at leaſt left by their Drummer at the Place ‘ where they kept their Randezvouze the Night ‘ before) where they ſaw our Veſſels riding at An- ‘ chor to their great Rejoicing, and when they had ‘ marched to the Water Side, there they ſat down ‘ in Quiet.

‘ Capt. *Patrick*[166] being there arrived (with our ‘ Veſſels) with forty Men ſent by the *Maſſachuſetts* ‘ Colony upon ſome Service againſt the Block ‘ Iſlanders or *Pequots*, came to the Shore in a ‘ Shallop, with ſome of his Men, as he ſaid, to ‘ reſcue our Army, ſuppoſing they had been pur-

164 “The Indians that then aſſiſted “ the Engliſh, waiting the Fall of “ the Pequets, (as the Dog watcheth “ the Shot of the Fowler, to fetch “ the Prey,) ſtill fetched them their “ Heads.” *Vincent*, 38.

165 Maſon ſays nothing about the Drum being loſt. He ſays it was left at the Place of their laſt Encampment. The Reaſon it was left is obvious. They had no Uſe for it. Every Man was wanted to wield the Weapons of Deſtruction. “ The “ Reaſon why the Engliſh wanted “ Amunition was, becauſe they had “ left that which they had for ſtore, “ with the Drum, at the Place of “ their Conſultation; but found it “ in their Return.” *Vincent.*

166 Daniel Patrick. He marched by Land to Providence, and arrived in the Neighborhood of Maſon and Underhill's Veſſels juſt in Time to get on board, and go round in them to meet the victorious Forces. The Time he marched is not mentioned.

'sued, although there did appear no Sign of any 'such Thing.[167]

'But Capt. Patrick could not be prevailed with 'by any Means to venture himself on Shore while 'our wounded Men were carried on board, which 'was troublesome, not only to our Souldiers, but 'to his own Men also, who manifested their dis-'like of his Carriage; at length our Men were 'fetched aboard our Vessels, to the great rejoicing 'of their Friends, where they did with one Heart 'bless the Lord for his Mercy and Goodness unto 'them.

[35] 'I might here relate a Contest that fel out 'between Capt. *Underhill* and Cap. *Patrick*, about 'Capt. *Underhil's* claiming an Interest in the Bark 'in which Capt. *Patrick* sailed, which by the 'Mediation of Capt. *Mason* was issued,[168] and that 'being the Place of Randezvouze, where Vessels 'were expected from the *Massachusets*, it was 'agreed that Capt. *Patrick* should there ride in 'that Bark, and secure the *Narraganset* Indians 'until our Vessel could carry our wounded Men 'to *Seybrook*, and our Pink return to carry home 'the *Narraganset* Indians.

[167] Both Mason and Underhill seem to have looked upon Patrick with Contempt or Envy; and so far as can now be perceived, without Cause. Patrick seems to have done his Duty like a good Soldier; not arriving in Time to be at the taking of the Fort was not his Fault, and had the Attack resulted unfavorably Mason would have been severely and justly censured for attacking without the coöperation of Patrick who was close at hand.

[168] The Particulars are in the original *Mason*, but being of slight Interest, hardly call for a Note, further than to direct Attention to the false Manner of dealing with the Work of Mason by the Copyist.

'After this Agreement, Capt. *Underhill* ſet Sail 'for *Seybrook* in our Bark, but before he was out of 'Sight, Capt. *Patrick* ſignified by writing to Capt. '*Maſon* that he could not attend that Service he 'had ingaged for he muſt with his Company wait 'at *Seybrook*, for ſome Veſſels he expected from the 'Bay,[169] adviſing Capt. *Maſon* ſeeing he had ob'tained the Honour of that Service, he would 'compleat it in ſecuring the *Narraganſet Indians*, '&c. Which indeed was a hard Taſk and difficult; 'for the Pink could not entertain them, and to 'march by Land was dangerous, it being near 'twenty Miles, and in the Enemies Country, and 'their Numbers being ſmall; for they had ſent 'home about twenty Men to help ſtrengthen the 'Plantations on *Connecticut*, for Fear of the *Pequods* 'invading of them, but at laſt, ſeeing they were 'neceſſitated to march to *Seybrook* by Land, they 'went Aſhoar with the Indians, and began their 'March; Capt. *Patrick* ſeeing what they were 'about, came Aſhoar alſo with his Men; and 'although Capt. *Maſon* told him he did not delight 'in his Company, yet he would and did march 'along with them.

'In this March about the Midway between that 'and *Seybrook*, they fell upon a People called *Nian'ticks*,[170] belonging to the *Pequots*, who fled to a

[169] The Force diſpatched under Capt. Iſrael Stoughton, which could not be got ready until after Patrick had left, as will be ſeen.

[170] Afterwards this Tribe appear to have ignored their Pequot Origin, and become, by Intermarriages with the Narraganſets, and having joined them againſt the Pequots, a Part of them. See *Book Inds.*, 131. Ninigret was their Chief.

'Swamp for Refuge; but when they heard or ſaw 'this ſmall Troop they fled, who purſued them 'awhile by their Tracks as long as they kept together; but the Day being much ſpent, Sabbath 'drawing on, and themſelves much ſpent with 'their former Travel, and Service, they left their 'Purſuit, and marched on towards *Seybrook*, 'and about Sun-ſet they arrived by *Connecticut* 'River ſide; where they were welcomed by Leiut. '*Gardner*, with many great Gunns, but were forced 'there to take up their Quarters that Night. On 'the Morrow Morning they were all fetched over, 'where they kept the Sabbath, and were nobly entertained by Leivt. *Gardner*, from whom they 'received meny Courteſies.

'And when they had taken Order for the ſafe 'Conduct of the *Narraganſet* Indians to their 'Country, Capt. *Maſon* with his Men returned to '*Connecticut*, the Place of their abode, where they 'were entertained with [36] great Triumph and 'Rejoycing and Praiſing of God, for his Goodneſs 'to us in ſucceeding our Endeavours, in crowning 'them with Succeſs, and in reſtoring our ſmall 'Army with ſo little Loſs.

'Thus was God ſeen in the Mount, cruſhing 'his proud Enemies, and the Enemies of his People, 'ſo that they who were ere while a Terror to all 'that were round about them, who reſolved to deſtroy all the Engliſh, and to root their very Name 'out of this Country, were by weak Meanes[171] thus

171 " Even ſeventy ſeven—there " being no more at the Fort."— *Omiſſion of the Tranſcriber.* Why ſuch an Omiſſion?

'vanquiſhed and deſtroyed, and the Miſchief they 'plotted, and the Violence they offered, was brought 'on their own Heads in a Moment: for the Lord 'burnt them up in the Fire of his Wrath, and 'dunged the Ground with their Fleſh, it was the 'Lords doing, and it was marvelous in our Eyes. 'It is he that hath made His Work wonderful, and 'and therefore ought to be remembered.

'Suddenly after this, the whole Body of the 'remaining *Pequots* repaired to that Fort where '*Saſſacous* the chief Sachim did reſide, and charged 'him that he was the only Cauſe of all their 'Troubles that befel them, and therefore they 'would deſtroy both him and his; yet by the 'Entreaty of his Counſellors, they ſpared his Life; 'conſulting what Courſe to take, concluded there 'was no Abiding any longer in their Country, and 'ſo reſolved to fly into ſeveral Parts. The greateſt 'Body of them went towards *Manadus*,[172] and in 'their Paſſage over *Connecticut* River, they met 'with three Engliſhmen in a Shallop going for '*Seybrook*, and fought them, who reſiſted them 'ſtoutly, and killed and wounded many of them, 'but their Shallop falling on Ground they were all 'three ſlain.[173]

172 *Manhatance*, in Prince's Maſon. *Manhattan*, where the City of New York is now.

173 I have not been fortunate enough to meet with the Names of theſe Sufferers. One of the Pequot Murderers of them was named *Pametſick*. The three Men were going in a Boat for Clay. One was killed, the other two were tortured, but in what Manner is not known—probably by burning them to Death in a ſlow Fire. See R. Williams in *Maſs. Hiſtorical Collections*, 36, 230-1.

'About a Fortnight after our Souldiers were 'returned Home from Mistick Fight, we heard of 'the Arrival of several Vessels from the *Massachu-'setts Colony* in *Pequot* River; Capt. *Israel Stough-'ton* being Commander in chief, and with him 'about 120 Men, who were sent by that Colony 'to prosecute the War against the *Pequots;* and 'although the main Body of the *Pequots* were fled, 'yet some Straglers remained in that Country, 'some of whom were discovered by the *Moheags,* 'and by them discovered to the Massachusetts 'Forces, by whom they were both surprised and 'taken, and several of which, to the Number of 'about twenty three, were put to Death; the Rest 'were sent to the Bay.[174]

'The Colony of *Connecticut* hereupon sent forth 'Capt. *Mason* again with forty Men, as also several 'Gentlemen, (as the Honour'd *John Haines* and

[174] For an Account of the Operations of the Massachusetts Troops we must recur to Hubbard. The above Paragraph is far more comprehensive than the corresponding one in Mason, and Hubbard has Facts not in either. His Paragraph runs thus: "It was "not long after Capt. Stoughton's "Soldiers came up, before News "was brought of a great Number "of the Enemy, that were discov-"ered by the Side of a River up "the Country, being first trepan-"ned by the Narhagansets, under "Pretence of securing them, but "they were truly hemmed in by "them, though at a Distance, yet "so as they could not or durst not "stir from the Place, by which "Means our Forces of the Massa-"chusets had an easie Conquest of "some hundreds of them, who were "there couped up as in a Pound; "not daring to fight, not able to fly "away, and so were all taken with-"out any Opposition: the Men "among them to the Number of "thirty were turned presently into "Charrons Ferry boat, under the "Command of Skipper Gallop, "who dispatched them a little with-"out of the Harbour; the Females "and Children were disposed of "according to the Will of the Con-"querors, some being given to the "Narhagansets and other Indians "that assisted in the Service."—*Narrative,* 127.

' *Roger Ludlow*, Efqrs.) to meet with thofe of the ' *Maffachufets* to confult and determine what was ' farther neceffary to be attended. Who meeting ' with thofe of the *Maffachufets* in the *Pequot* ' Harbour [37] after Confultation, concluded to ' purfue the *Pequots* (who as you heard before ' were fled towards the *Menados*) and fo began ' their March after them, and difcovered feveral ' Places where they had rendevowed and lodged ' not far diftant one from the other, for they could ' make but little Hafte, by Reafon of their ancient ' People and Children, and their Want of Provi- ' fion, being forced to gather Clams, and fuch other ' Things as the Wildernefs afforded for their Relief.

' The Veffels sailed along by the Shore. In the ' March fome were gleaned, but within the Space ' of three Dayes, or thereabouts, they arrived at a ' Place then called *Quinipiag* (now *New Haven*) ' and there efpying a great Smoke in the Woods, ' not far diftant, fuppofing the *Pequots* might be ' there, they went to difcover them; but they ' quickly difcovered them to be Connecticut Indi- ' ans. From them they fent a *Pequot* Captive ' (whom they named *Luz*) upon Difcovery, who ' brought them Tidings of the Enemy which ' proved real.

' The *Pequots* were fo terrified in their Flight, ' that a *Moheag* Indian (named *Jack Eaton*) meet- ' ing in this Perfuit with three *Pequots*, took two ' of them and brought them to the Englifh.

' But to return, they having Tidings where the

' *Pequots* were, haſtned towards the Place where ' they heard they were, and at laſt coming into a ' Corn Field, ſeveral of the Engliſh eſpyed ſome ' Indians, who fled from them. They purſued ' them, and coming to the top of an Hill, ſaw ' ſeveral Wigwams juſt oppoſite, only a Swamp ' intervening, which was almoſt divided in two ' Parts. One Serjeant *Palmor* haſtning with about ' twelve Men (who were then under his Com-' mand) to ſurround the ſmaller Part of the Swamp, ' that ſo he might prevent the Indians flying. ' But Lieut. *Davenport*, Serjeant *Jefferyes* &c. going ' up to the *Wigwams* were there aſſaulted by the ' Indians. In this Skirmiſh the Engliſh ſlew but ' few, two or three of themſelves were wounded, ' the Reſt of their Army coming up, the Swamp ' was ſurrounded.[175]

' Their Council being called, the Queſtion was ' propounded how they ſhould proceed? Capt. ' *Patrick* adviſed that they ſhould cut down the ' Swamp, (they having taken many Indian Hatch-' ets.) Others propounded to hedge in the Swamp, ' which others judged would be to no Purpoſe, ' and therefore ſtrongly oppoſed it. Some other ' adviſed to Force the Swamp, having Time enough

[175] The Pequots " flying into a " very thick Swamp, being unac-" ceſſible, by Reaſon of the boggy " Holes of Water, and thick Buſhes; " the Engliſh drawing up their " Company belagered the Swamp, " and the Indians in the mean Time " ſkulking up and down, and as " they ſaw Opportunity they made " Shot with their Arrows at the " Engliſh, and then ſuddainly they " would fall flat along in the Water " to defend themſelves from the re-" talliation of the Souldiers Muſ-" kets." *Wond. Work. Providences*, Page 115.

'(it being about three a Clock in the Afternoon), 'but that being oppoſed, it was then proupounded 'that the Men ſhould be drawn up cloſe to the 'Swamp, which would have leſned the Circum-'ference, and then to fill up the open Paſſages with 'Buſhes, that ſo they might ſecure them till the 'Morning, and then conſider farther about it. But 'neither of theſe would paſs, ſo different [38] were 'their Apprehenſions, which was very griveous to 'ſome, who concluded that the Indians would 'make an Eſcape in the Night, as eaſily they might, 'and did, the Swamp being large and their Num-'bers being ſo ſmall that they were forced to ſtand 'at a great Diſtance one from another, which 'made their Eſcape more eaſie.

'Capt. *Maſon* took Order that the narrow Paſ-'ſage in the Swamp ſhould be cut through, which 'ſhould much ſhorten the League, which was ac-'cordingly attended and reſolutely performed by 'Serjeant *Davis* and ſome others with him.[176]

[176] Johnſon ſays the Deciſion upon a Plan of Dealing with the enſwamped Indians was arrived at by the following Circumſtance: "Some of the Engliſh ſpyed an "Indian with a Kettle at his Back "going more inwardly into the "Swamp, by which they perceived "there was ſome Place of firm "Land in the midſt thereof, which "cauſed them to make Way for the "Paſſage of their Souldiers which "brought this Warre to a Period." *Wond. Work. Prov.; ibid.* P. 116.

In the Purſuit of the Enemy the following remarkable Feat, according to Johnſon, occurred: "As the "Souldiers were upon their March, "cloſe by a great Thicket, where "no Eye could penetrate farre, "ſome Souldiers lingering behinde "their Fellowes, two Indians watch-"ing their Opportunity, when they "ſuppoſed the laſt Man was come "up, who kept a double, double, "double Diſtance in his March, "they ſudden and ſwiftly ſnatched "him up, hoiſing him upon their "Shoulders, ran into the Swamp "with him. The Souldier ſtrove

'Mr. *Thomas Stanton*[177] a Man well acquainted 'with the Indians Language and Manners, per'ceiving the Counsell of War loth to destroy Wo"men and Children, (as also the Indians of that 'Place) freely offered his Service to go into the 'Swamp and treat with them, which the Councel 'were somewhat backward to, by Reason of some 'Hazard he might be exposed to, but his Impor'tunity prevailed, who going to them did in a 'short Time come to the Councel with near 200 'old Men, Women and Children, who delivered

"to free himself; but like a care"full Commander, one Captaine "Davenport, then Lieutenant of "this Company, being diligent in "his Place to bring up the Reare, "coming up with them, followed "with Speed into the Swamp after "him, having a very severe Cutlace "tyed to his Wrist, and being well "able to make it Bite sore when he "set it on, resolving to make it fall "foul on the Indians Bones, he "soone overtook them, but was "prevented by the Buckler they "held up from hitting them, which "was the Man they had taken: It "was Matter of much Wonder to "see with what Dexterity they "hurled the poore Souldier about, "as if they had been handling a "Lacedæmonian Shield; so that the "nimble Captaine Davenport could "not, of a long Time, fasten one "Stroke upon them; yet at last "they cast downe their Prey, and "hasted through the Thickets for "their Lives. The Souldier thus "redeemed, had no such hard "Usage, but that he is alive, as I "suppose, at this very Day." [1654.] *Wond. Work. Prov.*, 116. See also *Hubbard*, 129, who says "Lieut. "Davenport was sorely wounded "in the Body, John Wedgwood of "Ipswich in the Belly; was laid "hold on also by some of the In"dians." He was probably the *Buckler* above mentioned by Johnson. At the same Time Thomas Sherman, also of Ipswich, was wounded. "Others were in much "Hazard of being swallowed by "the miery Bogs of the Swamp, "wherein they stuck so fast, that if "Serjeant Riggs of Roxbury had "not rescued two or three of them, "they had fallen into the Hands "of the Enemy." *Ibid.*

177 We first hear of this important Personage by Lieut. Gardiner. He came to Saybrook in 1636, as an Interpreter; is probably the Thomas Stanton who sailed from England for Virginia the Year before. How he bacame Master of

'themſelves to the Mercy of the Engliſh, moſt of 'which brought their ſmall Preſent with them, and 'laid it down before the Councell. Now Night 'drawing on, they did beleaguer the Swamp as 'ſtrongly as they could.

'But above Halfe an Hour before Day the In- 'dians that were in the Swamp, attempted to break 'through Capt. *Patricks* Quarters, but were beaten 'back ſeveral Times. They made a great Noiſe, 'as their Manner is at ſuch Times, which ſounded 'round about the Leaguer; Capt. *Maſon* ſent Serjeant '*Stares*[178] to aſſiſt thoſe againſt whom the *Pequots* 'preſſed to come out by, at which Time alſo Capt. '*Traſk* came in to their Aſſiſtance, but the Tumult 'encreaſing, the Siege was raiſed, and they marching 'up to a Place at a Turning of the Swamp, the 'Indians were forcing out upon them, but they

the Indian Language does not appear. He ſetled in Stonington, and died in 1678, leaving a Wife and ſome nine Children. In all Troubles and Controverſies between the Engliſh and Indians Mr. Stanton was depended upon to interpret between them, yet at one Time the Indians greatly diſtruſted him; believing that he interpreted againſt them. He was ſaid to have been "groſſly "deluded" by the wily Wequaſchuck, "the Man (to my Know- "ledge) that ſheltered Audſah, the "Murtherer of Mr. Oldham." R. Williams in *Maſs. Hiſt. Colls.*, 36, 208, 216, 234, 246. Williams alſo ſays that Stanton was "groſſly "couſend and deluded by Wequaſ- "chuck, a Nayantaquit Sachim, as "himſelf confeſt to me at my "Howſe." *Ibid*, 208. Wequaſchuck had married the Mother of Saſacous. Genealogical Matters among Indians muſt have been very uncertain. Numerous are the Deſcendants of Thomas Stanton at this Day. Miſs Caulkins has laid them under many Obligations in this Behalf. See her invaluable *Hiſtory of New London*, 296, and elſewhere. Hubbard ſays "he was an exact "Interpreter."

178 Perhaps a Miſprint, as I do not find the Name of *Stares* in any of our Records; yet Prince has the ſame Spelling in his Edition of Maſon. Savage does not include him in his great Dictionary.

'fired upon them, and ſent them back by their 'ſmall Shot. Then they waited a little for their 'ſecond Attempt, but the Indians facing about, 'and preſſing violently upon Capt. *Patricks* Quar-'ters, brake through, and ſo eſcaped about ſeventy 'of them, as the Indians informed; the Swamp was 'ſearched; there were but few found ſlain. The 'Captives that were taken were about an hundred 'and eighty, which were divided between the two 'Colonyes, and they intended to keep them as Ser-'vants, but they could not endure the Yoke, for 'few of them continued any conſiderable Time 'with their Maſters.[179]

'Thus did the Lord ſcatter his Enemyes with 'his ſtrong Arm.

'The *Pequots* now become a Prey to all Indians: 'happy were they [39] that could bring in their 'Heads to the Engliſh, of which there came almoſt 'dayly to *Windſor* or *Hartford;* but the *Pequots* 'growing weary hereof, ſent ſome of the Chief 'that ſurvived to mediate with the Engliſh, offer-'ing that if they might but enjoy their Lives, they 'would become the Engliſh Vaſſals, to diſpoſe of 'them as they pleaſed.

'Whereupon *Uncas* and *Miantonimo* were ſent 'for, who with the *Pequots* met at *Hartford*; the '*Pequots* being demanded, how many of them 'were then living, they anſwered about an hundred 'and eighty or two hundred; Then were there 'granted to *Uncas* Sachim of *Moheag* eighty, and

179 Hubbard ſays the Swamp was a hideous one near the Place where Fairfield or Stratford now ſtands. *Indian Wars,* 129.

'to *Miantonimo* Sachim of *Narraganſet* eighty, and 'to *Ninnicraft* twenty Men, when he ſhould ſatisfy 'for a Mare of *Elwood Pomeryes*, killed by ſome of 'his Men; The *Pequots* likewiſe were by Cove-'nant bound, that they ſhould no more inhabit 'their native Countrey; nor ſhould any of them be 'called *Pequots* but *Moheags* and *Narraganſets* for 'ever; Shortly after about forty of them went to '*Moheag*, others went to Long Iſland, others ſet-'tled at *Pawcatuck*, a Place in the *Pequot* Country, 'contrary to their Covenant and Agreement with 'the Engliſh ſo lately made, which *Connecticut* ta-'king into Conſideration, and well weighing the 'Inconveniences that might enſue; for the Preven-'tion whereof, they ſent forth forty Men under 'the Command of Capt. *Maſon*, to ſupplant them 'by burning their Wigwams, and bringing away 'their Corn, except they would deſert the Place: '*Uncas* with about one hundred of his Men in 'twenty Cannoes alſo went to aſſiſt them in the 'Service; as they ſailed into *Pawcatuck* Bay, they 'met with three of thoſe Indians whom they 'ſent to inform the Reſt with the End of their 'coming, and alſo to tell them that they deſired to 'ſpeak with them or ſome of them, they promiſed 'to do the Meſſage, and ſpeedily to return; but 'they forgot to keep their Word for they came 'not.

'Then they went up into the River in their Veſ-'ſel, but by Reaſon of Flats were forced to land 'on the weſt Side of the River, their Wigwams 'being on the eaſt Side, juſt oppoſite; where they 'ſaw the Indians running up and down, jeſting at 'them.

'Then they landed, and went up into a narrow 'Place in the River between two Rocks, where 'they drew up the Indian Cannooes, and got ſud- 'denly over the River, ſooner than they were 'expected, and marched up to the *Wigwams*, where 'the Indians were all fled, except ſome old People 'that could not.

'They were ſo ſuddenly upon them, that they 'had not Time to convey away their Goods. 'There was plenty of Corn, it being the Time of 'Harveſt, [40] and when they had viewed it, they 'were paſſing to the Water ſide to the Pinnance, 'Half of *Uncas* his Men being with them, the reſt 'were plundering the Wigwams; and as they were 'marching they loked behind them, and ſaw 'about ſixty Indians running towards them, untill 'they came within forty Paces of the Indians, then 'they ran and met them, and fell on *pell mell*, 'ſtriking and cutting with Bowes and Hatchets 'and Knives, &c., after their feeble Manner. In- 'deed it did not deſerve the Name of Fighting. 'They then endeavoured to get between the In- 'dians and the Woods, that ſo they might prevent 'their flying, which the Indians perceived and 'endeavoured ſpeedily to get away under the Beach, 'but our Men made no Shot at them, but they laid 'hold on about ſeven of them, who were *Ninni- 'crafts* Men, who grew very outragious; the Cap- 'tain told them if they were not quiet they ſhould 'be made ſhorter by the Head; and when they 'were going to put it into Execution, *Otaſh* Sachim 'of *Narraganſet*, and Brother to *Miantonimo*, ſtep-'ped forth to Capt. *Maſon*, and told him, thoſe Men 'whom he was going to execute were his Brothers 'Men, who was a Friend to the Engliſh, and if 'their Lives might be ſpared, he would engage to 'deliver ſo many Murtherers Heads in lieu of them 'to the Engliſh; The Captain granted his Deſire, 'and the Men were delivered to *Uncas* to be ſecured 'till *Otaſh* his Engagement was performed.

'Then they drew up their Bark into a Creek 'the better to defend her, there being ſome hun-'dreds of Indians within five Miles, waiting their 'Motion.

'But there they quartered that Night. In the 'Morning as ſoon as it was Light, there appeared 'in Arms at leaſt *three hundred Indians* on the other 'Side the Creek, upon which the Captain com-'manded his Men to ſtand to their Armes, which 'the Indians perceiving, ſome of them fled, others 'crept behind the Rocks and Trees, not one of 'them were to be ſeen.

'They then called to them, ſaying, they deſired 'to ſpeak with them, and that they would lay 'down their Armes for that End, whereupon they 'ſtood up: The Captain told them that the Pe-'quots had violated their Promiſe and Covenant 'with the Engliſh, in that they were not there to 'inhabit, and that he was ſent to ſupplant them; 'the Indians anſwered, the *Pequots* were good Men, 'their Friends, and they would fight for them and 'protect them; which Words moved the Captain, 'who told them it was not far to the Head of the 'Creek, where he would meet them, and then they 'might try what they could do; [41] The Indians 'replied, *they would not fight with Englishmen, for 'they were Spirits*;[180] but they would fight with *Un-'cas*. The Captain told them that he thought it was 'too early for them to fight; but they might take 'their Opportunity and fight when they saw Cause, 'for they should be burning their Wigwams, 'and carrying their Corn aboard all that Day, and 'presently caused the Drum to be beat up, and 'fired their Wigwams in their View. But as they 'marched along, there stood two Indians upon an 'Hill jeering and reviling of them; Mr. *Stanton* 'the Interpreter marching at Liberty, desired leave 'of the Captain to make a Shot at them; the 'Captain demanded of the Indians, who they were; 'they answered that they were Murtherers; the 'Captain then gave Mr. *Stanton* leave to make a 'Shot at them, who did so, and shot one of them 'through both his Thighs, which was to the Won-'derment both of English and Indians, it being at 'such a vast Distance.

'They then proceeded and loaded their Bark 'with Indian Corn, and their Canooes, about thirty 'of them, with *Indian Trayes, Kettles, Mats*, and 'other Luggage, and then went on Board, and 'made homeward, and it pleased God to prosper 'them, so that in a short Time they all arrived in 'Safety at the Place of their abode; though they

180 It would have been gratifying if the Writer had told us what *Kind* of Spirits the Indians thought them to be.

'were in Hazard by the Veſſels ſtriking upon a 'Rock, and ſticking thereon a while in their Re-'turn, yet the Lord bore them in his own Armes, 'and preſerved them from Danger.

'Thus we may ſee how the Face of God is ſet 'againſt them that do Evil, to cut off their Re-'membrance from the Earth.[181]

'Our Tongues therefore ſhall talk of his Right-'eouſneſs all the Day long, for they are confounded, 'they are brought to Shame that ſought our Hurt, '*Bleſſed be the Lord God of Iſrael, who only doth* '*wondrous Things, and Bleſſed be his holy Name* '*forever, Let the whole Earth be filled with his* '*Glory*; for the Lord was pleaſed to ſmite our 'Enemyes in the hinder Parts, and to give us their 'Land for an Inheritance, who remembered us in 'our low Eſtate, and redeemed us out of our Ene-'myes Hands; Let us therefore praiſe the Lord 'for his Goodneſs, and wonderful Works to the 'Children of Men.

'Upon the whole it may not be amiſs to gather 'out ſome Specialtyes of Providence, that ſo the 'Goodneſs of God may be taken notice of, and our 'Hearts enlarged in the Praiſe and Service of that 'God who hath wrought ſo wonderfully for our 'Fathers and for us.

'Thoſe who were employed in this Service were 'not many, their Commons were very ſhort, there 'being then a general Scarcity throughout this 'Colony of all Sorts of Proviſion, it being upon our

181 Our Fathers were never at a Loſs for apt Scriptural Quotations which they fancied met each particular Caſe.

'very [42] Beginings on the Place, they had but 'little Refreſhment with them in their long March 'from *Narraganſet* to *Pequot;* but one Pint of 'Liquor which was moderately dealt out to ſuch 'as fainted in the Way, by Reaſon of the Extremity 'of the Heat and ſore Travel: after the Liquor 'was ſpent, the very ſmelling to the Bottle was 'effectual to the reviving of the fainting Souldiers. 'They walked in an unknown Path, yet God 'guided them *in the Way they ſhould goe,* though 'they knew not where the *Forts* were, nor how far it 'was to them, nor how far the Way that led to them 'otherwiſe than what they had from their Indian 'Guides, in whom they durſt not confide, and that 'in their ſo long a March among a treacherous 'People, who had ſeveral Relations amongſt our 'Enemies, and that in their March, and Allodge-'ment in the Enemies Country which was very 'populous, they ſhould not be diſcovered but 'brought to their Enemies in the fitteſt Seaſon, 'when none of them then uſually were together, and 'that they ſhould be ſo ſucceeded in their Deſign, '(as you have heard) is Matter of Wonderment.

'What ſhall I ſay? God was pleaſed to hide 'them in the Hollow of his Hand. It was a ſay-'ing of Mr. *Hooker*, that Man of God, in his 'Encouragements to the Souldiers, as they were 'going forth to thoſe Ingagements, that the *Pequots* 'ſhould be Bread for them; and the Lord made 'good his Sayings.

'It may not be amiſs here alſo to remember Mr.

'*Stone*[182] (the famous Teacher of the Church of '*Hartford*) who was ſent to preach and pray with 'thoſe who went out in thoſe Engagements againſt 'the *Pequots*; He lent his beſt Aſſiſtance and 'Counſel in the Management of thoſe Deſigns, and 'the Night in which the Engagement was, (in the 'Morning of it) I ſay that Night he was with the 'Lord alone, wreſtling with Him by Faith and 'Prayer; and ſurely his Prayers prevailed for a 'Bleſſing; and in the very Time when our Iſrael 'were ingaging with the bloud-thirſty *Pequots*, he 'was in the Top of the Mount, and ſo held up his 'Hand, that Iſrael prevailed.

'In thoſe Ingagements ſome Men had ſpecial 'Deliverances. There were two Men, being one 'Mans Servants, who were both ſhot in the Knots 'of their Neck-cloathes about their Necks, and 'received no Hurt.[183] Alſo Lieut. *Siely*,[184] was 'ſhot in the Eyebrow with a flat headed Arrow, 'the Point turning downward, the Captain himſelf 'pulled the Arrow out. Lieut. *Bull*[185] was alſo 'ſhot in the Back with an Arrow, which met with

182 Rev. Samuel Stone. He came to Boſton in 1633, and reſided at Cambridge till 1636, when he went to Hartford and ſettled, and died there 20 July, 1663. He was a Native of Hartford in England, and Hartford in Connecticut was ſo named on that Account (in 1637). *Trumbull*, i, 77.

183 Perhaps this refers to Wedgewood and Sherman, mentioned in a previous Note.

184 Lieut. Robert *Sieley*, Sealy, Seeley, or Seely. According to Savage, Capt. *Nathaniel* Seeley, Son of this Gentleman, was killed in Philip's War in the Narraganſet Fort Fight.

185 Lieut. Thomas Bull, before mentioned. He came to N. England in 1635, at the Age of 25.

'an hard Piece of Cheeſe and went no further, 'which may verify the old Saying *a little Armour* '*would ſerve if a Man knew where to place it.*

'Thus the Lord did great Things for his People 'among the Heathen whereof we are glad, *Praiſe* '*ye the Lord.*

[43] 'The Year following, the Colony of Con-'necticut being in great Want of Proviſion, Indian 'Corn being at twelve Shillings the Buſhel. The 'Court of *Connecticut* imployed Capt. *Maſon* and 'Mr. *William Wadſworth*, and Deacon *Edward* '*Stebbing*, to make a Trial what Providence would 'afford for their Relief, in this great Streight; who 'notwithſtanding ſome Diſcouragements they met 'with ſome Engliſh, went to a Place called *Pa-*'*comptuck*,[186] where they procured ſo much Corn at 'reaſonable Rates, that the Indians brought down 'to *Hartford* and *Windſor* fifty Cannoes laden with 'Corn at one Time, never was the like known to 'this Day, ſo that although the Lord was pleaſed 'to ſhew his People hard Things in their Begin-'engs, yet did he execute Judgment for the 'Oppreſſed, and gave Food to the Hungry, afford-'ing them his continued Protection and Bleſſing, 'in the bountifull Supply of the good Things of 'this Life, with the Continuance of his Goſpel and 'Ordinances, and a plentifull *Increaſe* of their 'Number, from *four* Plantations which was then 'the alone Number of the Colony of Connecticut; '*to twenty four Towns*,[187] which is the preſent

[186] Or Pecomptuck, ſince Deerfield.

[187] It muſt be remembered that this is what Mr. Allyn ſays and not

'Number of Towns in this Colony, *and from three* '*Churches to nineteen*, which is the Number now 'ſettled in this Colony."

Thus farr is Mr. *John Allyn* his Narrative of the *Pequot Troubles*, which I take to be the moſt perfect Account thereof that is extant, or that will probably be now attained.[188] ſince few of thoſe that were perſonally concerned in that *War* and who are fit to give a *Relation* thereof, are at this Day in the Land of the Living.

Neverthelesſs I have met with a Manuſcript in the Library of a learned and worthy Perſon deceaſed, wherein the Paſſages of the *Pequot War*, are deſcribed. The Author of the Script I know not, nor can conjecture, ſaving that it was one who had a particular and perſonal Acquaintance with thoſe Affairs. It doth in Subſtance agree with that of Mr. *John Allyn*: only in ſome Particulars, a more full Account of Proceedings is expreſſed. For this Manuſcript *Anonimus* doth *Relate* as followeth, *viz*. That in Anno 1634. a Bark wherein was Capt. *Stone*, and Capt. *Norton*, with ſix Men beſides going up Connecticut River were all killed by the *Pequot* Indians, and the Bark ſunk near a ſteep Rock, which to this Day bears the Name of Capt.

Capt. Maſon, for the Captain was dead before the Towns in Connecticut had increaſed to *twenty-four*. There appears to have been *twenty-ſix* Towns ſettled up to and including 1674. Maſon died "in "1672 or 1673." *Prince*.

188 This would be a ſingular Remark for a Hiſtorian to make in theſe Days, although I have heard within my Memory, a very good Writer of a Hiſtory of one of the important New England States, make the ſame.

Stones Rock. In the Year following a Bark going from the Bay, bound to *Virgina*, was by a Tempeſt caſt away at Long Iſland, certain Pequots there killed two Engliſhmen, the reſt eſcaping.

[44] In Anno 1636. A Veſſel going from Connecticut towards the Bay, putting in at Block-Iſland, the Indians coming aboard to Trade, killed the Maſter.[189] Another Veſſel coming from Connecticut, taken with a croſs Wind, intended to put in at *Narraganſet*, but could not; being therefore forced upon *Block-Iſland*, they ſaw a Bark with her Sayls up, driving too and fro, they hailed her, but no Anſwer was given; perceiving her full of Indians they ſuſpected the Engliſh belonging to the Veſſel were murdered, whereupon they diſcharged their Guns, ſhooting Bullets among the Indians, who, many of them immediately leaped overboard. The Maſter entered the Veſſel, and lifting up a Cloth ſaw an Engliſhman dead, and diſerning that many Indians were ſtill in the Hold, he returned to his own Veſſel again, from thence pouring in ſmall ſhot upon the Indians, for a while, untill the Wind coming fair; he ſailed away to *Boſton*, informing the Gouvernour and Council there, concerning what he had ſeen,[190] whence about an hundred

[189] This has Reference to the Murder of Capt. John Oldham, (See *N. E. Hiſt.-Gen. Reg.*, VII, 211), unleſs there was a previous and ſimilar Caſe and of which we have no other Account.

[190] This correſponds with an Account furniſhed the Author by the Rev. Thomas Cobbet of Ipſwich; which Account Mr. Cobbet ſays he had from the Mouth of Capt. John Gallup, who was preſent when the Indians were taken by his Father. Cobbet's Narrative was not printed till 1853, when it was publiſhed in the *N. Eng. Hiſt.-Gen. Reg.*, VII, 209-219.

Souldiers were forthwith ſent to *Block-Iſland*[191] As they were landing, the Indians came down and ſhot violently at them, wounding one Man, but as ſoon as one Engliſhman was landed, they ran away. The Engliſh purſued them two Dayes, burning their Corn and Wigwams, but the Indians betook themſelves to Swamps, thereby eſcaping with their Lives. After this they reſolved for the *Pequot* Country, having received ſome Intelligence of the Inſolency and Outrage of thoſe Indians. As they were ſailing up the River, many of the *Pequots* on both Sides of the River called to them, deſirous to know what was their End in coming thither, they were told that they deſired to ſpeak with *Saſſacus*, one of their Sachims; the Indians ſaid he was gone to *Long Iſland*; then it was demanded that *Moma-*

[191] The Expedition was under Endicott as General, and conſiſted of about 100 Men, which ſailed from Boſton near the End of Auguſt, 1636. The other principal Officers were Capt. John Underhill, Capt. Nathaniel Turner, Enſigns Jenyſon and Davenport. The Rev. John Higginſon of Salem, went as Chaplain. The Particulars of the Expedition may be found in Capt. Underhill's *Hiſtory*, Winthrop's *Journal*, Hubbard's *Indian Wars*, 120; but there is no Liſt of the Soldiers of which I am aware. I find on the Colonial Records that "George Munnings is granted five "Pounds in regard of the Loſſe of "his Eye in the Voyage to Block "Iſland." If an important Member of the Body was valued at £5, it might be intereſting to know what the whole was valued at in thoſe Days. But it appears that Munnings had ſome further Conſideration on Account of his Eye, though what it amounted to does not appear, as it was contingent on certain Fines, which might or might not have been remitted.

When Gen. Endicott went to chaſtiſe the Pequots they ſent their Women and Children to the Mohegans who protected them. This Miantonimo aſſerted to Roger Williams to ſhow that the Mohegans were not real Friends to the Engliſh.

nottuck[192] another of their Sachems ſhould appear. It was pretended that he was not at Home neither. The Engliſh went Aſhore, and required the Indians to deliver up thoſe that had murdered Capt. *Stone.* It was anſwered that they were alſo gone from Home, but they would ſend after them, and deliver them to Juſtice, and that they might the better keep the Engliſh in Parley, they ſaid that their Sachim would preſently come and treat with them. In the mean Time they tranſported Goods, Women and Children to another Place.

At laſt one of the Indians declared plainly, that *Momanottuck* would not come. Immediately a Skirmiſh followed, wherein one Indian was killed, and an Engliſhman was wounded. The Indians fled, the Engliſh purſuing, ſet Fire to their Wigwams, and deſtroyed their Corn, ſo did they return to their Veſſel. A few Days after this, going on Shore [45] again, as they were loading themſelves with Corn, the Indians violently aſſaulted them, ſo that they were forced to leave their Corn and ſtand to their Arms. At this Time an Indian was killed, and two Engliſhmen ſorely wounded. The Indians attempted the Veſſels, but were entertained with ſuch Volleys of ſmall Shot, as made them afraid to board any, ſo the Barks arrived ſafe at *Say-brook* Fort. The next Day ſome of the Fort going to the River to fetch Hay, the *Pequots* privily came

192 Since uſually written *Mononotto.* Roger Williams probably means the ſame Indian by *Maumanadtuck.* See *Maſs. Hiſt. Colls.*, 36, 192, 262. It was the Wife of this Chief that ſaved the Lives of the Captives mentioned in Note 148.

upon them took one Man and afterward roaſted him alive, another ſhot with five Arrows lived fourteen Weeks and dyed, the reſt eſcaped with much Danger.[193] After this the *Pequots* came near the Fort and deſtroyed many of the Engliſh Cattel. About two Miles diſtant from the Fort there was an Engliſh Houſe wherein were Souldiers. Their Commander charged them not to go out of doors, yet three of them would venture, and as they were a Muſket ſhot from the Houſe, the Indians encompaſſed them, and took two of them alive, the third being wounded did with his naked Sword eſcape through them to the Houſe, relating to the Company the ſad Event, and that one of thoſe Engliſh that were taken did firſt kill two Indians. The next Day all the Engliſh deſerted that Houſe, and repaired to the Fort. The Indians then quickly burned that, and two other Houſes. They made towards the Fort as if they would have done ſome great Matter; but a great Gun being diſcharged at them, they went quite away, and were no more ſeen at *Say-brook* for the greateſt Part of that

193 "Old Mr. Mitchell," ſays Gardiner, "was very urgent with me "to lend him the Boat to fetch Hay "from the Six Mile Iſland." Gardiner remonſtrated, ſaying he had not Men ſufficient, but was finally perſuaded to let the Boat go, and ſeveral Men ſet off. Part of them were enjoined to keep Guard, while the reſt loaded the Hay. This was neglected, and all went together on Shore. Suddenly the Indians roſe out of the long Graſs, killed three of them and took captive the Brother of Mr. Mitchell, Miniſter of Cambridge, and roaſted him alive. *Gardner*, 142-3. His Name was Butterfield. Savage ſays his Chriſtian Name was Samuel. Perhaps it was, but he gives no Evidence. The Place where Butterfield was taken was known for a Time as Butterfield's Meadow. It was on what is ſince called Calves Iſland. *Barber.*

Winter.[194] Only two Miles up the River two Men going in a Canoo to ſhoot Geeſe, the Indians hearing the Report of their Guns, came upon them. Thoſe two Engliſh ſought to ſave their Lives by padling, but the Indians purſued them with another Canoo ſhot at them and wounded one in his Head, who fell overboard, the other ſhot ſtoutly at the Indians, but at laſt being wounded and wearied, the Indians overtook him, he with his Paddle cleft one of the Indians Heads, but the reſt took him, and tortured him to Death.[195]

Feb. 22. The Lieut. with nine Souldiers well armed, went out of the Fort to burn the Woods thereabouts, being gone Half a Mile from Home they were beſett with about ſeventy Indians, who let fly their Arrows very fiercely; the Engliſh retreated, one Man preſently was ſhot in the Neck, and then did they lay Hands on him, he drew his Sword, but that was taken from him; Then would he (as the Indians afterwards teſtified) have killed himſelf, with his own Knife, but that alſo did the Indians deprive him of, and cut off his Noſe and Hands, and put him to a cruel Death; they ſhot down another Engliſhman with three [46] Arrows, and a third had one of his Ribs cleft with an Arrow, ſo that he died immediately. A fourth was mortally wounded, and though he got Home alive, he

194 This ſeems like an Abridgement of Gardiner's *Hiſtory*, without the Particulars.

195 "A Shallop coming down "the River in the Spring, [1636] "having two Men, one whereof "they killed at Six-mile Iſland, the "other came down drowned to us "Aſhore at our Doors, with an "Arrow ſhot into his Eye through "his Head." *Gardiner*, 143.

died within fourteen Hours, a fifth was sorely wounded, but afterwards recovered, and lived (the next Year) to behead that very Indian who had shot an Arrow into him. Yea, the Leiut. himself was wounded in this Skirmish. After this the Indians kept Leaguer before *Say-brook* Fort.[196]

March 9. A Body of Indians, consisting (as was conjectured) of two or three hundred come within Musket shot of the Fort, challenging the English to come out and fight, mocking and upbraiding them with such Words as the English used when by them tortured to Death, and bragged that

[196] Gardiner's Account of this desperate Adventure and furious Attack of the Pequots should be read in Connection. "In the 22d of "February I went out with ten Men "and three Dogs, Half a Mile "from the House [Fort] to burn "the Weeds, Leaves and Reeds, "upon the Neck of Land, because "we had felled twenty timber "Trees, which we were to roll to "the Water-side to bring home, "every Man carrying a length of "Match with Brimstone-matches "with him to kindle the Fire withal. "But when we came to the small "of the Neck, the Weeds burning, "I having before set two Sentinels "on the small of the Neck, I called "to the Men that were burning the "Reeds to come away, but they "would not until they had burnt "up the rest of their Matches. "Presently there starts up four "Indians out of the fiery Reeds, "but ran away, I calling to the rest "of our Men to come away out of "the Marsh. Then Robert Chap-"man and Thomas Hurlbut, being "Sentinels, called to me, saying "there came a Number of Indians "out of the other Side of the Marsh. "Then I went to stop them, that "they should not get [to] the Wood-"land; but Thomas Hurlbut cried "out to me that some of the Men "did not follow me, for Thomas "Rumble and Arthur Branch, threw "down their two Guns ran away; "then the Indians shot two of them "that were in the Reeds, and sought "to get between us and Home, but "darst not come before us, but "kept us in a Half-moon, we re-"treating and exchanging many a "Shot, so that Thomas Hurlbut "was shot almost through the Thigh, "John Spencer in the Back into his "Kidneys, myself into the Thigh, "two more were shot dead. But "in our Retreat I kept Hurlbut and "Spencer still before us, we de-"fending ourselves with our naked "Swords, or else they had taken us

they could kill Englishmen *all one Flyes:* but two great Gunns loaden with Carthages of Musket Bullets being fired at them, away they went, and hearing that the *Narragansets* were invading their Country, they visited *Seybrook* no more.[197]

After these Things, a Shallop coming down from Conecticut, with three Men rowing, was set upon by several Canoes of Indians, the English fought stoutly so long as they could, but one of them being shot through the Nose, so as the Arrow went out at the Crown of his Head, fell overboad and dyed; The other two were taken by the Indians, who ripped them up from the Bottom the Belly to the Throat, and cleft them down the Back

"all alive, so that the two sore "wounded Men, by our slow Re-"treat, got home with their Guns, "when our two sound Men ran "away and left their Guns behind "them. But when I saw the Cow-"ards that left us, I resolved to let "them draw Lots which of them "should be hanged, for the Articles "did hang up in the Hall for them "to read, and they knew they had "been published long before. But "at the Intercession of old Mr. "Mitchell, Mr. Higgisson, and "Mr. Pell, I did forbear. Within "a few Days after, when I had "cured myself of my Wound, I "went out with eight Men to get "some Fowle for our Reliefe, and "found the Guns that were thrown "away, and the Body of one Man "shot through, the Arrow going in "at the Right Side, the Head stick-"ing fast, Half through a Rib on "the Left Side, which I took out "and cleansed it, and presumed to "to send it to the Bay [Boston] "because they had said that the "Arrows of the Indians were of no "Force." *Hist. of the Pequot War,* 143-144.

"That very Indian" who was beheaded "the next Year" by the Man then desperately wounded, was named *Kiswas*, as will be elsewhere seen.

[197] This brief Episode is told at great Length by Gardiner in his History—too long for a Note in this Place. Gardiner mentions that Anthony Dike brought him a Letter, being "sent by Mr. Vane," then Governor, who required Gardiner to "prescribe the best way to quell "the Pequots, which I also did, and "with my Letter sent the Mans "Rib as a Token."

throughout, and afterwards hung them up by the Neck on a Tree by the River ſide, that the Engliſh might ſee them as they paſſed by; the Shallop they drew a Shore and ſet on Fire.[198]

May 15. 1637. Some of *Uncas* his Men being then at *Saybrook*, in order to aſſiſting the Engliſh againſt the *Pequots* eſpyed ſeven Indians, and ſlyly encompaſſing them, ſlew five of them, and took one Priſoner, and brought him to the Engliſh Fort, which was great Satisfaction and Encouragement to the Engliſh, who before that Exploit had many Fears touching the Fidelity of the Moheag Indians.[199] He whom they took Priſoner was a perfideous Villain, one that could ſpeak Engliſh well, having in Times paſt lived in the Fort, and knowing all the Engliſh there, had been at the ſlaughtering of all the Engliſh that were ſlaughtered thereabouts; he was a continual Spy about the Fort, informing *Saſacus* of what he ſaw or could learn. When this bloody Traitor was executed, his Limbs were by Violence pulled from one another, and burned to Aſhes: ſome of the Indian Executioners barbarouſly taking his Fleſh, they gave it to one another, and did eat it, withal ſinging about the Fire.[200]

198 This Shallop is that mentioned by Gardiner as belonging to "Mr. Michel," I ſuppoſe; and the Man ſo barbarouſly ripped in two was Maſter Tilly, of whom mention is already made.

199 The Mohegan Indians broke from the Pequots in the Year 1636. *Gardiner.*

200 The Indian thus barbarouſly executed was named *Kiſwas*, mentioned before. He had lived a Time at the Fort with Lt. Gardiner, as above remarked, but when the Expedition againſt the Pequots under Gen. Endicott cáme to Saybrook, he ran away; hence Gardiner called him a Traitor. The marked difference in the Narratives of this War

It is alſo reported that before the *Miſtick* Fight, a friendly Indian [47] that was ſent thither as a ſecret Spy, brought Word that the *Pequots* were ſinging, and dancing, and bleſſing their God, in that they ſuppoſed the Engliſh were gone from them; and that in the Night the Engliſh came upon them, they were fallen into a deep Sleep, by Reaſon of their long Dancing the Night before, and their Sentinel was gone out of his Place to light a Pipe of Tobacco, juſt as the Engliſh ſurprized them, and when our Souldiers gave Fire there was not one that miſſed; the *Pequots* ſo alarmed, in Horrour and Amazement crying *Wannocks Wannocks,*[201] i. e. Engliſhmen, Engliſhmen; ſome of the old Men taking hold of others that were willing to run away, and ſaying, as we have lived together, ſo let us dy together, the Wigwam which was firſt ſet on Fire, being to the windward Side carried all before it, (as is in the Narrative intimated). At that Time there were two Engliſh men ſlain, (one of which was thought to be ſhot by an Engliſh man) and twenty four wounded,

is obſervable throughout, and it is very apparent that the Jealouſies between the Heads of the different Colonies came near deſtroying them all; and the Man whom Hiſtory may decide ſaved them all, was the Founder of that Colony hated by all. But of this I have taken Notice in the Introduction.

The Account of the Execution of Kiſwas in Vincent's *Tract* correſponds with this in our Text, though it is more horrible, if poſſible. He ſays Capt. Underhill finiſhed the Execution by "ſhooting a Piſtol "through him to deſpatch him." *A True Relation of the late Battell,* 36.

201 In Maſon's *Hiſtory* the Pequot Word of Alarm is "*Owanux,* "*Owanux.*" Why Mr. Allyn changed the Orthography, he does not inform us. Mr. Prince in his Edition of Maſon's Work ſets the Matter right. See Note 156.

whereof one dyed within few Dayes.[202] Alſo fourty Indians that were Friends to the Engliſh were hurt in that Engagement. It was ſuppoſed that no leſs than five or ſix hundred Pequot Souls were brought down to Hell that Day.[203] Moreover it is therein added, that as the Engliſh marched towards their Veſſels in the River, ſtill as they came near any Swamp, they ſent in a Volley of Shot leſt the Enemy ſhould haply be in Ambuſh in thoſe dark Places of the Earth, and ſome Indians have related that the Engliſh did by that Means kill more Men of War in their marching away, than in the Fight at the Fort, whereby alſo *Saſſacous* his Plot to cut off the Engliſh as they paſſed by Swamp-ambuſhments was utterly and happily fruſtrated.

It is further ſaid, that an Indian called *Wequaſh* did direct the Engliſh to the Fort at *Miſtick*,[204]

202 Underhill mentions a very remarkable Circumſtance connected with the firſt Attack on the Fort—that at the Word—Fire—every Gun went off at the ſame Moment—which he thus relates: "So re-" markable it appeared to us, as we" could not but admire at the Pro-" vidence of God in it, that Soldiers" ſo unexpert in the Uſe of their" Arms, ſhould give ſo complete a" Volley, as though the Finger of" God had touched both Match" Flint," P. 23.

203 This ſeems to have been a favorite Expreſſion of our Author. It will be met with again in the Courſe of the Work.

204 The other Hiſtorians of the War do not give this Indian Credit for this moſt important Service. He lived till about 1643, and was in great Favor with Roger Williams. See his *Key*, P. 22 (*R. I. Hiſt. Colls.*, i). See alſo *Book Indians*, 166. It appears from Roger Williams's Letters, that there was another Indian named Wequaſchuck, whoſe Name with the Engliſh ſlid into Wequaſh Cook, and became confounded with that of Wequaſh. But Wequaſh was a Pequot, and Wequaſhchuck was a Nyantick, and "the Man," ſays Williams, "to my Knowledge, that ſheltered" Audſah, the Murtherer of Mr." Oldham. *Maſs. Hiſt. Soc. Colls.*,

which *Wequash* was by birth a Sachim of that Place but upon ſome Diſguſt received he went from the Pequots to the Narraganſets, and became a chief Captain under *Miantonimo;* and that there were with thoſe eighty Engliſh Souldiers, who engaged in this Expedition againſt the *Pequots*, at firſt four hundred Indians, whereof three hundred were *Narraganſets*. The Day before the Fight there was ſome Agitation which Fort ſhould be firſt aſſaulted, whether that of *Miſtick*, or another eight Miles further, where *Saſſacus* himſelf reſided. The Engliſh were an End to be upon *Saſſacus*, but the Indians were afraid ſaying, that *Saſſacus* was *all one God*, and nobody could kill him; this made the Engliſh yet more deſirous to try what Power was in this *imaginary Deity*, and that was the Concluſion, whereupon many of the *Narraganſets* withdrew and returned all Home, reporting that the Engliſh were cut off by the Indians; the Fame of which was quickly at [48.] Boſton; to the great Affliction of the Engliſh untill ſuch Time as the Truth of Things was certainly known.[205] In this *Interim* one of Capt. *Underhils* Souldiers fell lame,

36, 208, 242. For other curious Particulars in the Life of *Wequaſh*, ſee *Ibid*, 198. See alſo *Note* 177. Mr. Williams recommended Wequaſh for a Guide in the Expedition. Many other intereſting Facts reſpecting this Indian are brought to Light by the newly publiſhed Letters of Williams.

205 "Preſently upon this [May "25] came News from the Narra"ganſett, that all the Engliſh, and "two hundred of the Indians "were cut off in their Retreat, for "Want of Powder and Victuals. "Three Days after, this was con"firmed by a Poſt from Plimouth, "with ſuch probable Circumſtances, "as it was generally believed."— Winthrop, *Journal*, i, 225. See alſo Bradford, 358-359.

not being able to go ſo far as the Place where *Saſſacus* was ſuppoſed to be; whence the Captain changed his Purpoſe, and determined for *Miſtick*;[206] and Capt. *Maſon* was not willing they ſhould part aſunder, ſo did they agree to make their Aſſault there; few or none of the Indians which were in the Fort eſcaped, whole Companyes of them gathered together and were burnt to Death; thoſe that eſcaped the Fire, the Engliſh without the Fort ſlew them with the Sword, ſo that round about the Fort, dead Men lay hideous to behold.

The *Indians Goliah*, even their only Champion, being a Man of huge Stature was then ſlain, he brake through the Souldiers, and although one *Sergeant* ſtroke him on the Neck with his Cutlaſh, he got by him and by five Souldiers more, but the ſixth killed him.[207]

And thoſe that eſcaped the Sword, the friendly Indians that encompaſſed the Engliſh took as Captives to the Number of eighteen.[208]

This was done upon Friday, May 26. Anno 1637. A memorable Day.[209]

Upon this notable Victory, *Saſſacus* his Heart failed him, his Men of War being many of them

[206] If this were true, it would be very remarkable indeed, that through the Failure of a ſingle Soldier the Plan of the Campaign was changed.

[207] This was the Nameleſs "ſtout "Indian" mentioned by Vincent. See Note 160, and 161. Johnſon alſo heard ſomething about the Feat of this *Indian Goliah*, as is ſhown in Note 158.

[208] This does not agree with the other Accounts as will have been ſeen.

[209] Winthrop records the Attack on the Fort on May 25th; but the 26th is doubtleſs the actual Date. Bradford does not give any Date.

cut off, ſo that he fled his Country, breaking down his Forts, and burning his Wigwams himſelf, he marched away by Land, with ſome Men, Women and Children, their Goods being ſent away in the *Cannoo's*. The Engliſh at *Say-brook* had Notice of the *Cannoos*, and an Advantage to ſtop their Paſſage, but Capt. *Kilpatrick*[210] delayed untill the Opportunity was gone, ſo that *Saſſacus* with his routed Train, coming up to his *Cannoos* ſix Miles from *Say-brook* Fort, was tranſported over the River, and fled towards *Quinipiack*. Being now inraged he ſollicited his Men of War, that they might go, and fall upon the Engliſh at *Connecticut*, but ſome of them not conſenting, that Deſign was not put in Execution; he therefore fled to the *Mohawks*, who (being as is ſuppoſed excited thereto by the revengefull *Narraganſets*) cut off his Head.[211]

Many of the *Pequots* before *Saſſacus* his Death

210 Why Capt. Daniel *Patrick's* Name is thus transformed muſt be left to conjecture.

211 It appears that the Mohawks ſent the Head and Skin of Saſſacus to the Engliſh;—for Winthrop ſays, under date of Auguſt 5, that Mr. Hooker, Mr. Stone, Mr. Wilſon, Mr. Ludlow, Mr. Pinchon, and about twelve more arrived at Boſton from Connecticut by way of Providence, bringing with them as a Trophy, "a Part of the Skin and lock "of the Hair of Saſſacus and his "Brother and five other Pequot "Sachems, who being fled to the "Mohawks for Shelter, with their "Wampum, (being to the Value of "£500,) were by them ſurpriſed "and ſlain, with twenty of their "beſt Men." *Journal*, i, 235.

Records of the Reception at Boſton of the Heads and Hands of the Indians ſeems to have been made as coolly as almoſt any other matter-of-courſe Affairs. Yet there were ſome in the Land who did not approve of ſuch Barbarities. "Thoſe "dead Hands,,' wrote Roger Williams, "were no pleaſing Sight. . . . "I have alwaies ſhowne Diſlike to "ſuch diſmembering the Dead."—*Maſs. Hiſt. Colls.*, 36, 207.

returned to their Country again; but Souldiers being ſent from the *Maſſachuſets* the returned *Pequots* were preſently diſreſted, ours ranſacking their Country, and ſetling a Garriſon therein, quickly came back to *Sey-brook*, with one of the *Pequot* Sachims, and other *Indian* Captives. After which a Supply of Men from *Connecticut* coming to the Maſſachuſets Souldiers, they ſailed Weſtward in Purſuit of the *Pequots* who were fled that Way, ſailing along to the Weſtward of *Mononowuttuck*,[212] the [49] Wind not anſwering their Deſires, they caſt Anchor, where two Sachems from *Long-Iſland*[213] came to them, deſiring Peace and promiſing to deliver up whatever *Pequots* ſhould fly to them for Shelter, ſome ſcattering *Pequots* were then taken and ſlain, as alſo the Pequot *Sachem*, before expreſſed, had his Head cut off, whence that Place did bear the Name of *Sachems Head*[214] Being

[212] Like moſt other Indian Names, this has been variouſly written. Uſually now Menunkatuc; the preſent Town of Guilford in Connecticut. In two Years after this purſuit of the flying Pequots—1639—it was ſettled by the Engliſh. Roger Williams, writing in Sept. 1637, ſays the Place where the laſt Fight was, was called *Saſquankit*. See *Maſs. Hiſt. Colls.*, 36, 213.

[213] Theſe Long Iſland Indians are very ſlightly paſſed over, while their Services probably ſaved the Engliſh Settlers from Deſtruction, if Lieut. Gardiner may be allowed to have known the Indian Policy of that Day, and has faithfully narrated it in his *Hiſtory of the Pequot War*, 153, *et ſeq.*

[214] Though moſt of the Forces went from the Fort at Saybrook by Water, a Number of Soldiers with Uncas and his Indians ſcoured the Shores near the Sea, leſt any of the Pequots ſhould lurke there. Not a great Way from this Harbor they came acroſs a Pequod Sachem with a few Indians, whom they purſued. As the ſouth Side of the Harbor is formed by a long narrow Point of Land, the Pequods went on to this Point, hoping their Purſuers would have paſſed by them. But Uncas

come near to *Quinipiack*[215] obſerving a Smoak, it was conjectured that the Enemy might be thereabouts, whereupon Indians were ſet on Shore to hunt after them, but they could find no more then two, one of which was the Sachems Son of that Place, ſuppoſed to be Confederate with the *Pequots*. They promiſed to conduct the Engliſh to the Enemy, but failed in Performance. After that they took another Indian Captive, who likewiſe engaged to lead the Engliſh upon the Pequots, but he directed them into a quite contrary Way, for which his Life was deſervedly taken from him.[216] But an Indian called *Luz*, who was before taken Captive by our Souldiers in the Pequot Country, with two other Indians that were his Kinſmen, promiſed that if the Engliſh would give him and his Kinſmen their Lives, he would conduct them

knew Indian's Craft, and ordered ſome of his Men to ſearch that Point. The Pequods perceiving they were purſued, ſwam over the Mouth of the Harbor, which is narrow; but they were way-laid, and taken as they landed. The Sachem was ſentenced to be ſhot to Death. Uncas ſhot him with an Arrow, cut off his Head, and ſtuck it up in the Crotch of a large oak Tree near the Harbor, where the Skull remained for a great many Years. Thus from this extraordinary Incident, the Name of Sachems Head was adopted to the Harbor. Ruggles's *Hiſt. Guilford*, in Barber's *Hiſt. Colls.*, 216.

[215] New Haven, which Name it received three Years after the War, namely, in 1640. Hoadly's *New Haven Records*, i, 40. It does not appear why this Name was made Choice of, yet very likely it was conferred in Remembrance of New Haven in Suſſex, England. The Engliſh began the Settlement at Quinipiack late in the Fall of 1637, and the next Year bought the Lands thereabouts of the Indian Claimants.

[216] It is not very concluſive Evidence that theſe Indians favored the Pequot Murderers, becauſe they failed to lead the Engliſh to their hiding Places; but a Thirſt for Indian Blood is rather more concluſive, now that their Hand was in.

to the Enemies they ſought after. He did ſo, the Pequots with other Indians belonging to thoſe Parts, were found near a Swam, into which they did betake themſelves for Safety, upon the Approach of the Engliſh Souldiers. After a while, an Indian came out of the Swamp unarmed, with a Preſent of *Wampam*. The Engliſh declared to him that they came not to take away the Lives of the Indians nor their Goods, if they would deliver up the Murtherers that were amongſt them. After which ninety nine came forth with their Sachim, who offered as a Preſent all the Eſtate he had to diſpoſe of, and that was nothing but the Coat on his Back, being a Bears Skin. He was ſent into the Swamp again to ſignify to the Pequots there lurking, that if they would bring forth the Murderers it ſhould be better for them, which they would not do, but at laſt profeſſed they had lived together, and would dy together.

There were about ſeventy or eighty Indians in the Swamp, amongſt whom there were twelve Murderers. So then the Engliſh beſett the Swamp; and ſhot in upon them, and the Indians at them, ſome of which were furniſhed with Guns.[217] One in ſpecial that was climbing up a Tree to ſhoot at the Engliſh, was eſpyed by a Souldier, who ſent a Bullet into him before the other could make his Shot. In the Night time the Indians brake away. Diligent ſearch was the next Day made in the

[217] It was aſcertained that the Pequots had, in all, among them, about ſixteen Guns, and a due Quantity of Ammunition. The Engliſh ſay they were ſupplied by the Dutch at Manhattan,

Swamp for dead Indians. Not many (as ſome have made Narration) but ſeven, and no more could be found. As for the Captives a [50] Guard was appointed to look after them, they were charged upon Peril of their Lives not to Attempt running away; yet one of them betook himſelf to his Heels, but a Souldier ſhot after him, and killed him, which ſtruck a Terror into the Reſt of the Captives, that no Man durſt make an Offer to eſcape. Theſe Things do I find related by *Anonymous.* There is not much more additional to what is expreſſed in Mr. *Allyns* Narrative. Some of theſe Particulars inſiſted on confirming the Truth of that. Only one Thing more is contained therein which I have not elſewhere met with, which therefore it may not be amiſs here to take Notice of. It is this, whereas on April 23. 1637.[218] The Indians coming upon the Engliſh at *Wethersfield,* killed nine Perſons, and took two young Women alive, and carried them away Captives, Means were uſed to effect their Deliverance, but at firſt, in vain.

On May 8. A Dutch Sloop eame by *Saybrook* Fort, having on board an Indian Captive, who ſaid ſhe was *Momonottocks* Squaw. The Engliſh there deſired the Dutchmen to let them have the Squaw in order to redeeming the Engliſh Captives, offering to give them to the Value of two hundred Pound, provided that thoſe Captives might be ſet at Liberty. The Dutchmen hoping to gain much by ſuch an Indian were ſome of them loth to part

218 See Note 148.

with her. In Conclusion Capt. *Underhill* (who then commanded the Fort) having obtained the Consent of the Master of the Vessel, did *vi et armis* take the Squaw out of the Sloop. Afterwards when the *Moheags* came to *Saybrook* that Squaw appeared to be one belonging to them, whom the *Pequots* had captivated, and she made the Dutch believe she was *Momonottucks Squaw*, hoping that thereby she should obtain the more courteous Usage amongst those into whose Hands she was fallen, so that the Contest between the English and Dutch about her was needless. In the *Interim* the Dutch Governour sent another Sloop, with Order to redeem the Engish Captives if possible, and those Dutch did in Conclusion wilily accomplish their Design. For being arrived in the *Pequot* Country, certain Indians coming aboard to trade with them after they had been Trafficking they were clapt under Hatches, and told they should not be set at Liberty, except they would deliver the English Maids that were captivated, and presently hoysted Sayle, as if they would be gone. The *Pequots* on Shore called to them, declaring that if they would come to an Anchor, the English Captives should be brought to them, which was done, and the Men whom the Dutchmen had secured in their Sloop given in Exchange for the English Captives, who were also brought safe to *Saybrook*, May 16. when our Souldiers waited for a Wind to carry them to engage with [51] the *Pequots*, and that Wind which for a few Dayes kept the English from going upon their Expedition, brought that Dutch Sloop to redeem thoſe Captives, concerning whom there was no other Hope (and that was a Trouble to ſome) but that the Engliſh would be neceſſiteted to deſtroy them amongſt the Indians, in the Day when their Fort ſhould be attacqued.

Some have thought that in theſe Narratives, there is not due Notice taken of what was done by the *Maſſachuſets* Forces. The Truth is, the Conqueſt obteined over the *Pequots* was wonderfully the Lords doing, nor may we aſcribe much to Man therein, yet muſt it be acknowledged (and the Narratives deny it not) that Capt. *Vnderhill* (and thoſe under his Command) who was ſent from the *Maſſachuſets* did acquit himſelf worthily, when the Indians at *Miſtick* Fort were cut off. It muſt alſo be owned that the *Maſſachuſets* Souldiers did glean the *Pequots* after that, (and we know who, to pacify thoſe that were unreaſonably diſſatisfied, was ready to ſay, *Is not the Gleaning of Ephraim better than the Vintage of Abiezer;*) Likewiſe they had an equal Hand with others in the Service done at the Swamp, where ſuch a Multitude of Indians were either ſlain or taken as Captives.[219]

And beſides theſe Things inſtead on, there are who have taken Notice of ſome other Specialtyes of Divine Providence relating to thoſe Commotions

[219] Our Author ſeems to have learned in ſome Way, that Jealouſy had prevailed among the Men who were ſent againſt the Pequots. It is apparent from the different Accounts, that the Connecticut Men were not very modeſt in their Claims of the Honor of deſtroying thoſe Indians, as is ſufficiently apparent from Maſon's Story.

which have been of momentous Confiderations, to the People inhabiting this Wildernefs, which it may not be amifs here to remark. It is then worthy our Obfervation, that the guilty bloody *Pequots* after they had treacheroufly murthered Capt. *Stone* and his Company, brought Prefents of *Wampum* and *Bever* to the Englifh at *Bofton*, defiring their Friendfhip, pleading that *Stone* had (who was like enough to do it) offered fome Abufe to them, in furprizing divers Indians, and binding them, and forcing them to fhew him the Way up the River, &c.[220]—wherefore a Peace was concluded upon Condition they would fuffer the Englifh who defired to inhabit *Connecticut*, there quietly to live, and alfo deliver up thofe Men who had been guilty of *Stones* Death. Thefe Things were not performed by the Pequots. The Reafon why they were the more willing to have Peace with the Englifh was, in that they were fallen out with the Dutch at *Monhatus*, as alfo with the *Narraganfetts* who were then potent and numerous; and at firft they thought Scorn to make Overtures of Peace to them, proudly defigning the Subjugation of all their neighbor Indians, which wrought well for the Englifh. Howbeit not unlike him that faid: *Flectere fi nequeo fuperos Acheronta movebo.* When they faw they could not attain [52] their

220 This agrees with Winthrop's Record as found in his *Journal*, i, 148. The "&c." in our Text is thus explained in the fame Place: "This was related with fuch Confidence and Gravity, as, having "no Means to contradict it, we "inclined to believe it." Thomas Dudley was Governor of Maffachufetts, at that Time (1634).

Ends with the Englifh, except they would let Juftice have a free Paffage, and having contracted frefh bleeding Guilt upon themfelves by new and outragious Murthers, and Crueltyes, they earneftly folicited the *Narragănfets* to joyn with them in their wicked Confederacy againft the Englifh, *Satan* fuggefting to them fuch Arguments as did almoft prevail. For they told the *Narraganfets* that if they joyned with the Englifh, they did but make Way for their own Ruine, fince after the *Pequots* were conquered, they would find an Occafion to fall upon the *Narraganfets*, and that they fhould not need to come to open battel with the Englifh, only fire their Houfes and kill their Cattel, and lye in Ambufh to fhoot them as they went about their Occafions, fo would they quickly be forced to leave this Country, and the Indians in the mean while not expofed to any great Hazard.[221] Had the *Narraganfets* been overcome by thefe Arguments, it would have occafioned far greater Trouble and Hazard to all the

[221] The above is very fimilar to what Hubbard had ftated, in his *Hiftory of the War*, p. 121. But that elegant Writer inimitably adds: " Michiavel himfelf, if he had fat " in Counfel with them, could not " have infinuated ftronger Reafons " to have perfwaded them to a " Peace. It is faid, that fo much " Reafon was apprehended in thefe " Motives, that the Narraganfets " were once wavering, and were " almoft perfwaded to have granted " an Ear to their Advice and Per " fwafion, and joyned all againft the " Englifh; but when they confid- " ered what an Advantage they had " put into their Hands by Strength " and Favour of the Englifh, to take " a full Revenge of all their former " Injuries upon their inveterate " Enemies: the Thought of that " was fo, fweet, that it turned the " Scale againft all other Confiderations whatever." *Ibid.*

Neither our Author nor Mr. Hubbard was aware probably, of the perilous Efforts of Roger Williams to prevent the Alliance of the Pequots and Narraganfets. See *Hiftory and Antiquities of Bofton*, 204.

Englſh Colonyes, newly ſettled in this Land. But therefore God in Mercy to his People prevented it. Commiſſioners were then ſent from *Boſton* into the *Narraganſett* Country, to endeavour that thoſe Indians might be kept from Complyance with the Enemy. There is one who having a little enquired into theſe Things, doth *Relate* that the old *Kanonicus* did diſſwade the Pequots from War, adviſing rather to deliver up the Murderers. They made believe as if they would do ſo, and when a Band of Souldiers was ſent into the *Pequot* Country for that End, they bid them ſtay awhile and the Murderers ſhould be brought to them, and certain Indians converſing with our Souldiers, did very much obſerve the Armor which was upon them, and would point where they ſhould hit them with their Arrows, notwithſtanding. In fine, when a great Body of Indians appeared on an Hill not far off, thoſe that were with the Souldiers went over to them, when they all came together, they gave a ſcornful Shout, and ſo ran all away, making their Boaſt to others, how they had deluded the Engliſh; ſo that *Canonicus* his Adviſe to the *Pequots* took no Effect. After which the *Narraganſets* were not only prevailed with to decline joyning with the Enemy, but (as is intimated in the above written Narrative) they pretended they would fight for the Engliſh; albeit when it came to in good earneſt, they proved themſelves Cowards, doing little againſt the Enemies, except in unmanly Inſultations when they ſaw them in Miſery: For whereas it was cuſtomary with the *Pequots*, when they had overcome their Enemies, inſultingly to triumph, ſaying, *O brave Pequots!* The *Narraganſets* ſeeing them wounded or conſuming to Death in their burning Wigwams, would taunt [53] at them and vaunt over them, ſaying, *O brave Pequots! O brave Pequots!* The more of a Divine Hand is there to be taken Notice of in overcoming the *Pequots* by a ſmall Number of Engliſh and Indians. Alſo the *Pequots* were more furniſhed with Armes then before times they had been: ſince the Dutchmen had ſold ſome Guns to them; and beſides their Bowes and Arrows they had an Abundance of ſmall Hatchets, and *Mohawgs*-hammers[222] made of Stone, yet God would not ſuffer them to find their Hands.

What ſpecial Acts of Valour were manifeſted by any of our *Commanders* or Souldiers in this Expedition, beyond what is expreſſed in the fore-mentioned *Narrative*, I am not able to *Relate;* Nor am I (though willing that Mens Vertues ſhould be duly acknowledged) diſpoſed to ſay much on thoſe Accounts, reſpecting ſuch as are yet alive, as knowing that however it may pleaſe ſome by nouriſhing a proud Humour, it would be nauſeous to others, and deemed adulatory by wiſe and impartial Readers.

Only I remember Capt. *Davenport* (that good

[222] Doubtleſs what are ſince called *War-clubs*. Theſe were ſometimes made by forcing a well wrought Stone of ſome four Inches in Length, of a conical Form into a ſmall green Tree near the Roots. After remaining thus for two or three Years the Wood would become tightly bedded into a groove made in the Stone, and thus a very formidable Weapon was produced. Different Tribes had different War Clubs.

Man, who was afterwards Commander of the Caſtle at *Boſton*, and there ſlain by Lightning)[223] once told me, that himſelf with two or three more, engaged with no leſſe than thirty Indians, and that there were ſeventeen Arrows ſhot into his Coat, but having on a Coat of Male, none of thoſe Arrows hurt him, only one that happened to ſtrike where he was not defended by his Coat.

Alſo he reſcued a poor Souldier, that was in extream Danger of being devoured by thoſe Wolves; For two Maſtive-Indians that lay in Ambuſh, as a Party of Souldiers paſſed by, ſuppoſing they had all paſt, ſnatched hold of him whom they thought to be the laſt Man, and were running away with him upon their Shoulders, Capt. *Davenport* followed them with his drawn Cutlaſh, but ſtill as he lifted up his Hand to ſtrike at them theſe *Gigantine Salvages* held up the poor Man they were running away with, whereby for a while they ſecured their own Bodyes from the Blow, until at laſt mſſing the Engliſhman, Capt. *Davenport* ſmote one of the Indians, whereupon they threw down their Prey, and ran for their Lives.[224]

He that giveth Account of this laſt Paſſage, doth alſo *Relate* another Particular no leſſ pleaſant; namely, that whereas the *Pequots* obſerved, that the Engliſh, being willing to ſhow as much Mercy as would ſtand with Juſtice, did only captivate and not kill the *Squaws*, ſome great Indian Boyes would

[223] He was killed as he lay upon his Bed, July 15th, 1665, aged 59; having lain down to Reſt in the Heat of the Day.

[224] See *ante*, Note 176.

cry, *I Squaw, I Squaw,* thereby to eſcape with their Lives.[225]

[54] But to be Serious, That which Governour Winthrop writeth in his Letter, publiſhed by Mr. *Morton*[226] is very memorable, *viz.* that in one Fight though the Indians coming up cloſe to our Men, ſhot their Arrows thick upon them, ſo as to pierce their Hat brims, and their Sleeves, and Stockings, and other Parts of their Cloaths, yet ſo miraculouſly did the Lord preſerve them, as that (excepting three that raſhly ventured into a Swamp after them) not one of them was wounded. And truly to ſet aſide caſual Conſiderations, there were two Reaſons obvious, that may be aſſigned as Cauſes of that glorious and ſpeedy Succeſs, which God gave to the Euglish againſt the *Pequot* Indians.

I. Blaſphemy of thoſe Enemies. For ſome of them ſaid, that Engliſh mans God was one Flye, which execrable Blaſphemy the bleſſed God would not bear from thoſe his Enemies. Alſo when ſome Engliſh were cruelly tortured to Death by them, they would in a Way of Diverſion bid them call upon God now, and blaſphemouſly mock at them when they did ſo. Therefore did the Lord bring thoſe bloody Blaſphemers in a Moment down to Hell, yea, and damned them above Ground, when they lay frying in the Fire that was kindled in their Houſes, and making horrible outcries.

2. There was a mighty Spirit of Prayer and

[225] With *Mourt's Relation* before him the Author could have ſeen that this Story had its Origin ſeveral Years before the Pequot War. That it might have happened again is not altogether improbable.

[226] In Morton's *Memorial.*

Faith then ſtirring, both in thoſe that ſtaid at Home, and in ſome that ventured their Lives in the high Places of the Field. That Reverend Man of God Mr. *Wilſon*, (who excelled in thoſe Graces of Faith and Love) went forth with the Souldiers that went from this Colony. I think I have myſelf heard him ſay, (or if I have not, others have) that *he was before he went out, as certain that God would give the Engliſh the Victory over thoſe Enemies, as if he had ſeen the Victory already obteined.* Such great Faith did the Lord ſtir up in the Heart of that Holy Man, and of other his Servants; and by Faith did they *turn to Fight the Armyes of the Aliens.* So then, thoſe Enemies being ſubdued, in ſuch Wayes and by ſuch Means as hath been expreſſed, the Terror of God fell upon all the Heathen round about, and the Engliſh were dreadful to them: when they heard that the Engliſh had ſlain, and taken Captive ſeven hundred Indians, and killed thirteen *Sachims* (who are their Kings) there was no more Spirit left in them. The *Pequots* beſt Friends were afraid to receive ſuch as fled to them for Refuge. But happy was he counted that could make Friendſhip with the Engliſh, ſo that two of the *Sachims* in *Long-Iſland*[227] came to that worthy Gentleman Captain (afterwards Lieut. Colonel)

[227] Theſe were the Sachems, without Doubt, induced to aid the Engliſh by Lt. Gardiner. The Name of one of them was *Waiandance.* Winthrop ſays, "the Indians about "ſent in ſtill many Pequot's Heads "and Hands from Long Iſland and "other Places, and Sachems of "Long Iſland came voluntarily, and "brought a Tribute to us of twenty "Fathom of Wampum, each of "them." *Journal*, i, 247.

Stoughton [228] entreating that they might be under our Protection. Alſo two of the *Napannet* Sachims, addreſſed themſelves to Governour *Winthrop*, [55] ſeeking to be in Favour with the Engliſh. Theſe Things deſerve to be mentioned among the *Magnalia Dei*, which he hath wrought for his *New-England-People*.

Matters being again reduced to this peaceable State, that Land reſted from War, and that for the Space of almoſt forty Years together. Howbeit Jealouſies amongſt the Engliſh grounded upon Treacheries and Conſpiracies amongſt the Indians, (and ſome particular Acts of Hoſtility and Outrages by them committed) there have been, more than once or twice, ſince the *Pequot-Troubles* were ended.

For in Anno 1638, the publick Peace was endangered by Occaſion of a Murder committed by an Engliſh man upon an Indian. Thus it was, One *Arthur Peach* a young Deſperado, who had been a Souldier in the *Pequot* War, and done notable Service, being bold and forward in any deſperate Attempt, after he was returned Home he was loth to go to Work, wherefore he reſolved to go to the Dutch Plantation, and enticed three Perſons, that were other Mens Servants, to run away with him. As they were travailing through the Woods, they met a *Narraganſet-Indian*, and deſired him to take

[228] His Lieut. Colonelcy was obtained in England; he having returned to that Country and ſerved in the Civil War. He did not return again to New-England. He was Father of William Stoughton, Lt. Governor and Chief Juſtice of Maſſachuſetts.

a Pipe of Tobacco, which the Indian was willing to do, *Peach* told his *Comrades*, he would kill him; they were afraid to do that, but let him alone to do as he would. When he ſaw his Time, he ran the Indian through with his Rapier, and took away his *Wampam* from him, ſuppoſing he had left him dead, but after they were gone, the Indian made a Shift to get Home, where he dyed of his Wound within few Dayes; But told other Indians that ſuch and ſuch Engliſh-men had mortally wounded him; The *Sachims* therefore preſently found out theſe Men (only one of them eſcaped) who had done the Murder, and carried them away to the Engliſh at *Aquidnet* Iſland, where they were examined and committed. In the mean Time the *Narraganſets* were about to riſe in Arms, ſome of them conceiving that they ſhould find the *Pequots* Words true, that the Engliſh would fall upon them, now the other were vanquiſhed. To be ſhort, the Murder being confeſſed by the Partyes guilty, the Court in *Plymouth* did by Advice from Magiſtrates and Elders in the *Bay*, condemn and ſee Execution done upon thoſe three *Engliſh men* for murdering that one Indian; whereupon the other Indians magnifyed the Juſtice which they ſaw among the *Engliſh*, and Peace was continued.[229] Yet after this new Fears and Troubles did ariſe upon other

[229] The three Engliſhmen were executed at Plymouth, Sept. 4th, 1638. Their Names were—Arthur Peach, Thomas Jackſon and Richard Slinnings. An exceedingly intereſting Letter of Roger Williams, detailing the Particulars of the Murder may be ſeen in the *Maſs. Hiſt. Colls.*, Vol. 21, p. 170, &c.

Accounts. For although the *Narraganſets*, and the *Moheags* did Anno 1638. come under ſolemn Promiſe that they would not engage in a War, either amongſt themſelves, or with other Indians, until they had adviſed with, and obtained Approbation [56] from the Engliſh. Neverthelеſs *Miantonimo*, the chief *Narraganſet Sachim*, was continually picking Quarrels with the *Moheags*, deſigning to make them become his Vaſſals. Some (*viz.* Mr. *Gorges* and Mr. *Johnſon*)[230] have related that *Miantonimo* was ſet on by certain *vagabond Engliſh*, known by the Name of *Gortonians*,[231] who being deep Apoſtates from, and bitter Enemies unto the Wayes of Chriſt, profeſſed by our Fathers, might eaſily be induced to animate Motions of that Nature. However *Miantonimo* choſe rather to accompliſh his Ends upon the *Moheags* by Treachery, than by open War; and hired a *Pequot* Indian who was ſubjected to *Vncas* (the *Moheags Sachim*) to aſſaſſinate him that was become his Lord, which the Indian attempted accordingly; inſomuch as on a certain Evening as *Vncas* was paſſing from one Wigwam to another, he was ſhot into the Arm by

230 This Confuſion of Authors requires ſome Elucidation. Johnſon's *Wonderworking Previdence*, &c., printed in London in 1654, appears to have been taken by Sir Ferdinando Gorges the younger, who by cancelling its Title-page and ſubſtituting one with his own Name as Author, impoſed upon the Public. It would ſeem that our Author was aware of the Fact, and yet makes a Reference as if there were two Works. See Prince, *Preface to his Annals*

231 For a rational View of the much abuſed Gortonians and the more abuſed Narraganſet Chief Miantonimo, the Reader is referred to the able and lucid Pages of the *Hiſtory of Rhode Iſland*, by Gov. Arnold, Vol. 1, 115, *et. ſeq.*

an Arrow, but recovered the Houſe he intended without receiving further Hurt.[232]

The Indian who was ſuſpected about this Matter, being called to an Account about a great Sum of *Wampam-peag*, by him poſſeſſed, could not give any tolerable Account, how he came by his Money, which augmented Jealouſies of his being hired by *Miantonimo* to kill *Vncas*. *Vncas* then made his Complaint to the Engliſh; the Iſſue was, that *Miantonimo* and the ſuſpected Indian came to *Boſton*, where he was examined, at firſt in the Preſence of *Miantonimo*, by whoſe Help he had framed an *Artificial Lye*, ſaying that one Night as he came out of a thick Swamp, *Vncas* deſired him to ſay that he was hired by *Miantonimo* to kill *Vncas*, and that therefore he cut his Arm with the Flint of his Gun, that Men might think he had been ſhot with an Arrow. This pittiful Story made the Engliſh ſuſpect *Miantonimo* more vehemently than ever, and upon a further private Examination (much againſt *Miantonimo's* Mind) they ſaw Cauſe to believe that he was ſecretly deſigning Miſchief againſt the Engliſh, as well as againſt *Vncas*. Neverthele ſs, it was thought beſt to diſmiſs him for the preſent, only with an Engagement to remit the ſuſpected *Pequot*

[232] It is ſcarcely neceſſary to remark, after the Reference in the laſt Note, that from exiſting Documents the Reverſe of what our Author has delivered is the Truth; Uncas was the Scamp and Miantonimo was the upright and honourable Man. But Uncas's Sins were forgiven by the Perſecutors of Roger Williams and his Followers, becauſe he was always ready to do their Bidding, right or wrong; while Miantonimo adhered to the Treaty he had made at Boſton, in the Beginning of the Pequot War. There ſhould be written a Life of the much injured Miantonimo.

to his Mafter *Vncas:* He contrary to his Promife, as he was returning Home cut off the poor *Pequots* Head, whereby he was made uncapable of difcovering any thing further about Matters between *Miantonimo* and him.

Being come Home, he forthwith refolveth to be revenged upon *Vncas*, and with a thoufand *Narraganfets* gave him Battel, but the *Moheags* (though not half their Number) worfted the *Narragansets*, and took *Miantonimo*, their chief Sachem, Prifoner, and brought him to the Town of *Hartford*, defiring Advice from the Englifh concerning the Difpofal of him. The Commiffioners of the United Colonyes [57] confidering that *Miantonimo* had fhed Blood by raifing an unjuft War againft the *Moheags* their Friends, to whom they had engaged Protection, and that he was treacherous to the Englifh, and Peace not like to be fettled among the Indians, nor continued with the Englifh except he were difpatched (together with fome other Reafons, more fully expreffed in the Declaration publifhed by the Commiffioners, Anno 1645.)[233] they counfelled *Vncas* to put him to Death, withal prohibiting him to ufe any Crueltyes in the Manner of his Execution, it being cuftomary with barbarous Indians (who like their Father the Devil are delighted in Crueltyes) to put their Enemies to the

[233] This "Declaration" may be feen in the *Records of the United Colonies*, i, 50, &c., as printed by the State of Maffachufetts, 1859; alfo in Hazard's *Hift. Colls.*, ii, 48, &c. It would feem that the Commiffioners publifhed it at the Time, but if fo I have never met with a Copy. It is by no means the conclufive Argument for which it was intended.

greateſt Tortures they can deviſe, when they kill them.[234] The Advice was followed. *Vncas* led away *Miantonimo* as if he would carry him to another Place, for Cuſtody and Safety, and by the Way very fairly cut off his Head, as he not a Year before had ſerved one of *Vncas* his Men.[235] Theſe Things hapned Anno 1643.

[234] I apprehend it will not be difficult for future Hiſtorians to determine which had the largeſt Share of the Devil in them, thoſe who adviſed the Murder of Miantonimo or thoſe who committed it. The Record of the Dealings againſt the noble Indian Chief by our People, forms one of the blackeſt Pages in the Hiſtory of New England. Mr. Arnold ſays (*Hiſt. R. I.*, i, 117), "A juſtly ſevere Criticiſm on the "Authors of the Outrage is penned "by Mr. Savage [in his Edition of "*Winthrop's Journal*]. The ſcath-"ing Remarks of the Editor, hon-"ourable alike to himſelf and to "humanity, come with a better "Grace from a Maſſachuſetts Man "than any Comments from a Son "of Rhode Iſland could do—who "will find enough beſides to de-"nounce in the Conduct of the "Puritans towards his State, although "nothing more needleſſly cruel than "the clerico-judicial Murder here "recorded." See alſo Gov. Hopkins's Remarks in *Maſs. Hiſt. Colls.*, XIX, 202.

My own Comments, with all the Particulars of this Tranſaction and the Cauſes which led to it, will be found in the *Book of the Indians.*

[235] The ſince well known *Sachems Plain* near Norwich is the Place of the Murder of Miantonimo, as it was the Place where the Battle was fought in which he was taken Priſoner. A ſquare Block of Granite marks the Spot where it is ſuppoſed he was buried. For many Years after the rude Interment of the noble Chief, a conical Heap of Stones marked the Site of his Remains. That *Monument* was *raiſed* by the Indians, who, from the Time of Miantonimo's Death to a comparatively recent Period, always in paſſing his Grave placed a Stone upon the Pile. But when the Engliſh ſettled about Norwich, the Land was cleared, and the Monument to Miantonimo was removed and uſed in erecting a ſtone Fence. I viſited Sachem's Plain many Years ago, and ſought for the Sachem's Grave, but nothing marked its Site. On inquiring of a neighboring Farmer if he could tell me where the Grave of Miantonimo was, ſaid "he could not, but he had heard "that an old Indian was buried "over there ſomewhere"– pointing to an indefinite Part of the Plain.

It is quite remarkable that our Author takes no Notice of the War

In the next Year the Peace of two of theſe Colonies, *viz*, thoſe of *Connecticut* and *New Haven* was diſturbed by the *Indians.*[236]

For, firſt an Engliſh man running away from his Maſter, out of the *Maſſachuſets* was murdered in the Woods near *Connecticut* by an Indian; and about ſix Weeks after was diſcovered by another Indian, a Sagamore in thoſe Parts promiſed to deliver the Murderer bound to the Engliſh; and having brought him to *Vncaway* a Connecticut Sachim, he was there unbound it ſeems by their joynt Conſent, and left to Shift for himſelf whereupon ten Engliſh men, who were forthwith ſent by Mr. *Ludlow* to the Place, ſeeing the Murderer was eſcaped, laid hold on eight Indians there preſent, amongſt whom there was a Sagamore or two, and kept them in hold two Dayes, until four *Sagamores* ingaged themſelves within one Moneth to deliver the Malefactor to Juſtice; About a Week after which Agreement an Indiam came preſumptuouſly, and in the Day time murderouſly aſſaulted an

of 1643, in which Mrs. Hutchinſon and her Family were maſſacred. I have given the Events in the *Book of the Indians*, and it is therefore unneceſſary to recount them here. See alſo Dr. O'Callaghan's *Narrative.*

236 The Records of Connecticut and New Haven appear to be ſilent reſpecting any Troubles of the Nature here indicated; but Dr. Dwight ſays in his *Hiſt. of N. Haven*, 35: "Sept 30, a Pequot is hanged at "New Haven for ſome of his Con- "duct in the Pequot War." And Mr. Goodwin has copied a Court Record ſhowing that the Indian hanged was named *Nepaupuck*, and that he was proved to have been one of thoſe who committed the Murders at Wethersfield in April, 1637, which brought on the Pequot War. See *Foote Genealogy*, xxv. See *Note* 138. The Indian called *Wampbanck* by Roger Williams is doubtleſs the ſame as *Nepaupuck.*

Englifh Woman in an Houfe in *Stamford* and by three Wounds (fuppofed mortal) left her for dead, and robbed the Houfe.[237] The Indians generally in thofe Parts demeaned themfelves after an hoftile Manner, refufed to come to the Englifh, or to attend Treaties of Peace, departed from their *Wigwams*, left their Corn unweeded, and fhot off Guns near fome Englifh Plantations in a tumultuary Way, and fome Indians informed that there was a Purpofe to fall upon the Englifh; fo that there was Watching and Warding Day and Night. *New-Haven* and *Hartford* were fent unto, that Relief might be afforded the weaker Towns, alfo Application was made to the other Colonyes for Affiftance. At laft the Indians were perfwaded to deliver the Murderers up to Juftice. So did thefe dark Clouds blow over.

[58] Neverthelefs, in this Year (*viz.* in Anno 1644.) the Rage of the *Narraganfets* againft the *Moheags* did break out again in greater Violence than ever before, infomuch that *Vncas* was forced to betake himfelf to a Fort, and was there furrounded with Multitudes of thofe Indians.[238] The Englifh thought it their Concern, not to fuffer

237 According to a Record made by Winthrop in his *Journal*, this was a moft foul Attempt to murder an unfufpecting Woman by an Indian named *Bufheage*. He was afterwards tried and executed, though the Woman furvived her Wounds, but loft her Senfes. Hoadley's *New Haven Col. Records*, i, 135, 146. This Attempt at Murder was in the End of Auguft, 1644.

238 A pretty correct Notion of the Severity of the Fighting between the Narraganfets and Mohegans may be obtained from a Letter of Thomas Peters, printed from the original MS, in the *Book of the Indians*, 133. See alfo Johnfon, *Wonder Working Providences*, 184-5.

him, to be ſwallowed up by thoſe Adverſaryes, ſince he had (though for his own Ends) approved himſelf Faithful to the Engliſh from Time to Time. The *Narraganſets* perceiving that the Engliſh did (as they had Reaſon to) favour *Vncas*, began to be high and inſolent in their Expreſſions and Actions, threatning to deſtroy the Engliſh (only as to the Engliſh at *Povidence* and *Rhode-Iſland* the *Narraganſet Sachims* concluded a Neutrality) as well as the *Moheags*.[239]

Before theſe Things, there being four Colonyes of Engliſh Inhabitants ſettled in this Country, *viz.* *Maſſachuſets*, *Plymouth*, *Connecticut* and *New-Haven*, (which is ſince become a Part of *Connecticut* Colony) who were ſenſible of the common Danger they were expoſed unto, by Reaſon of Indians throughout this Land, as alſo in that *Dutch* and *Swedes*, and *French* had ſeated themſelves not far off, who might ſome of them probably prove evil Neighbours, and withal conſidering that, as he in the famous Poet expreſſeth.

Συμφερτη δ'αρετη πελει ανδρῶ καὶ μαλα λυγρῶν
Νῶι δέ και'κ' ἀγαθοισιν' επιςάιμεσθα μαχεσθαι.

Vis unita fortior, if they were all Confederate it would tend to the Safety of the Whole: Articles

239 It was ſufficient Cauſe for Maſſachuſetts to declare War againſt the Narraganſets, that the latter were the Friends of the People of Rhode Iſland and Providence. Upon the ſad Concluſion of this War, and the Death of Miantonimo, Mr. Arnold remarks: "To Miantonomi and his Uncle, the ſage "Canonicus, who ſurvived him four "Years, Rhode Iſland owes more "than to all others, Chriſtian or "Heathen, for the Preſervation of "the Lives of her Founders." *Hiſt. Rhode Iſland*, i, 118. This Deciſion will probably ſtand.

of Confederation were agreed upon, whence theſe were called the *Vnited Colonyes:*[240] And now was there an Opportunity for them to Act as became ſuch; wherefore each of the Colonyes did proportionably firſt ſend out Souldiers to keep Garriſon with *Vncas*, and after that raiſed an Army in order to War with the *Narraganſets*.[241]

When a War was with good Advice[242] concluded on, forty Men were immediately ſent out of the *Maſſachuſets* to relieve *Vncas*, who upon the departure of *Connecticut* Souldiers (their Time appointed them to keep Garriſon with *Vncas* being expired) was preſently ſet upon by the *Narraganſets*; but further Attempts upon him were prevented by the coming of thoſe from the *Maſſachuſets*. Alſo before the other Colonyes could expedite what concerned the whole Deſign, Forces were ſent out of Plymouth under the Command of Capt. *Standiſh*, and marched as far as *Rehoboth*, that being near the Borders of the Enemy.

That worthy Commander, Major *Edward Gib-*

240 Deputies from the four Colonies met at Boſton, and the Articles of Confederation were ſigned on the 19th of May, 1643. Thoſe Deputies were—JOHN WINTHROP, Governor of Maſſachuſetts, THOMAS DUDLEY, GEORGE FENWICK, THEOPHILUS EATON, EDWARD HOPKINS, and THOMAS GREGSON.

At the Meeting of the Commiſſioners at Boſton on the 7th of Sept. following, the Fate of Miantonimo was determined. Edward Winſlow and William Collyer were ſent as Commiſſioners from Plymouth, and thoſe for the other Colonies were the ſame as before. Winthrop was Preſident.

241 It was ordered by the Commiſſioners of the United Colonies, that Maſſachuſetts ſhould raiſe 100 Men; the other Colonies each 45.

242 This has Reference to the Advice of the Miniſters.

bons,[243] was appointed a *General*. Mr. *Thompson*[244] Paſtor of the Church in *Braintree*, being in [59] diverſe Reſpects eminently fitted for ſuch a Service, was to ſound the ſilver Trumpet along with this Army. They did ſolemnly take their Leave of their Friends, and were ſolemnly commended to the Bleſſing of the God of Armies: But as they were juſt marching out of *Boſton*, (their Baggage being ſent before towards the Enemies Quarters) many of the principal *Narraganſet* Indians, *viz*, *Peſſicus*, *Mexano*, and *Witawaſh* Sagamores, and *Awaſequin* Deputy for the *Nianticks*; theſe with a large Train came to *Boſton*, ſuing for Peace, being willing to ſubmit to what Terms the Engliſh ſhould ſee cauſe to impoſe upon them.[245]

It was demanded of them that they ſhould defray the Charges that they had put the Engliſh to,[246]

243 Gen. Gibbons was in New England in 1639, but how, whence or where he came is not certain. He appears to have been among the Coloniſts who came early to the ſouth Shore of Maſſachuſetts Bay, poſſeſſed a good Eſtate for thoſe Times. Settled in Boſton where he held various honorable Offices, and had a Family of Children. He died 1654. Johnſon gives him a high Character. See *Won. Work. Prov.* 191.

244 Members of this Family uſually ſpelled their Name *Tompſon*. Mr. Tompſon was one of the moſt diſtinguiſhed Miniſters in New England. He was the Father of the not leſs diſtinguiſhed Benjamin Tompſon, the Poet and Mathematician. There is a Pedigree of the Family in the *New Eng. Hiſt. and Gen. Regiſter*, xv, 112-116. William Tompſon died 10 Dec., 1666.

245 Some Additions to theſe Facts may be found in the *Book of the Indians*, 133-4.

246 This ſeems to have been a prepoſterous Demand, as the Indians were notoriouſly without any Means to perform ſuch Obligations. In Caſe of War with them Johnſon ſays: "The naked Natives have "neither Plunder nor Caſh to bear "the Charges." *Wonder Working Prov.*, 182. Perhaps their Land was in Proſpect.

and that the *Sachims* ſhould ſend their Sons to be kept as Hoſtages in the Hands of the Engliſh until ſuch Time as the Money ſhould be payed. All this did the *Narraganſets* yeild unto.

Mel in ore, verba lactis Fel in corde fraus in factis.

Notwithſtanding the *Narraganſets* have diſſembled Friendſhip with the Engliſh, yet Venome hath been in their Hearts ever ſince theſe Motions: Nor was there any other then *Fides Græca* obſerved by them, in the performance of their Engagements.

In the firſt Place they endeavoured to play *Leger de main* in their ſending Hoſtages. For inſtead of *Sachems* Children, they thought to ſend ſome other, and to make the Engliſh believe thoſe baſe *Papooſes*, were of royal Progeny, but they had thoſe to deal with, who were too Wiſe to be ſo eluded. After the expected *Hoſtages*, were in the Hands of the Engliſh, the *Narraganſets*, notwithſtanding that, were ſlow in the Performance of what they ſtood engaged for. And when upon a partial Diſcharge of the Debt, their Hoſtages were reſtored to them, they became more backward than formerly; until they were by hoſtile Preparations again and again terrified into better Obedience. At laſt Major *Atherton*, (then Capt. *Atherton*) of Dorcheſter[247] was ſent with a ſmall Party of Engliſh Souldiers to demand what was due. He at firſt

[247] Major Atherton was accidentally killed by his Horſe ſtumbling over a Cow in the Duſk of the Evening, as he was returning Home from a military Parade, June 16th, 1661. See *Hiſt. and Antiqs. Boſton*, 361; *N. Eng. Hiſt. Gen. Reg.*, ii, 382; v, 393.

entered into the *Wigwam* where old *Ninnigret* (the *Nyantick* Sachim) reſided, with only two or three Souldiers, appointing the Reſt by Degrees to follow him, two or three dropping in at once, when his ſmall Company were come about him that Indians in the meantime ſuppoſing that there had been many more behind, he caught the Sachim by the Hair of his Head, and ſet a Piſtol to his Breaſt, proteſting who ever eſcaped, he ſhould ſurely dy, if he did not forthwith comply with what was required. Hereupon a great Trembling and Conſternation ſurprized the Indians, albeit Multitudes of them were then preſent, with ſpiked Arrows[248] at their Bow ſtrings ready to let fly. The Event was, the Indians [60] ſubmitted and not one Drop of Blood was ſhed; nor was there (ſo far as I am informed) after this any open Diſcovery of Enmity in the *Narraganſets* againſt the Engliſh until ſuch Time as *Philip* began his great Rebellion. Yet it is evident that there hath been Treachery, and ſecret Treaſon againſt the Engliſh, amongſt them.

Aſtutum vapido ſervant ſub pectore Vulpem.

I have been told that a Man of God (viz. Mr. *Street*,[249] who formerly lived not far from thoſe Parts) obſerving the Perfidiouſneſs of thoſe *Narra-*

[248] After the Indians became acquainted with Europeans they procured of them by Purchaſe whatever they could of Iron. Nails, Spikes, iron Hoops were greatly coveted. They ſoon found the Superiority of their Arrows when pointed with Iron. Hence the "ſpiked Arrows," mentioned in the Text.

[249] Mr. Nicholas Street of New Haven was early ſettled in Taunton, Maſſachuſetts, but removed to New Haven, and died there, April 22d, 1674. Emery's *Miniſtry of Taunton*, i, 156-7.

gansets, and their Enmity against the Gospel, publickly declared that he foresaw the Destruction of the *Narraganset* Nation, solemnly confirming his Speech in saying, *If God do not destroy that People, then say that his Spirit hath not spoken by me.*

Surely that holy Man was a Prophet, Μάντις γ' αριστοσ όςισ εικαζει καλῶς. *Qui bene conjiciet hunc Vatem.* And this is a summary Account of what hath in former Years hapned between us and the *Narragansets*.

Considering that the *Narraganset Troubles* have been of no small Concernment, it would be worth the while a little more fully to relate the Truth about those Motions. Only it is already done in good Part by that Declaration which was published by the Commissioners of the United Colonies, Anno. 1645. (together with the Articles then consented unto, and subscribed by the *Narraganset* Sachims[250]). Who so pleaseth to consult those Things will receive Satisfaction concerning the *War* which was at that Time fully intended, but not actually prosecuted by Reason of the Indians Complyance as hath been specified.

In Anno 1646. They failed in the Performance of their Covenants, above expressed, as to every Particular therein contained.[251]

It is also evident that they had by presents of *Wampam* been practicing with the *Mohawks*, and

[250] Contained in Plymouth Colony Records, ix, 47-8.

[251] All the Allegations of the short Comings of the Indians are set down in the *Records of the Commissioners of the United Colonies, Plymouth Col. Records*, ix, 75-6.

other Indians to engage them againſt *Vncas*, unto whom they knew the Engliſh had promiſed Protection. So that the Engliſh according to the Rules of Righteouſneſs, might have righted themſelves by the Juſtice of *War*, yet being deſirous rather to manifeſt Long-ſuffering towards theſe Barbarians, the Commiſſioners of the United Colonies contented themſelves with ſending a Declaration to the *Narraganſet* and *Niantick* Indians, ſignifying that they ſhould no longer delay the Performance of what they had bound themſelves unto, as ever they would not be look'd upon as a treacherous and perfidious People, no more to be treated with.[252]

252 At the Meeting of the Commiſſioners of the United Colonies at Boſton on the 26th of Jnly, 1647, they ſay: "One principall Cauſe "of their meetinge together at this "Time being to conſider what "Courſe ſhould be held with the "Narraganſett Indyans and their "Confederates who haue not onely "broken their Covent ſolemnly "made at Boſton A° 1645, But as "the Commiſſioners haue been en-"formed credibly, haue bene plot-"tinge by p'ſents of Wampam, in-"gaging the Indyans rounde aboute "to combine with them againſt "the Engliſh Colonies in War." Therefore it was reſolved to ſend Meſſengers to them, who were inſtructed to aſcertain why they had not fulfilled their Agreement. The Meſſengers were Thomas Stanton, Benedict Arnold, and Seargeant Waite. On the 31ſt of July they made their Report: That they had ſeen Paſſacus, the Chief of the Narraganſets, and that he made divers Excuſes for not performing his Engagements. One of the moſt reaſonable ſeems to have been, that when he mode them, he did not dare to do otherwiſe, as an Army ſtood ready with Guns in their Hands to compel him; that he did not meet the Commiſſioners at New Haven as they allege he was ordered, becauſe he had no Notice of the Meeting; and becauſe he was ill and had left the whole Affair to Ninigret. "In which Anſwere the "Commiſſioners founde ſeuerall "Paſſages of Vntruth, and were "vnſatisfied."

On the 3d of Auguſt Ninigret and ſome of the Nianticks, and two of Peſſacus's Men came to Boſton. Being queſtioned by the Commiſſioners, Ninigret did not corrobo-

This Year also there was Trouble and Fears raised in the Country, by Reason of the *River-Indians*, at *Waranoke*,[253] *and Norwoottuck*,[254] who it seems were secretly contriving the Death of those famous Worthyes [61] Mr. *Hopkins*, Mr. *Hains*, and Mr. *Whiting*, Magistrates in *Connecticut* Colony. For I find upon publick *Record*, that Complaints and Informations about that Matter (in September, 1646) were brought before the Commissioners then assembled at New-haven, where an Indian testified that *Sequasson* the *Sachim* of *Waranoke*, had given him a Sum of Money on Condition that he would murther the Gentlemen mentioned.[255]

rate Pessacus's Statements; and to their Question, "Why they (the "Narragansets) had not paid the "*Wampan* to the English according "to Covenant, he being by his "Deputy one of the Covenanters?" He expressed Ignorance of the Covenant, and asked "For what the "Narragansets should pay so much "*Wampam?*" He said "he knew "not that they were indebted to the "English." See more of this onward.

From all which it is pretty evident that the Indians understood but little about Covenants and pecuniary Obligations, especially when they had received nothing for which Payment was demanded.

253 Westfield in Massachusetts. It is found spelled several different Ways. *Waranot* and *Warranok*, in *Recs. Commissioners U. Colls.*. i, 67, 69.

254 Probably the same abridged to *Nonatuck*, Northampton. See Williams's *Hist. Northampton.*

255 What the Records of the U. Colls. afford relative to this Matter of an Attempt to murder "those "famous Worthyes," may be seen in Vol. 1, 66, &c.

Complaints of all Shades were continually made against the Indians. The following is a Specimen of many of them: "Mr. Pelham on behalf "of Richard Woddy [Woody or "Wooddy] and Mr. Pincham "[William Pinchon] by Letter "complayned of some Thefts com- "mitted by some of the Narragan- "sett Indyans; the like Complnt "was also made by Mr. Browne "in the Behalfe of Wm. Smith of "Rehoboth, but in the Absence "of the Indyans nothing could "p'ceede." *Records of the C. U. C.*, i, 80.

Before the Commiſſioners convened, Mr. *Haines* had twice ſent to *Sequaſſon*, but he neglected to make his Appearance: Wherefore *Jonathan Gilbert* was ſent to him again, to ſignifie from the Commiſſioners that they expected *Sequaſſons* Appearance before them, and to anſwer what he was accuſed with, and they promiſed him free Paſſage both to and from *Newhaven*, withall intimating that his withdrawing himſelf would greatly augment the Suſpition of his Guilt.

The Meſſenger quickly returned, bringing Word, that he could not ſpeak with *Sequaſſon*, who he ſuppoſed had received Notice of his coming by other Indians, and was thereupon fled.

But a few Days after, *Nipniſoit* and *Naimetayhu*[256] two *Sagamores*, came with ſome other Indians to *Newhaven*, declaring that they were Friends to *Sequaſſon*, and pretended great Reſpect to the Engliſh, and that they had brought *Sequaſſon* to clear himſelf, and that although one of them had him by one Arm, another by the other, when he was come near the Town,[257] he brake from them and was eſcaped.

The Commiſſioners told them they intended *Sequaſſon* no Hurt; but deſired to bring him and his Accuſers Face to Face, that he ſhould have a juſt Hearing in their Preſence.

256 In the Records theſe Names are *Nepinſoyt*, and *Naimataigue*.

257 " Yet when he was neare " New Haven, almoſt at the Towne " Fence, he brake from them." They added alſoe, that " he was " aſhamed to come becauſe he had " brought no Preſent." *Records*, *ib.* i, 67.

Some other Indians informed that *Sequaſſon* was within a Mile of *Newhaven*, and it was conceived that he would gladly make his Peace by ſome other Means, rather then by a due Examination and Trial. The two *Sagamores* ſaid he was much afraid, and durſt not come, though they confeſſed it was juſt he ſhould come and clear himſelf, if innocent; all which being conſidered, the Commiſſioners conceived that *Sequaſſon* whether guilty or afraid of the Engliſh, would ſtill be Plotting againſt them and ſo prove dangerous; wherefore they thought fit, and ordered that all juſt and prudent Means ſhould be uſed (his Life being preſerved) to bring him to a Tryal, that the Matter might be ſome Way iſſued. In the mean Time they thought good to examine *Wotchiborow*[258] a *Pocatuck* Indian, *Sequaſſons* Accuſer, who waited to give in Evidence againſt him. He (being warned by *Thomas Stanton* the Interpreter, to ſpeak nothing but Truth) affirmed, that being this laſt Spring at *Waranoke*, in a Wigwam with *Sequaſſon*, and ready to depart, *Sequaſſon* perſwaded him to [62] ſtay three Days, thence he drew him to the *Falls* above Mr. Pinchons; when they had been there four Dayes, *Wotchiborow* would have been gone to *Moheag*, to ſee ſome Friends; *Sequaſſon* told him it was dangerous Travelling that Way, he would be killed, walked along with him to a Spring, and there told him if ever he would doe the ſaid *Sequaſſon* a Kind-

[258] *Watchibrok, Wontibrou and Wotchibrough* in the Records. See *Vol.* i, 68. *Pocatuck* in the Records is *Potatuke.* Now *Pawcatuck* or *Paugatuck.* Weſterly in Rhode Iſland.

neſs now was a Time, he was almoſt ruined, and the Engliſh at *Hartford*, the Cauſe of it: He ſhould therefore go to *Hartford* and kill Mr. *Hopkins*, Mr. *Hains* and Mr. *Whiting* and he would give him a Reward, and thereupon pluckt out of his Bag, three Girdles of *Wampam*, and gave them to him, with a Piece of a Girdle of *Wampam* to play, and promiſed him much more. *Wotchiborow* ſaid it was dangerous to kill an Engliſh *Sachim*, they would find out the Murderer and purſue him to Death, what could then *Wampam* doe him good? *Sequaſſon* ſaid he had Store of *Wampam*, when the Thing was done they would fly to the *Mohawkes*, but in the Way, when they came to the *Wampeag-Indians*,[259] he ſhould give it out that *Vncas* had hired him for ſo much *Wampam*, and that would ſet the Engliſh *againſt Uncas*, and then he the ſaid *Sequaſſon* ſhould riſe again.

He further told this Examinate, that *Naymetayhu*, one of the forementioned *Sagamores* that came on the Behalf of *Sequaſſon*, and his Father, knew and approved of the ſaid Murther.

Wotchiborow further ſaith that having taken the aforeſaid *Wampam*, he remembered that himſelf had formerly taken *Buſheag*,[260] and brought him to the Engliſh, who for a murderous Attempt at *Stamford* was put to Death at *Newhaven*, that if he ſhould kill any Engliſh Sachim, he ſhould goe

259 There was a Place called *Wamkeag*, two Miles N. E. of Greenville in R. I. But whether this refers to Indians living *there*, or to the *Wampanoags*, or othe Indians, it is uncertain. See *Parſons*, 29.

260 See *Note* 232.

in Fear of Death all the Dayes of his Life, and that for bringing in *Busheag*, he had a Gratuity from the English, and for the Discovery of this Plot he should have their Favour, and he thought the Favour of the English with Security would be better to him than *Sequassons Wampam* with Fear and Danger; he therefore came first to *Tunksus*[261] and the next Day to *Hartford*, and discovered *Sequassions* Practice.

He said further that *Sequassion* hearing of the Discovery, spake to *Romanoke* an Indian, and he sent another Indian called *Sixpence* to this Examinate, desiring him to hide and conceal as much of the Plot as he could and not to lay all open, but he in Anger bade the said *Sixpence* hold his Peace, he had discovered it, and would hide nothing.

Thus much do I find upon Record, relating to *Sequassons* Plot. What afterwards came of this Business, or how it issued, I cannot say.[262] There was also another Trouble about the Indians this Year.

[63] For whilst the Commissioners were sitting

[261] *Tunxis*—Farmington in Connecticut.

[262] It would seem by the "*Acts* "*of the Commissioners*," of Sept. 1650, that Sequason had fled to the Mohawks for Protection, and that at their Request "that he might "haue Libertie without Offence to "returne to his former Habitation, "alledging how reddy and willing "they haue been to gratify the "English in what they have re-"quested"—"they thought meet "that an Answare bee returned to "this Purpose,—That the English "neither formerly haue nor yet doe "p'hibite his Returne, soe that hee "carry himselfe inoffenciuely, for "the Future hee may come at his "Pleasure, and that they are now "the more free for it being requested "by them." *Records Commissioners U. C.*, i, 170.

at *Newhaven*, Petitions were presented from[263] *Edward Elmere* and some others, complaining that Indians had willfully and maliciously burned some Quantity of Pitch, and Tarr of theirs, together with some Bedding, and a Cart with its Furniture, and Tools &c. in Value about an hundred Pounds. And particularly they complained of one *Wasemose*, a *Waranoke*[264] Indian as guilty therein, as by sufficient Evidence they thought they could prove; and that he hath since avoided all the English Plantations; and that he being sent for by a Warrant from one of the Magistrates of *Connecticut*, fled; but being overtaken and seized by some of the English, he was rescued by some of the Indians, and the English by them jeered and abused, and particularly by *Chickwallop* Sachim of *Norwootuck*. Whereupon *Jonathan Gilbert* and *John Griffin*, were sent to *Chickwallop* and *Manasanes*.

At their Return, they informed that they could not meet either with *Chickwallop* or *Manasanes*, but the *Sagamores* and Indians at *Waranoke* carried it insolently towards the English, vaunting themselves in their Arms, Bows and Arrows, Hatchets and Swords, some with their Guns ready charged, before and in the Presence of the English Messengers, they primed and cockt them ready to give Fire, and told them, that if they should offer to carry away any Men thence, the Indians were

263 "John Griffin, Edward Elmar and others. *Acts of the Commissioners*, i, 69.

264 "*Wabannos* a *Waranot* Indian." *Ibid.* In the same Page *Wanbannos* is called *Mahanose*.

resolved to Fight,[265] yet the next Morning the *Sachim* with some others offered the English Messengers eight Fathom of *Wampam*, towards Satisfaction, and promised to provide more. The Messengers not having any thing to that Purpose in their Commission, advised the *Sachim* to send to the Commissioners, but he refused. Hereupon, *Naymetayhu*[266] one of the *Sagamores* of *Wananoke*, who, as before, came on *Sequassons* Behalf, was questioned by the Commissioners about these proud Affronts to the English; At first he denyed what was charged, and excused some Part, but one of the English Messengers being present, and he hearing the Rest should be sent for, he fell under most of the Charge, professing that he intended no Harm to the English. Thus concerning Disturbance by the Indians in the Year, 1646.[267]

In Anno, 1647. New Fears and Troubles arose by Reason of the *Narraganset* Indians, there being credible Informations that they were Plotting, and by Presents of *Wampam*, ingaging the Indians round about to combine with them against the

265 "And if they should stay but "one Night at the English trading "House [with a captured Indian] "neare all the Country would "come to rescue any such Indian "seized." *Ibid*, p. 70.

266 *Noynetacha*.

267 Besides this there are numerous Entries in the Records showing that an evil Spirit constantly stirred up Uncas to do Mischief. Having laid the Connecticut and Massachusetts English under singular Obligations, they had to shuffle very adroitly to keep their Temper with that miscreant Indian. It is a desperate Game which requires the employment of a Rogue to play an important Part of it. Indian History scarcely affords a Parallel in Perfidy to Uncas.

Englifh Colonyes, infomuch that a Meeting of the Commiffioners was called before the ordinary Time; Being therefore convened at *Bofton*, July 26. A Meffenger was fent to *Narraganfet*, fignifying to *Pefícus* and other *Sachims* there, that the Englifh Commiffioners expected their Appearance at *Bofton*, and that if they [64] did refufe or delay, they fhould no more be fent unto, withal promifing them fafe Conduct, in Cafe they only attended. The Meeffnger being returned informed that *Pefícus* excufed his not meeting the Commiffioners at *New Haven* the laft Year, from his Ignorance of the Time, when he fhould attend, though that was falfely pretended by him. He alfo defired Excufe for his not appearing at this Time, becaufe he faid he was fick and not able to come, (but the Meffengers could not perceive that he was fubject to any fuch Sicknefs or Difablement) Neverthelefs, he had given full Power to *Ninnigret* to act on his Behalf. Moreover, he excufed his not performing the *Articles* he had fubfcribed at *Bofton*, two Years before, by pretending that he was frighted into that Engagement, with the Sight of the Englifh Army, which was then ready to invade the *Narraganfet* Country, and he thought they would follow him Home, and there kill him if he did not promife to do as the Englifh would have him.

Auguft 3. *Ninnigret* with fome *Niantick* Indians, and too of *Peffícus* his Men came to *Bofton*. At firft he (though againft his Confcience) made as if he were ignorant, and had never been informed of the Covenants which the Indians had made to the Englifh, and feemed to wonder that the Englifh fhould afk fuch a Sum of *Wampam*, faying that he knew not that the Indians were in the Englifhmens debt. He was then put in mind, how that formerly Satisfaction had been demanded of the Indians for the Breach of Articles; and how the Englifh Meffengers had been ill intreated by them, and particularly by himfelf, who had ufed threatening and infolent Language, faying to the Meffengers, that he knew the Commiffioners would endeavor to keep them from warring upon *Vncas*, but they were refolved they would do it for all that, and nothing but *Vncas* his Head fhould fatisfy them; and that if the Englifh did not withdraw their Garrifons from the Defence of *Vncas*, they would heap up their Cattel as high as their *Wigwams*, and that he was the Man that had given out that an Englifhman fhould not ftep out of Doors to pifs but they would kill him. *Ninigret* not being able to deny thefe Charges, and fomewhat appalled thereat, began to comply with the reafonable Demands of the Englifh.[269] A Dayes Time was

[269] The Author has omitted as important a Part of the Records as that he has given, but the Omiffion is too long for a Note. See *Records of the Commiffioners*, i, 88. But in order to underftand the Refources of the Indians the following Extract is given. I imagine however that fome allowance fhould be made as to their Ability to pay a large Sum, for it does not appear that this Debt was ever cancelled. "Ninigret not "able to deny this Charge [that "an Englifhman fhovld not ftep out "of Doores," &c.] "pretended "that the Englifh Meffengers pro- "voked him, but that appeared a "falfe and weake Excufe. He "affirmed that the Some was fo "great, that the Narraganfets had "not Wampam enough to pay it— "it being well knowne to the Co-

allowed him for Confideration and Advice with the Reft of the Indian Deputyes that were then in *Bofton.*

The next Day he declared that he was refolved to give the Englifh Colonies due Satisfaction in all Things, and that he would forthwith fend fome of his Men to gather up the *Wampam* which was yet behind hoping that within ten Dayes it might be obtained, and that himfelf [65] would ftay with the Englifh as Security, untill the Money was paid. Accordingly he difpatched his Meffengers home for that End, who not many Dayes after, came back to *Bofton,* bringing with them two hundred Fathom of *Wampam,* towards Satisfaction of what they owed to the Englifh. This falling very much fhort of what was expected, *Ninigret* pleaded that his perfonal Abfcence from Home was the Caufe of that Defect, and therefore defired Liberty to go Home, withal adding, that if the Whole were not paid by next Spring, the Englifh fhould take his Head, and fieze his Country. The Commiffioners let him depart, and fince he pretended fo fair, did deliver to him the Children which were kept as

" miffioners that the Narraganfets " are a greate People, and can reafe " a greater Quantity of Wampam " vpon a fhort Warninge when they " pleafe." Finally, Ninigret, feeing that pleading Poverty would not overcome Cupidity, agreed to fuch Terms as was demanded of him. What had been offered by Peffacus was in Kettles and Wampam, in all, £17:9:6, but it was called " a con- " temptible fum," and was refufed, fo the Meffenger fold the Kettles to Mr. Samuel Shrimpton for £14:5. In our View this was not fo " contemptible" a Sum as might be imagined. This laft Amount being raifed from the Sale of the brafs Kettles taken from the Families of the Indians'! The Weight of thefe Kettles was 285 lbs. See *Book of Indians.*

Hoſtages, expecting from him, the more Care to ſee Engagements performed; and if they did find him real, that then former Neglects ſhould be charged upon *Peſicus*, and that they ſhould expect his Aſſiſtance, when it ſhould be required, in recovering the whole Remainder from *Peſicus;* all which Things were cheerfully accepted by *Ninigret*.[270]

This Year other *Troubles* hapned by ſome of *Vncas* his Indians, who committed ſeveral Outrages upon the Engliſh in the *Pequot* Country. Mr. *John Winthrop*, and ſome with him, complained

[270] The Failure of the Chief to perform his Promiſe ſhows plainly enough two Facts: firſt, that the Indians were unable to raiſe ſo large an Amount of Money; and ſecond, that a Sachem's Power to compel his People to part with what they poſſeſſed did not amount to anything like arbitrary Power. The Commiſſioners were evidently fully aware of theſe Facts, and wiſhed to uſe their own Power to keep the Indians under their Control. The original Records add: "Not thinking it meet "to begin a pr'ſent War, if Satisfac- "tion (though with a little forbear- "ance may be had otherwiſe) by "their Interpreter acquainted Nina- "gratt, that ſince he p'tended the "Wampam had bene gathered and "paid, if himſelf had been at home, "they would giue him free leaue to "returne, and twenty Dayes more "from hence to collect and ſend "the Reſidue yet behinde; and "tho' 500 Fathome of the Wam- "pam now due ſhould fall ſhort in "his Payment 20 Dayes hence, "they would forbeare it till next "planting Time; and in the meane "Time accept both the 200 Fathom "now brought, and the 105 F. "intended for a preſent, in pt. "Paymt, but if they brought not "1000 Fathome more within 20 "Dayes, the Comiſſrs. would ſend "no more Meſſengers, but take "Courſe to right themſelves as they "ſee Cauſe." This is accompanied with the further Threat, that if they ſhould reſort to Armes, the Indians need not expect to eſcape Vengeance as hitherto, by a little Wampam; that though they (the Engliſh) would be juſtified in putting the Hoſtages to Death, they "would forthwith "deliver the Children to Ninegratt, "expecting from him the more Care "to ſee Ingagements fully ſatisfied." *Records U. C.*, i, 106.

that *Wowequay*[271] (*Vncas* his Brother) with about forty *Moheags*, behaved themſelves inſolently, hovering againſt the Engliſh Plantation in a ſuſpicious Manner, to the Afrightment of the Inhabitants there; Alſo, although *Vncas* at firſt ſeemed gladly to entertain the Engliſh Plantation at *Pequot*, yet his Carriage ſince was ſuch as if he deſigned by *Alarums* to diſturb and break that Plantation. In fine *Vncas* was cenſured, and required to acknowledge his Fault to the Engliſh Plantation, (which he did) and pay an hundred Fathom of *Wampam* to make amends for Wrongs ſuſtained.[272]

In *September* 1648. New Complaints were brought before the Commiſſioners of the United Colonyes, (then ſitting at *Plymouth*) againſt the *Narraganſet* Indians. *Henry Bull* of *Rhode-Iſland* petitioned for Relief, informing that thoſe Indians had beaten him, and other Wayes been injurious to him. Alſo Meſſengers from the Town of *Warwick* came with Complaints in Behalf of the whole Town,[273] alledgeing that their Neighbour Indians did kill their Cattel,[274] abuſe their Servants when they took them alone, and ſometimes would

271 Written *Nowequa* in the Records.

272 The Records here are too much abridged to give the Reader a correct Idea of the Tranſactions intended to be noticed. As they cannot be abridged intelligibly the Reader is only referred to them. See *Records Coms. U. C.* i, 101-2.

273 The Meſſengers were Mr. Randall Houlden and Mr. John Warner. They had "a Writing "vnto vs [ſay the Commiſſioners] "from the Towne or Plantatiō of "Warwicke, as they call it, ſub-"ſcribed by Mr. John Smith, Aſ-"ſiſtant in behalfe of the whole "Towne, dated the 4th of the 7th "Mo. 1648."

274 And "about a hundred hoggs," &c.

make forcible Entry into their Houſes, yea, and ſtrike the Maſters thereof, and ſteal and purloyn their Goods at Pleaſure. At the ſame Time, Informations were brought before the Commiſſioners, that the *Narraganſet* Indians inſtead of paying the *Wampam* that was due to the Colonyes, had improved their *Wampam* to hire Indians to invade *Vncas*, and in Caſe the Engliſh ſhould defend [66]
him, to fight with them alſo. Particularly, that *Ninigret* had given, out that if the Engliſh did protect *Vncas*, he would quickly burn the Houſes at Connecticut. The *Narraganſets* were withdrawing their old Men, Women, and Children into Swamps, hiding their Corn, &c. The mercenary *Mohawks* were ſaid to be about four hundred in Number, all armed with Guns, and three Pound of Powder for every Man.

Theſe Counſils were ſo far ripened and prepared for Execution, as that *Thomas Stanton* and other Meſſengers from Connecticut, goeing to the Indians to enquire into, and (if might be) ſtop Proceedings, found them met at *Pacomptuck* their Rendezvouze, who acknowledged that they had received *Wampam* from the *Narraganſets* to invade *Vncas*, and that they were met together to that Purpoſe, expecting *Mohawks* and other Indians to make up their full Numbers: But hearing that two *Mohawk* Sachims, were lately killed by the Eaſtern Indians, and that the Engliſh, who, they thought were a juſt and warlike People, would defend *Vncas*, they did therefore ſtop their intended Proceedings at this Time. But theſe Things made it yet more evident, that the *Narraganſets* were a falſe and treacherous People, not to be truſted, nor worthy to be treated with.

Anno 1649. *Newhaven* Colony was in apparent Danger of being involved in Trouble by Reaſon of the Indians there: For at *Stamford* a Man going forth to ſeek his Cattel returned not home as was expected, nor could be found by the Engliſh that ſought for him; but quickly after the Son of a *Sagamore* who lived near *Stamford*, came into the Town, and told the Engliſh that *John Whitmore* was murthered by an Indian called *Toquattos*, and to prove it, told them that *Toquattos* had ſome of his Cloathes; and particularly his Shirt made of Cotton-linnen. Hereupon the Engliſh and ſome Indians went into the Woods to ſeek the murthered Body for burial, but though they beſtowed much Time and Labour, they could not find it. Diverſe of the Engliſh at *Stamford* ſuſpected the *Sagamores* Son to be either Author or Acceſſory to the Murther, but had not ſatisfying Grounds to ſeize and charge him.

About two or three Months after, *Vncas* coming to *Stamford*, calling the Indians thither, and enquiring after the murdered Body, the forementioned *Sagamores* Son, and another ſuſpected Indian called *Kehoron*[275] fell a trembling, and hereby confirmed the Suſpition of the Engliſh, and wrought a Suſpition in ſome of the *Mohegin* Indians, ſo that they ſaid theſe two Indians were *Matchet*, meaning they

275 *Reboron*, according to the printed Records. I find this Indian nowhere elſe mentioned, under either Name.

were Guilty. Notwithſtanding the Indians thereabouts excuſed the *Sagamores* Son, and accuſed [67] *Toquattos*, and intimated that if the Sagamores Son ſhould upon Suſpition be ſeized on by the Engliſh, the Indians would doe the like by ſome Engliſh, untill he ſhould be ſet at Liberty.[276]

Likewiſe at *South-hampton* in *Long-Iſland*, the Engliſh were expoſed to great Difficulties and Dangers by Reaſon of a Murder committed in that Town, ſo that they were neceſſitated to arm themſelves and ſtand upon their own Defence for many Dayes; the Indians being gathered together in an hoſtile Poſture.[277]

This Year alſo *Vncas* renewed his Complaints againſt the *Narraganſet* Indians, that notwithſtanding all former Engagements, they are ſtill undermining his Peace, and ſeeking his Ruine, and in particular that to their late Endeavour to bring the

276 "The Comiſſioners being "minded [July 1649] that Aſquaſh, "a Murtherer of an Engliſhman "ſome Yeares ſince in or neare the "Bounds of Fairfield lived yet (ac-"cording to general Report) among "Indians neare to ſom of the Eng-"liſh Plantations in thoſe Parts, and "that the non p'ſuite of ſo notorious "a Malefactor is like to proue pre-"iudiciall to the Engliſh by giveing "incurragment to the Indians in "other malicius and murtherous "Attempts. It is therefore thought "fitt that the two weſtern Colonies "vſe the beſt Means they can to "take him, and then p'ceed with "him according to Righteouſneſs." *Records of the Commiſſioners*, i, 142.

277 "An Information being alſo "given of ſom Indians at Long "Iſland that (by the Accuſation of "a Native that ſuffered lately at "Hartford for a Murther) are "guilty of the Death of ſom Eng-"liſh who ſuffered boatwracke ſome "Yeares paſt in a Veſſell belonging "to one Cope at or near Long "Iſland. It was deſired and thought "expedient that all Opportunities "p'ſenting bee improved for mak-"ing Inquiry and ſearching after "the Truth and (if Evidence ap-"peere) the Murtherers be proſe-"cuted to Juſtice." *Ibid*, i, 142.

Mohawks upon him, when that failed, they ſought by Witchcraft to take away his Life. A *Narraganſet* Indian (called *Cuttaquin*) in an Engliſh Veſſel in *Mohegin* River,[278] ran a Sword into *Vncas* his Breaſt, whereby he received to all Appearances a mortal Wound, which murderous Act, the Aſſailant then confeſſed, he was for a conſiderable Sum of *Wampam*, by the *Narraganſet* and *Niantick* Sachems hired to attempt. *Ninnigret* when examined utterly denyed his having an Hand in that Fact but, affirmed that *Cuttaquin*, who accuſed himſelf, and the other Sachims, was drawn thereunto by Torture from the *Moheags*.[279]

[278] A Part of Pequot River, probably that Part of the Thames above Montville.

[279] The Records continue: "but "he was tould that the Aſſalent "before hee cam into the Hands "of the Moheges, p'ſently after the "Fact was comited, layed the charg "vpon him [Ninnigret] with the "Reſt, which hee confermed the "Day folowing to Captaine Maſon "in the p'ſence of the Engliſh that "were in the Barkque with him . . . "that hee was p'ſented to Vncas "vnder the notion of one appertaining to Vſſamequin wherby hee "was acknowlidged as his Frend "and no Provocation giuen him." . . . . . "Theire Indeavours to diſturbe the Peace by theire Confederaſy with the Mowhawkes "was ſo euident by Mr. John Winthrope and Mr. Williams Relation the laſt Year, together with "the Confeſſion of the Mowhawks "themſelves to Thomas Stanton." The Commiſſioners then recount the Indebtedneſs of Ninigret, and "expreſſed themſelves altogether "vnſatisfied in the whole Frame of "his P'ceedings," and recommended "to all the Colonies to bee in conſtant Readineſs either for Defence "or Offence as the State of Occaſions may call for, which is like "to be terbulent and difficult, which "they the rather p'ſent to concideration from an Information thay "receved ſence theire ſiting, of a "Marriage ſhortly intended betwixt Ninegrets Daughter and a "Brother or Brothers Soone of "Saſſaquas, the mallignant furious "Pequot, wherby p'bably their "Aimes are to gather together and "reunite the ſcattered conquered "Pequates into one Body and ſett "them vpp againe as a diſtinct "Nation which hath alwayes been

About four Years after this (*viz.* in Anno 1653.)[280] there were great *Troubles*, and Commotions raiſed in the Spirits of Men with reference to the Indians, it being generally believed that there was an horrid Conſpiracy amongſt the Indians throughout this Land to cut off all the Engliſh, and that they were animated thereto by the Dutch; there being at that Time war between England and Holland.[281] An Indian *Squaw* was ſent by other Indians (that profeſſed Love and Friendſhip) to one in *Wethersfield* on *Connecticut* informing that there was a Confederacy between the Dutch and the Indians, to deſtroy the Engliſh Colonyes, and that the Day of

" wittneſed againſt by the Engliſh, " and may haſſard the Peace of the " Colonies." Here Affairs appear to haue reſted for that Time. Whether the *fearful* Marriage took place we are not informed, although an Inference that it did is drawn from the Commiſſioners' Records of the next Year (1650), i, 169.

Yet the Commiſſioners do not ſeem to have troubled themſelves about Uncas's Marriages, one of whoſe Wives was Siſter to Saſſacus.

280 Notwithſtanding the Author ſkips nearly four Years, there were conſtant Troubles with the Indians during that Time; one Tribe complaining of another to the Engliſh. At the Meeting of the Commiſſioners in Sept. 1650, Uncas complained that " the Mohanſick Sachem in " Long Iſland had killed ſome of" his Men, " bewitched diuers and " himſelf allſo," and deſired that he might be " righted therein." But the Complaint could not be acted on becauſe the Long Iſland Sachem was not preſent to anſwer or defend himſelf. So it was adviſed that the Governor of Connecticut commiſſion Capt. John Maſon, Mr. Howell, Mr. Goſmer and Thomas Benedict of Southhold to attend to the Caſe. What the Cmmiſſioners thought of Uncas being bewitched they do not inform us; but from their Silence on that Point it may reaſonably be concluded that they thought the Devil had more to do with him than Witches.

281 Whatever Grounds there may have been for ſuſpecting a Combination of Indians with the Dutch againſt the Engliſh Coloniſts at this Period, there ſeems not to be found any reliable Facts of ſuch Combination or Conſpiracy. All the Teſtimony elicited is vague and uncertain.

Election of Magiſtrates in the ſeveral Juriſdictions was intended for Execution, becauſe then the Towns would be left naked and leſs able to defend themſelves. This Squaw moreover deſired the Engliſh to remember, how dear their ſlighting of her former Information of the *Pequots* coming had coſt them.[282]

Alſo, *Vncas* addreſſed himſelf to the Governour of *Connecticut* Colony declaring that *Ninnigret* had that Winter been at *Manhatos*, and that he had given the Dutch Governour a great Preſent of *Wampam*, and received from him twenty Gunns, with Powder and Shot anſwerable; [68] and that during his ſtay in thoſe Parts, he went over *Hudſons* River, gathered as many *Sachims* together as he could, made ample Declaration againſt the Engliſh, deſiring their Aid and Aſſiſtance againſt them.

Yea moreover, there were no leſs than nine Indian *Sagamores*, who lived near *Manhatos*, did voluntarily without any Notice or Reward from the Engliſh, ſend their Meſſengers to *Stamford* declaring and affirming (even after they were urged by the Engliſh to teſtifie nothing but the Truth) that the Dutch had ſollicited them by promiſing them Gunns, Swords, Powder, Wampan, Waſt coats and Coats to cut off the Engliſh. The Meſſengers added that they would not lye, and were as the Mouth of the nine Sagamores, who *All ſpeak they no lye*, they would affirm it to the Dutch Govern-

282 This refers to the Maſſacre at Watertown (afterwards called Wethersfield), and to the Agency of the Wife of Mononotto, probably.

ours Face, and if the Dutch were angry, and ſhould fight with them, *No Force &c.* The next Day, one of thoſe Sagamores, with the Son and Brother of another of them came themſelves to *Stamford*, and confirmed what their Meſſengers in their Names had before reported.

This Spring alſo the Indians in the northern and eaſtern Parts generally grew inſolent, and their Cariage very Suſpitious, and they gave out threatning Words, ſo that many Alarms were made, the Peace of the Engliſh through the whole Country diſturbed, they wearied with extraordinary Watchings and Wanderings, hindered in their Plowing, Sowing, preparations for Planting and other Occaſions, to their exceeding great Damage. Theſe Things cauſed many ſad Thoughts of Hearts, and ſome warlike Preparations; but when the Partyes accuſed were enquired of about theſe Matters they would own nothing; as for *Ninigret* he pretended that his wintering amongſt the Dutch was on the Account of his Health, and not at all out of Deſign againſt the Engliſh. The Reſt of the *Narraganſet Sachims* made themſelves very ignorant of any Plot; the Dutch Governour likewiſe profeſſed great Abhorency of ſo vile a Thing as that would be, to hire barbarous Indians to murder Chriſtians; withall adding, that if the Colonyes fell upon him on that Account, the righteous Judge would be his Defence,[283] and that,

. . . . . . Hic murus aheneus eſto
Nil conſcire ſibi nullâ palleſcere culpâ.

[283] Peter Stuyveſant was Gov- ernor of the Dutch at New Am-

Alſo glad Tidings of Peace between the Nations at Home arrived here; ſo did theſe Troubles vaniſh.[284]

Albeit not many Years after theſe Things, the Indians in thoſe Parts made an horrible Slaughter, not of Engliſh-men but Dutch-men, who were treacherouſly maſſacred by them.[285]

[69] In the latter End of this Year it was that the *Montauket* or *Long-Iſland* Indians who were Friends and Tributaryes to the Engliſh, complained that *Ninnigret* and the *Nianticks* had aſſaulted them, killing and taking captive diverſe of them. They were ſo far hearkned unto, as that the Com-

ſterdam (N. York) and there has nothing ſince been diſcovered in the Character of the Dutch Governor to warrant any other Concluſion, but that he was malignantly traduced by the vagabond Indians. Plymouth, Connecticut and New Haven ſeemed inclined to believe the Stories; but Maſſachuſetts, leſs intereſted, did not credit the Tales.

284 The Treaty of Peace with Holland was ſigned the 5th April, 1654; the News of which was received in Boſton, 23d June following. See Holmes, *Annals*, i, 301.

285 New England has never ſeen ſo diſtreſſing a Time as was experienced by the Dutch Settlers adverted to in the Text. Tolerably minute Accounts may be read of thoſe Troubles in O'Callaghan and Brodhead's Hiſtories and their Authorities indicated. The Invaſion by the Indians is ſaid to have began on the 13th of September, 1655. But if ſo there muſt have been another Invaſion the ſame Year; for, on the ſame Day the Commiſſioners of the United Colonies, who had met at New Haven on the 6th of Sept., 1655, ſay, that on "the 15 of the "p^r^ſent September, by the Returne "of the Meſſengers whom they had "ſent forth for Inquiry, received "certaine Intelligence of a great "Maſſacar perpitrated by the Wampeage and other Indians vpon the "Dutch at the Monhatoes," who had taken ſeventy of the Dutch Priſoners; that as they were about to take Means to ranſom the Captives, Mr. Allerton's Ketch arrived at Newhaven from Manhattan, bringing News that the Indians had offered to make Peace, and a Treaty was entered upon. They therefore thought any Action on their Part unneceſſary *Records Commiſſioners U. C.*, ii, 144. See alſo *A Narrative* juſt iſſued by Dr. O'Callaghan.

miſſioners of the United Colonies did apprehend themſelves called of God to wage War againſt *Ninigret* and ſuch Indians as ſhould adhere to him in his bloudy Proceedings, and accordingly did by Vote conclude and determine the ſame, and that two hundred and fifty Souldiers ſhould be forthwith raiſed, and ſent forth by the ſeveral Colonies. But the Council of *Boſton* not concurring in thoſe Concluſions, the intended Expedition failed at that Time;[286] Neverthele ſs the next Year, it being known that *Ninnigret* perſiſted in his warring upon the Long Iſlanders, and that he brake his Covenant, refuſing to pay Tribute for thoſe *Pequots* that were by the Engliſh formerly placed under him, and that the Lenity of the Colonies was abuſed to heighten his Pride and Inſolency; upon theſe Conſiderations it was agreed by the Commiſſioners that there ſhould be two hundred and ſeventy Foot Souldiers, and forty Horſe, raiſed out of the ſeveral Colonyes, in order to reducing *Ninnigret* to Subjection and better Obedience. Accrdingly Forces were forthwith levied, and a ſmall Army ſent forth under the Chriſtian and Couragious Major *Willard* as Commander in Chief.[287]

286 If thoſe who are now maintaining the abſurd Doctrine of Seceſſion only knew how Matters ſtood in the United Colonies in 1653, they might uſe the Facts to fortify their Poſition The General Court practically nullified the Action of the Commiſſioners by a Reſolution that "no Act of theirs, though they "ſhould all agree, ſhould bind the "General Court to join in an "offenſive War." This Proceeding on the Part of Maſſachuſetts came near breaking up the Confederacy; and that probably would have been the Reſult had Affairs turned out as the Majority of the Colonies ſuppoſed they would.

287 There was ſtrong Diſſatisfac-

Upon the Approach of the Engliſh Army, *Ninnigret* fled from the Place of his uſual Reſidence, and got into a Swamp, where it was not eaſie to purſue him. Moſt of the Pequots under his Juriſdiction then deſerted him, and came to the Engliſh.[288] Meſſengers were ſent to demand a Treaty with him, but he was afraid to appear.

In fine, two Gentlemen, viz. Capt. *Davis* and Capt. *Siely* went to him requiring the Delivery of the Reſt of the *Pequots;* to whom he replyed that they were gone on Hunting, but ingaged that within ſeven Dayes they ſhould be delivered to Mr. *Winthrop.*[289] He was moreover charged to forbear

tion with Major Willard's Proceedings againſt Ninigret. It was unaccountable to the war Party that he ſhould have returned from his well planned Expedition, having inflicted no Chaſtiſement on the Nianticks; when as Ninnigret fled on his Approach leaving his Country, Corn and Wigwams unprotected, which might have been deſtroyed without Moleſtation. It is evident that the Major did not think ſuch a Courſe was the beſt one; and that Ninigret and his Nianticks did not deſerve ſuch Severity; and although he was gravely cenſured at the Time by ſome, and perhaps even by a Majority of the Engliſh, yet Poſterity will doubtleſs ſuſtain him. He did excellent Service afterwards in the War with Philip, and died in the Midſt of it. See Mather's *Brief Hiſtory*, 153. His Report of the Expedition, and the Action of the Commiſſioners upon it may be ſeen in the *Records of the United Colonies*, ii, 145-9. The Epedition ſet out from Boſton the 9th of October, 1654, and returned on the 24th of the ſame Month.

288 About one hundred of them, according to Maj. Willard's official Report. Theſe all ſubſcribed certain Conditions drawn up for that Purpoſe. The Subſtance of ſaid Conditions are contained in the Major's Report, but the Originals are probably not preſerved.

289 This Interview tranſpired on the 18th of October, 1654. The Number of Engliſhmen ſent to treat with Ninigret was ſix. He refuſed to meet them becauſe they were ſo many, but ſent Word that he would meet two of the Engliſh. Accordingly Capt. [William] Davis and Capt. [Robert] Seily were met by the Chief, who inquired—" Why

all Acts of Hostility against the Long-Islanders, or any other Indians that were in Amity with the English;[290] and plainly told, that if he did not hearken to the Advice and Charge laid upon him, he must expect that ere long his Head would be set upon an English Pole.[291]

So did the Messengers return and the Army also. These Things hapned in October Anno 1654.

After the English Forces were withdrawn, *Ninnigret* did according to his usual Manner, observe *Fidem punicam* in keeping the Promises which at that Time he made and set his Hand unto.

[70] Not many Years after this the Indians in

" do you demand the Pequots? You " have them already. I have but " three or four. The rest are abroad " hunting and elsewhere." Finally the "seven Days" Arrangement was made, as mentioned in the Text

290 Ninigret had been made war upon by the Long Island Indians, who had killed several of his Chiefs and other Men. He therefore thought it singularly unjust Interference on the Part of the English that he should not be allowed to "right himself;" while at the same Time the New Haven People had been sending Powder and Shot to his Enemies, the Long Islanders. And we do not wonder that when he was told that he must desist from attacking those Indians, that "he " was silent for a Time, but after, " said this—'Shal such a Prince " and two Captains lose theire Lives " and theire Bloud not to bee re- " venged?'" The English again repeated the Command, but Ninigret said no more. They next demanded that he should defray the Expense of the Expedition upon which they had now come. To this he answered, in Effect, that he had not caused the Expedition; that if it was on Acconnt of the Long Islanders they might look to them. Here the Matter appears to have rested, so far as payment for the Expedition was concerned. See *Records Coms. U. Cols.*, ii, 147.

291 Ninigret was living in the Time of Philip's War, and rendered some Service against those Indians who brought it on; but he must at that Period have been very old, for we hear of him as early as 1632. The Time of his Death is not known. Several Anecdotes concerning him will be found preserved in the *Book of the Indians.*

the ſouthern and weſtern Parts of this Land were involved in Broyles amongſt themſelves, raging with implacable Feudes and Wars one againſt another. The *Nianticks*, *Mauntaukets*, *Mohegins*, *Norwootucks*, all engaged in cruel and bloody Quarrels. And the Peace of theſe Colonyes was not a little diſturbed and endangered thereby, inaſmuch as the Indians would purſue one another to the Engliſh Plantations, and ſometimes into the Engliſh Houſes, and there kill one another.[292] Some Engliſh at *Wethersfield*, and ſome inhabiting in the *Moheag* Country were by Means hereof put into ſad Frights.[293] In ſpecial, in Anno 1658. ſundry

[292] It was not an uncommon Thing, when Diſputes and Difficulties occurred among the Indians themſelves, that one Party would fly to the Neighborhood of the Engliſh, thinking thereby to eſcape the Fury of the other Party. But this did not often ſhield the Fugitives; for if the Engliſh had the Ability to ſhield them, they could know nothing as to who was the originally agrieved Party. Hence deadly Skirmiſhes took place ſometimes in the very Encloſures of the Engliſh, and Bullets often paſſed through their Houſes. Sometimes even one Indian has purſued another into their Houſes and Murders were committed on the Floor and before the Eyes of the Family. An Inſtance of this Kind once occurred in Cambridge.

[293] Sometime in the Month of May, 1660, the Government of Connecticut ſent a Letter to the Commiſſioners of the United Colonies, dated June 9th, ſaying, among other Things, that "not many "Weeks now paſt, wee are by ſuf-"ficient Information certified, that "one Night, at the new Plantation "at Munheage, ſome Indians (as "will appeare) of the Narraganſets "ſhot eleven Bullets into a Houſe "of our Engliſh there, in Hopes, "as they boaſted, to have ſlain him "whom we have Cauſe to honour," who appears to have been Deputy Governor Major Maſon. "As alſo "ſlew another at Robert Layes, "to the great Affrightment and "Terror of Goodwife Lay. We "intreat you to conſider how in-"cogruous and croſs it would haue "bin 20 Yeares agoe to an Engliſh "Spirit to beare ſvch Things as "now we are forct to beare, or "whether the Indians would not "haue expected a Viſitation upon

English in divers Places were disquieted by the Insolence and Outrage of the *Pacumptick* Indians.[294]

" less Occasions then these that haue " of late bene met with by several " of ours. We cannot but conceaue " it is high Time to renew vpon " the Memory of these Pagans the " obliterate Memorials of the Eng- " lish." At the next Meeting of the Commissioners it was resolved, in View of these Complaints, " to " require and force the Narrogan- " setts to a just Satisfaction." See Trumbull's *Col. Recs. Ct.*, i, 576-7. Conformably to this a Demand was made on the Narragansets for " att " least foure of the chiefe of them " that shott into the English House," or to pay 500 Fathom of Wampum. The Matter appears to have been setled by the Wampum.

At the same Time a Complaint was considered about an Outrage committed at the House of Mr. Brewster by those Indians who besieged Uncas, " by theire forcable " attempting to enter his House and " theire violent Intrusion and taking " away som Goods and stealing his " Corn." Besides, the last Spring (1659) " som Narragansett Indians " did assault and kill a Mohegan " Indian in his Seruice who flying " to Mistris Brewster for Succor; " yet they violently tooke him from " her and shott him by her Side to " her great Affrightment." The Commissioners said this was " an " intolerable and impudent Miscar- " riage," and for which they demanded 80 Fathom of Wampum. *Recs. U. Cols.*, ii, 227. The Pocumtucke Indians were concerned in the Siege of Uncas's Fort, one of whose Chiefs was a principal Leader. *Ibid*, 223. The Brewster Family so vaguely mentioned in the *Records*, was probably that of Mr. Jonathan Brewster, eldest Son of Elder William of the Pilgrim Band. Mr. Brewster established a Trading house on the Thames in 1649, at a Point on the east Side of the River, still called Brewster's Neck. Of this he had a Deed from Uncas, dated 25 April, 1650. His Wife's Name was Lucretia. See Miss Caulkins's *New London*, 66, 331, &c. Mr. Brewster was one of the Defenders of Uncas, and was with him in his Fort when it was attacked by the Mohegans, and thus was saved the Life of the deceitful Uncas. His Fort was at the Head of Nahantick River. See *Ibid*, 127.

294 In the Records of Connecticut mention is made of the Session of the General Court in April, 1657, of " a horid Murder committed by " some Indians at Farmington."— (Trumbull, *Col. Rec. Ct.*, i, 294.) But on whom the Murder was committed no mention is made. I infer from subsequent Actions of the Court that the Murder was among the Indians themselves, and that during the Affair a House was burnt; " and " though Mesapano seems to bee " the principall Acter, yet the Ac- " cessories are not yet clearly dis- " coured, and none brought to a

But when the *Sachims* were called to an Account about it, they pretended that they were ignorant of what Diſorders were committed by their Men, nor allowed of by them who deſired to live in Amity with the Engliſh, and were willing to give Satisfaction for paſt Injuryes, and to prevent the like Abuſes for the Future. So did thoſe Troubles paſs over. Not very long before this, at *South-Hampton* in *Long-Iſland* ſome Houſes had been burned by a wicked Indian (and a Negro Woman) who it ſeems after he had done this Wickedneſs, deſperately killed himſelf, to prevent juſt Execution. It was at firſt thought that more of the Indians there had had an Hand in that burning, whence they were condemned to pay ſeven hundred Pound in ſeven Years, but afterwards that Penalty was taken off, ſince it was judged unreaſonable that thoſe Indians who were not proved to act in, or conſent to the Miſchief that was done, ſhould be made to ſuffer as Guilty.

In Anno 1662, *Plymouth* Colony was in ſome Danger of being involved in Trouble by the *Wampanoag* Indians. After *Maſſaſoit* was dead, his two Sons called *Wamſutta* and *Metacomet*, came to the Court at *Plymouth* pretending high Reſpect for the Engliſh, and therefore deſired Engliſh Names might be impoſed on them, whereupon the Court there named *Wamſutta* (the elder Brother) *Alex-*

" legall Triall." At the Seſſion in Auguſt of the ſame Year the Tunxis Indians agreed to pay for the Damage done at Farmington, " occaſioned " by *Meſupeno*" (as he is then called) eighty Fathom of Wampum, " well ſtrungd," for ſeven Years. See alſo Trumbull's *Hiſt. Conn.*, i, 230.

ander, and *Metacomet* (the younger Brother) *Philip*; this *Alexander* (*Philips* immediate Predeceſſor) was not ſo faithful and friendly to the Engliſh as his Father had been.[295] For ſome of *Boſton* having occaſionally been at *Narraganſet* wrote to Mr. *Prince* who was then Governour of *Plymouth*, that *Alexander* was contriving Miſchief againſt the Engliſh, and that he had ſolicited the *Narraganſets* to ingage with him in his deſigned Rebellion. Hereupon Capt. *Willet* (who lived near to *Mount Hope*, the Place where *Alexander* did reſide) was appointed to ſpeak with him, and to deſire him to attend the next Court in *Plymouth*, for their Satiſfaction, and his own [71] Vindication, he ſeemed to take the Meſſage in good Part, profeſſing that the *Narraganſets* who (he ſaid were his Enemies) had put an Abuſe upon him, and he readily promiſed to attend at the next Court. But when the Day of his Appearance was come, inſtead of that, he at that very Time went over to the *Narraganſets* his pretended Enemies; which compared with other Circumſtances, cauſed the Gentlemen at *Plymouth*, to ſuſpect there was more of Truth in the Information given, than at firſt they were aware of.

[295] The Treaty made with Philip at this Time may be ſeen in the *Plymouth Col. Records*, iv, 256. The Subſtance of it is alſo contained in Morton's *Memorial*, *Sub. an.* 1662. But Morton omits Part of the Signers of the Treaty. They are theſe: "The Marke —&— "PHILLIP, allis METACUM, "Sachim of Pocanakett, The Marke "y—c—ʊ VNCOMPOWETT, "Vnkell to the abouesaid Sachem. "Witneſſe, John Saſomon. "The Marke of ——ɲ Francis, "the Sachem of Nanſet. "The Mark of Nimrod —-—, "allis Pumpaſa, "Marke –L– of Punckquaneck, "The Marke —ઈ— of Aquete-"queſh."

Wherefore the Governour and Magiſtrates there, ordered Major *Winſlow* (who is ſince and at this Day Governour of that Colony) to take a Party of Men and fetch down *Alexander*. The Major conſidering that *ſemper nocuit differre paratis*, he took but ten armed Men with him from *Marſhfield*, intending to have taken more at the Towns that lay nearer *Mount Hope*. But Divine Providence ſo ordered, as that when they were about the Midway between *Plymouth* and *Bridgewater*, obſerving an hunting Houſe they rode up to it, and there did they find *Alexander* and many of his Men well armed, but their Guns ſtanding together without the Houſe, the Major with his ſmall Party, poſſeſed themſelves of the Indians Arms, and beſet the Houſe; then did he go in amongſt them, acquainting the *Sachim* with the Reaſon of his coming in ſuch a Way, deſiring *Alexander* with his Interpreter to walk out with him, who did ſo a little Diſtance from the Houſe, and then underſtood what Commiſſion the *Major* had received concerning him The proud *Sachim* fell into a raging Paſſion at this Surpriſe, ſaying that the Governour had no Reaſon to credit Rumors, or to ſend for him in ſuch a Way, nor would he go to *Plymouth* but when he ſaw Cauſe. It was replyed to him, that his Breach of Word touching Appearance at *Plymouth* Court, and inſtead thereof going at the ſame Time to his pretended Enemies, augmented Jealouſies concerning him. In fine, the Major told him that his Order was to bring him to *Plymouth*, and that (by the help of God) he would do it, or elſe he would dy on the Place; Alſo declaring to him that if he would ſubmit, he might expect reſpective Uſage, but if he once more denyed to go, he ſhould never ſtir from the Ground wheron he ſtood, and with a Piſtol at the *Sachims* Breaſt, required that his next Words ſhould be a poſitive and clear Anſwer to what was demanded. Hereupon his Interpreter (a diſcreet Indian, brother to *John Sauſaman*) being ſenſible of *Alexanders* paſſionate Diſpoſition entreated that he might ſpeak a few Words to the *Sachim* before he gave his Anſwer. The prudent Diſourſe of this Indian prevailed ſo far as that *Alexander* yielded to go, only requeſting that he might go like a *Sachim*, with his Men attending him, which (although [72] there was ſome Hazard in it, they being many, and the Engliſh but a few) was granted to him. The Weather being hot, the Major offered him an Horſe to ride on, but his Squaw and diverſe Indian Women being in Company, he refuſed, ſaying he could go on Foot as well as they, entreating only that there might be a complying with their Pace, which was done, and reſting ſeveral Times by the Way, *Alexander* and his Indians were refreſhed by the Engliſh; no other Diſcourſe hapning while they were upon their March, but what was pleaſant and amicable. The *Major* ſent a Man before, to entreat that as many of the Magiſtrates of that Colony as could; would meet at *Duxbury*; wherefore having there had ſome Treaty with *Alexander*, not willing to commit him to Priſon, they entreated Major *Winſlow* to receive him to his Houſe, untill the Governour (who then lived at *Eaſtham*) could come up. Accordingly he and his Train were courteouſly entertained by the Major. And albeit not ſo much as an angry Word paſſed between them whilſt at *Marſhfield;* yet proud *Alexander* vexing and fretting in his Spirit, that ſuch a Check was given him, he ſuddenly fell ſick of a Fever. He was then nurſed as a choice Friend. Mr. *Fuller* (the Phyſitian) coming providentially thither at that Time, the Sachim and his Men earneſtly deſired that he would adminiſter to him, which he was unwilling to doe, but by their importunity was prevailed with to doe the beſt he could to help him and therefore gave him a Potion of working Phyſick, which the Indians thought did him good; but his Diſtemper afterwards prevailing, they entreated to diſmiſs him, in order to a return Home, which upon Engagement of Appearance at the next Court was granted to him, ſoon after his being returned Home, he dyed.[296]

And this is the Truth and Subſtance of what concerns Tranſactions with *Alexander*, concerning which ſo many fabulous Storyes have been ſpread abroad.[297]

Alexander being dead, his Brother *Philip* (of late

[296] Judge Davis has a long Note in his Edition of Morton's Memorial on this Affair of Alexander, in which he compares the various Accounts of the Tranſaction, indulging in ſome probably juſt Criticiſms upon them.

[297] Whether the Author intended to inc ude Mr. Hubbard's Account among the "many fabulous Storyes" which had been in Circulation is not poſitive, but probable; and yet what Mr. Hubbard does relate is much to the ſame Purport as this, and his Work had juſt been publiſhed. Perhaps it had been out near ſix Months.

curſed Memory)[298] roſe up in his ſtead, and he was no ſooner ſtyled *Sachim,* but immediately in the Year 1662. there were vehement Suſpitions of his bloudy Treachery againſt the Engliſh: yet he profeſſed otherwiſe, and making his perſonal Appearance at a Court holden at Plymouth, renewed that Covenant which his Father and Brother had confirmed with the Engliſh there.[299] This Covenant he perfidiouſly brake: For in Anno 1671. it was evident that he with other of his Confederates had been conſpiring againſt the Colony, under whoſe Protection and Juriſdiction he had ſubmitted himſelf. He then armed himſelf and acted like a Rebel that intended a ſpeedy Riſing, yea, he ordered (as ſome Indians [73] have ſince confeſſed) that if the Engliſh did ſend Meſſengers to treat with him, if above four came in Company together they ſhould be ſhot down, and appointed ſome to ly in Ambuſh for that End; and behaved himſelf after a ſurly and provoking Manner towards Meſſengers that deſired Treaty with him,[300] and refuſed to appear, and give Anſwer for his Inſolencyes, his

298 "The Idea was too much "cheriſhed, that they [the firſt Settlers] were themſelves the People "of God—the choſen Iſraelites, "and that the Natives, being Heathen, were in the Situation of the "Canaanites whom the Children "of Iſrael had a Right, by the "Command of God, to extirpate "them;" Rev. John Taylor of Deerfield, in his *Appendix* to Williams's *Redeemed Captive,* Ed. 1800, p. 199.

299 This has Reference to the Treaty in the *Plymouth Col. Recs.* as before cited in *Note* 295. It was doubtleſs owing to the Death of Alexander, that Philip gave Occaſion for the Authorities of Plymouth to ſuſpect him of a treacherous Deſign againſt the Colony.

300 This Matter of the Treatment of Meſſengers is touched upon in the *Brief Hiſtory,* p. 220.

Covenant notwithſtanding. Neverthelefs, he at laſt conceded to meet the Governour and Magiſtrates of *Plymouth*, at *Taunton*, where ſundry Commiſſioners of *Boſton* were deſired to be, and to hear the Matters of Difference between the Engliſh of *Plymouth* and this *Philip* Sachim. This Meeting was attended in April, 1671. when *Philip* confeſſed his Breach of Covenant, and that he had groundleſſly taken up Arms againſt them, whom he had always found friendly to him; And ſurrendered ſome of his Arms, engaging for the delivery of the Reſt in due Time.[301] The Engliſh being tender of ſhedding Blood, let him go upon Promiſe of better Behaviour for the Future. Soon after this, *Philip* (with ſome of his Counſellors) repaired to *Boſton*, endeavouring to poſſeſs the Engliſh there, with lying Informations about Injuryes done to him by thoſe of *Plymouth*. Wherefore the Council of that Colony entreated that Commiſſioners from *Boſton*, and from *Connecticut* alſo might be ſent to *Plymouth*, that ſo a fair Hearing of Differences before all the World might be attended. So then in *September* following the Governour of *Connecticut*, and ſeveral Magiſtrates from the *Maſſachuſetts*, and ſome other Gentlemen met at *Plymouth*,[302] where *Philip* appeared, and all his

301 The Treaty of Taunton is given in the *Brief Hiſtory*, p. 223. It is alſo contained in Hubbard's *Narrative*, 11-12. It bears Date, April 10th, 1671.

302 Theſe Proceedings are entered upon the *Records* of *Plymouth*. The Names of thoſe appointed to treat with Philip were Gov. John Winthrop of Connecticut, Maj. General John Leverett, Mr. Thomas Danforth and Capt. William Davis of Maſſachuſetts. The Names of "ſome other Gentlemen," do not appear in the Records.

Allegations were heard to the Conviction of *Philip* himſelf, and great Satisfaction of all that Audience. The Concluſion was, *Philip* acknowledged his Offence and was appointed to give a Sum of Mony to defray the Charges which his inſolent Clamours had put that Colony unto. The Particulars which *Philip* then covenated to were theſe.

1. That he would for the Future be ſubject to the Government of *Plymouth*, and to their Laws.

2. He engaged to pay the Colony an hundred Pound towards reparation of ſuch Wrong as they had ſuſtained by his Miſdemeanors.

3. He was under Obligations to ſend five Wolves Heads every Year to the Governour of *Plymouth* in Token of his Fealty.

4. That he would not make War with any without the Approbation of that Government.

5. In Caſe any future Difference ſhould ariſe between him and the Engliſh, he would repair to the Government there to rectify Matters, before ingaging in any hoſtile Attempts.

[74] 6. That he would not diſpoſe of any of his Lands but with the Approbation of the Engliſh Government there—So was he diſmiſſed.[303] Some

303 Plymouth had now, in Promiſes, all ſhe required of the Wampanoags. In Caſe of Diſobedience, ſhe had only to call upon the Commiſſioners to aid, if ſhe needed Aid, to coerce any refractory Spirit among her neighbouring Indians. Thoſe who made their Marks to the Treaty were PHILIP, Sachem; WOHKOWPAHENITT; WUTTAKOOSEEIM; SONKANUHOO; WOONASHUM, alias NIMROD; WOOSPASUCK, alias CAPTAINE. The Treaty was ſigned 29 Sept. 1671.

On the 3d of November following Philip came again to Plymouth with the Sachem of Saconet, named

of theſe Covenants were in Part obſerved by him, and ſome Particulars not at all—Thus did Things reſt between the Engliſh and him, until the Year 1674. when in *January* an Indian Preacher, known by the Name of *John Sauſaman*,[304] addreſſed himſelf to the preſent Governour of *Plymouth*, informing him that the Indians were complotting the Deſtruction of the Engliſh, and that not only the *Wampanoags*, but the *Narraganſets*, yea, and the *Mohegins* were involving themſelves in this Conſpiracy. This *Sauſaman* was by Birth a *Maſſachuſet*, his Father and Mother living in *Dorcheſter*, and they both died Chriſtians. This their Son did for ſome Time apoſtatize from his Chriſtian Profeſſion, and lived like an Heathen, being *Philips* Secretary (for he could write a very legible Hand) and one of his Counſellors, untill at laſt God convinced him of his Miſery, and he manifeſted ſuch evident Signs of Repentance as that he was, after his Return from Pagan *Philip*, reconciled to the praying Indians and baptized, and received as a Member in one of the Indian Churches, yea and imployed as an Inſtructor amongſt them every Lords Day. Nevertheleſs, his Information (becauſe it had an Indian Original, and one can hardly believe them when they ſpeak Truth) was not at firſt much regarded,

TAKAMUNNA, who alſo ſigned an Article binding him to the Obſervance of the Treaty of the 29th of September preceding. He alſo agreed to pay one Wolf's Head per annum "into the Treaſury of Plymouth," Philip becoming his Security. *Plym. Col. Recs.*, v, 67-80.

[304] His own Signature upon a Document in my Poſſeſſion is *Wuſſauſman*; a Fac Simile of which may be ſeen in the *Hiſt. and Antiquities of Boſton*, 397.

untill by Relation of Circumſtances, he made it too apparent that *Philip* was really hatching Miſchief. The Effect was, the Governour of *Plymouth* adviſing with his Councill, reſolved once more to ſend for *Philip*, and to enquire into the Truth of Things: But before that could be accompliſhed, an Indian called *Tobias*, with his Son, and another Indian named *Mattaſhinnamy*, meeting with *John Sauſaman* at a Pond, cruelly murdered him; and that their Villany might not be diſcovered, they cut an Hole through the Ice, and put in the dead murthered Body, leaving his Hat and Gun upon the Ice, that ſo others might think that he had drowned himſelf. It being rumored that *Sauſaman* was loſt, the dead Body was ſought after, and found in the Pond, and taken up and buried.[305]

Jealouſies being on the Spirits of Men that the other Indians had murthered him, on Account of revealing their Conſpiracyes to the Engliſh: The Governour of *Plymouth* ordered the Conſtable of *Middlebury*[306] (that being the neareſt Town to the Place where the Murther was committed) to cauſe *John Sauſamans* Body to be taken up again, and to empanel a Jury as a *Coroners Inqueſt*, to make Enquiry how he come by his Death:[307] And they

[305] Aſſawomſet Pond in Middleborough was the Place where Sauſaman's Body was found. He was murdered on the 29th January, 1674-5.

[306] Middleborough; ſaid to have been ſo called becauſe it was about Midway between Plymouth and a noted Point on Taunton or Tehticut River.

[307] The Names of the Jurymen were WILLIAM SABINE, WILLIAM CROCKER, EDWARD STURGIS, WILLIAM BROOKES, NATHANIL WINS-

found that he had been murthered, for his Neck was broken by twiſting of his Head round; which is the [75] Way that the Indians ſometimes uſe when they practice Murthers; alſo his Head was extreamly ſwollen, and his Body was wounded in ſeveral Parts of it, and when it was firſt taken out of the Pond, no Water iſſued out of it, which argued that the Body was not drowned, but dead before it came into the Water.

Moreover, when *Tobias*, (the ſuſpected Murtherer) came near the dead Body, it fell a bleeding on freſh as if it had been newly ſlain, albeit it was buried a conſiderable Time before that.[308]

Afterwards an Indian called *Patuckſon*, came and teſtified to their Faces that he ſaw *Tobias* and the other Indians murthering *Sauſaman*: He alſo himſelf before his Death had declared, that he was

LOW, JOHN WADSWORTH, ANDNEW RINGE, ROBERT VIXON, JOHN DONE, JONATHAN BANGS, JONATHAN SHAW, and BENJAMIN HIGGINS.

"Itt was judged very expedient by "the Court, that together with this "Engliſh Jury aboue named, ſome "of the moſt indifferenteſt, graueſt "and ſage Indians ſhould be ad-"mitted to be with the ſaid Jury, "and to help to conſult and aduice "with, of, and concerning the "Premiſes. Their Names are as "followeth, viz[t]. one called by an "Engliſh Name, HOPE, and MAS-"KIPPAGUE, WANNOO, GEORGE, "WAMPYE, and ACANOOTUS; theſe "fully concurred with the aboue "written Jury in theire Vedict." *Plymouth Col. Recs.*, v, 168.

[308] The Practice of this Method for the Diſcovery of a Murderer is very ancient, and dates probably near the Beginning of the human Family. King James alludes to it in his *Demonology*—he ſays, "if the "dead Carkaſe bee at any Time "thereafter handled by the Mur-"therer, it will guſh out of Blood, "as if the Blood were crying to the "Heaven for Reuenge of the Mur-"therer, God having appointed that "ſecret ſupernatural Signe for triall "of that ſecret unnatural Crime." This is certainly worthy of the Author of the *Demonology*.

It may be preſumed that there were few Occaſions when this Teſt was required, or if required the Murderer was not found.

afraid thoſe very Indians would at laſt prove his Murtherers.

They were therefore apprehended and kept in Durance untill Plymouth Court, which was held in June, 1675. and being found guilty of *Sauſaman's* Death, they were (one of them before his Execution confeſſing the Murther) condemned and executed.[309] And then did *Philip*, being (as was verily ſuppoſed) privy to what *Tobias* (his Counſellor) and thoſe with him had perpetrated upon *John Sauſaman*, fell to open Rebellion and bloodſhedding amongſt the Engliſh at *Swanzy*, who were his next Neighbours.

But of the ſpecial Occurrences attending the late (and not yet ended) *War* between the Engliſh and the Indians, I have elſewhere given a brief Account, and therefore ſhall not here add anything, that not comporting with my preſent Deſign.[310]

The Particulars which have been mentioned, are

[309] Their Names were Tobias, Wampapaquan his Son, and Mattaſhunannamo. Tobias and his Son were executed by being "hanged "by the Head," on June 8th, 1675. "But the ſaid Wampapaquan, on "ſome Conſiderations was reprieued "vntil a Month be expired." He was however ſhot within the Month —probably owing to the Commencement of Hoſtilities by Philip; for it will be remembered, that within ſixteen Days from the Time Tobias and his Son were hanged, the War began in Swanzey. Tobias was a Chief and one of Philip's Counſellors, whoſe Death doubtleſs exaſperated Philip and his other Chiefs, and was the immediate Cauſe of the War that followed.

The Indians underſtood very little of Agreements made by a few Scratches upon Paper with Pen and Ink. And they looked upon it that it was no buſineſs of the Engliſh to puniſh one Indian for killing another. See *Old Indian Chronicle*, 5-6.

[310] The Author here refers to the *Brief Hiſtory* which he publiſhed the previous Summer or Autumn, ſo fully noticed in this Volume.

the chief (if not the only) Troubles[311] which have hapned by the Indians in *New England*, from the firſt Planting thereof by the Engliſh till the late Commotions. Some few private Murthers there have been, which are not inſiſted on in this Narrative, as namely thoſe at *Nantucket*,[312] and that by *Matoonas* his Son, and that at *Woburn*,[313] but the publick Peace was not ſo endangered by thoſe clandeſtine Revenges, as by the Conſpiracyes, the Relation whereof hath been deſcribed.

It is eaſy to obſerve; from the Hiſtory of theſe *Troubles*, that whereas there have been two Sorts of Men deſigning Settlement in this Part of *America*, ſome that came hither on Account of Trade and worldly Intereſts, by whom the Indians have been ſcandalized, others that came hither on a religious and conſcientious Account, having in their Eye the Converſion of the *Heathen* unto Chriſt; the former have [76] been attended with blaſting ruining Providences,[314] theſe latter have been ſignally owned

311 This is hardly expreſſed as it ſhould be by one who had read the *Records of the Commiſſioners of the United Colonies* as the Author muſt have done, as theſe *Notes* ſhow.

312 Perhaps the Nature of the Affair at Nantucket may be learned from Macy's Hiſtory of that Iſland. See *Macy's Work*, 42-44. In the Year 1665, King Philip purſued a Fugitive to Nantucket, putting the Inhabitants into a great Fright. All that has been learned reſpecting this Raid of Philip will be found in the *Book of the Indians*, 202.

313 "That by *Matonas* his Son, "and that at Woburn" I judge to refer to the ſame Tranſaction. Compare what is ſaid in the *Old Indian Chronicle*, 137-8, with a Communication of the Rev. Samuel Sewall, D. D., publiſhed in the *Book of the Indians*, 698-9. See alſo Hubbard's *Nar.*, 7. According to the *Chronicle*, the Murder at Woburn was about 1669 or 1670.

314 Had the Author been able to extend his prophetic Viſion a hundred Years in advance of his own Age, his Views reſpecting the Ob-

by the Lord Jeſus, for the like hath been rarely known in the World, that a Plantation ſhould be raiſed out of nothing, and brought to ſuch conſiderableneſs in ſo ſhort a Time, whereas in the Cloſe of the laſt *Century*, there was not ſo much as one Chriſtian in this Land, there are now above *Fourſcore* Engliſh, and *ſix* Indian *Churches*, therein, beſides many other Congregations calling upon the Name of the True God in Jeſus Chriſt, although as yet not brought into Church eſtate, according to the Order of the Goſpel.

This is the Lords doing, and it is marvellous in our Eyes.

jects of our Fathers would have been ſomewhat modified. That any Settlement was, or could have been made independent of Trade is preposterous. That the Plymouth Settlers were Traders, is as plain as that they were generally a ſuperior Company of Emigants to ſome of thoſe who preceded, as well as many who followed them.

FINIS.

An

HISTORICAL DISCOURSE

Concerning the

PREVALENCY

OF

PRAYER.

Wherein is ſhown that *New-Englands* Late Deliverance from the Rage of the Heathen is an Eminent Anſwer to Prayer.

By INCREASE MATHER,

Teacher of a Church in Boſton *in* New-England.

Pſal. 102. 18. *This ſhall be written for the Generation to come.*

Jam. 5. 17. 18. *Elias was a man ſubject to like paſſions, as we are, and he prayed earneſtly that it might not rain, and it rained not on the Earth by the ſpace of three years and ſix moneths; and he prayed again, and the heaven gave rain, and the earth brought forth her fruit.*

Preces et Lachrimæ ſunt Arma Eccliſiæ *Ambroſius.*

Oratio eſt vis Deo grata. *Turtul.*

Boſton, printed and ſold by *John Foſter.* 1677.

[iii] TO THE READER.

MY *Design in the Subsequent Discourse, is not to enumerate all the Particulars which might be mentioned, that doe evince New-Englands late Deliverance to be a great Answer of Prayer: only to take Notice of some more eminent Passages of Divine Providence, whereby it doth appear that the God of our Salvation hath answered us by terrible Things in Righteousness, against our Heathen Adversaryes. There is now Cause for an Holy Sollicitude lest Security should be the Effect of these Dispensations; lest we should now say, our Mountain is made strong, and we shall never be moved. Howbeit there is little Reason for such Imaginations, if Things be duly laid to Heart: we cannot but remember how near this Tree was to cutting down a Year or two agoe; but the Lord of the Vineyard hath at the earnest Intercession of his Servants* let it alone this Year also. *But who can say, how far the Lord may cut and lop and mar our Vine branches before many Years be expired? To this Day we see not the End of our late bleeding Distresses,*[315] *and when this Day of Trouble*

[315] It will be noticed that this Preface was written amidst Alarms and Desolations. Philip had been dead a Year, but there were fearful Ravages in the East and in the West. Only in the previous July many fishing Vessels had been surprised and their Crews carried into Captivity, and Men were killed at Black Point. And, only a Month later, twenty-four People were killed and carried away from Hatfield and Deerfield.

ſhall be over, I for my part, muſt ſolemnly profeſſ and declare, that I look for another ſeven times greater, though what it ſhall be, or how it ſhall come to paſs I cannot tell; for I pretend not to any Revelation, beyond what they that diligently compare the Word and Works of God together, may attain unto. It grieveth me not a little that I ſhould ſo frequently write and ſpeak in ſuch a Strain, but I cannot forbear, the Lord hath ſpoken, who can but prophecy? *There are many Conſiderations, which are enough to cauſe ſad Expectations of ſome more fatal Changes of Providence not far off, but eſpecially theſe two.*

[iv] I. *There is not a general Reformation in New England ſo much as in any one Particular, notwithſtanding the Lord hath tryed us by all Manner of Wayes that may be thought of, even by leſſer and greater Judgments, and by ſignal Mercyes and Deliverances: and that which aggravateth our unreformedneſs, is, that in the Time of our Trouble we have ſaid,* ariſe and ſave us.

2. *There are Evills prevailing amongſt us, which if they be not reformed, the Lords Controverſy will not be ended, ſuch as notorious Self ſeeking, reigning Pride, ſhameful Drunkenneſs, with the Occaſions Leading thereunto; wofull Apoſtacy, the bleſſed Deſign of our Fathers in coming into this Wilderneſs not being minded and attended as ought to be: and as Things are circumſtanced, there is no Hope that theſe and other Evils ſhould be reformed, untill God ariſe and ſhake terribly the Earth. So that* Nil niſi vota ſuperſunt. *On theſe Accounts, it concerns us, to be*

crying unto the Lord Day and Night. If wee look abroad upon the Face of the Earth, in other Parts of the World, the Children are come to the Birth, and there is not Strength to bring forth. We behold 'αρ'χήν 'ωδίνων the Begining of travailing Sorrows, even *ſuch Things as Evidence that ſome great Birth is at Hand. And in our* Horizon *dark Clouds gather apace, and the Heavens are covered over with blackneſs. Surely in theſe Reſpects, we may truly ſay as ſometime that Martyr did,* Pray, Pray, Pray, never more need than now. *And conſidering the bleſſed Encouragement God hath given us, whatever come on us, let us be found ſo doing.*

BOSTON, *N. E.*
Auguſt. 16. 1677.

Increaſe Mather.

An HISTORICAL DISCOURSE Concerning the Prevalency of PRAYER.

IT was a great Word (and if rightly underſtood, a true Word) which *Luther* ſpake when he ſaid, *Eſt quædam precum omnipotentia*, there is a kind of Omnipotency in Prayer; and the Reaſon is obvious, *viz.* In that the Almighty doth ſuffer himſelf to be prevailed upon and overcome by Prayer. Had not Jacob in this reſpect Power with God? Yea when he made his Supplication, he had Power, and prevailed over the Angel, even that Angel who is the Lord of Hoſts, the Lord is his Memorial. Where do we find in all the Books of God a more wonderfull Expreſſion, then that of the Lord to praying Moſes, *Now let me alone?* That ever the eternal God ſhould become thus a Petitioner to a poor mortal Man! *Feriendi licentiam petit a Moſe qui fecit Moſen.* Prayer then is like the Sword of Saul, or the Bow of Jonathan, which never returned empty from the Battle. Prayer is ſtronger than iron

See Mr. Hall. *Pſalm* 82, p. 183, 184.

Gates. At the Prayers of the Church the iron Gates fly open, and the Apoſtles Fetters fall off. Sometimes the Prayers of one Man that hath an eminent Intereſt in God, are a Means to preſerve a whole Town, yea a whole Land from Deſtruction, wel might the Antient ſay, *Homine probo orante nihil potentius.* How far did Abrahams Prayers prevail for Sodom? Did not Elijahs Prayers open and ſhut the Windows of Heaven? Did they not bring down Showers when the gaſping Earth was ready to dy for Thirſt? When a [2] fiery Drought had like to have devoured the Land of Iſrael, and the Prophet Amos prayed and cried to the Lord, ſaying, *O Lord God, Ceaſe I beſeech thee, by whom ſhall Jacob ariſe? for he is ſmall; the Lord repented for this, and ſaid this ſhall not be.*

Chryſoſtom.

Wars, when juſtly undertaken, have been ſucceſsful through the prevalency of Prayer.

Moſes in the Mount praying, is too ſtrong for all the Armies in the Valley fighting. When the Philiſtines went up againſt the Children of Iſrael, *Samuel* ceaſed not to cry to the Lord for Iſrael, and the Lord thundered with a great thunder that Day upon the Philiſtines, and diſcomfited them, that they were ſmitten before Iſrael. *Jehoſhaphat*, when ſurrounded by a Multitude of heathen Enemyes, by Prayer overcame them. When *Zera* the Ethiopian came againſt the Lords People with an Hoſt of a thouſand thouſand Men, Aſa by Prayer and Faith overcome them all. *Hezekiah* and *Iſaiah* by their Prayers brought an Angel down from

Heaven, who ſlew an hundred and fourſcore and five thouſand Aſſyrians, in the Hoſt of Sennacherib in one Night.

And beſides theſe and many Scriptural Examples in eccleſiaſtical Story, Inſtances to this Purpoſe are frequently obſerved. The History of the thundering Legion is famouſly known. Thus it was.

Cluverius *in Hiſtoriarum totius Mundi Epitome*, p. 304.

The Emperour *Marcus Aurelius* going to war againſt the *Quads*, *Vandals*, *Sarmats* and *Germans*, who were nine hundred ſeventy and five thouſand fighting Men; The Imperialiſts were ſo cooped up by their numerous Enemies, in ſtrait, dry, and hot Places, that the Souldiers having been deſtitute of Water for five Days together, they were all like to have periſhed for thirſt. In this exremity, a Legion of Chriſtian Souldiers being in the Army, withdrew themſelves apart from the Reſt, and falling proſtrate on the Earth, by ardent Prayers prevailed with God, that he imediately ſent a moſt plentiful Rain, whereby the Army that otherwiſe had periſhed, was refreſhed and dreadfull Lightnings flaſhed in the Faces of their Enemies, ſo as that they were diſcomfited and put to flight. The Effect of which was, that the Perſecution which before that the Emperour deſigned againſt the Chriſtians, was diverted; and that *praying Legion* did afterwards, bear the Name of κερυνοβολος the *Lightning Legion.*

Conſtantine the Great, being to join the Battle with the Heathen Tyrant *Licinius*, ſingled out a Number of godly Miniſters of [3]

Ereſebuus *in vita* Conſtantii.

Chriſt, and with them betook himſelf to earneſt Prayer and Supplication, after which God gave him a notable and glorious Victory over his Enemies. But *Licinius* himſelfe eſcaped at that Time, and raiſed another Army, which was purſued by *Conſtantine*, who before he would engage with the Enemy, cauſed a Tent to be erected, wherein he did ſpend ſome Time in Faſting and Prayer, being attended with a Company of holy praying Men round about him, after which marching againſt his Enemies, he fought them, and obtained a more glorious Victory than the former, and the Grand Rebel *Licinius* was then taken Priſoner.

Theodoſius[316] being in no ſmall Danger by Reaſon of the potent Army of Adverſaryes he had to do with, in his Diſtreſs cryed unto Heaven for Help, and behold! the Lord ſent ſuch a terrible Tempeſt, as the like was not known, whereby the Darts of the Enemy were driven back upon themſelves, to their own Confuſion, which cauſed *Claudian* the Poet, (though no great Friend to the Chriſtian Name) to ſay concerning *Theodoſius*,

Lego Theodoſi *vitam.*

Auguſt *De Civitate Dei Lib.* 5. 6. 26.

> *O nimium dilecte Deo cui militat Æther,*
> *Et conjurati veniunt ad Claſſica Venti.*[317]

[316] Theodoſius, Senior. He died A. C. 397.

[317] The Author has made Claudian appear to great Diſadvantage, by quoting him in a blundering Manner. The Lines he intended to quote are;

> O nimium dilecte deo, cui fundit ab antris
> Æolus armatas hyemes, cui militat æther,
> Et conjurati veniunt ad claſſica venti.

Cl. Claud. Paneg. Lib. vi. F. 123, Ed, Paris, 1530.

It is ſtoried concerning the City of *Niſibis* that being ſtraitly beſieged by *Sapores* King of Perſia, the diſtreſſed Citizens deſired a devout and holy Man amongſt them (whoſe Name was *James*) to be earneſt with the Lord in their Behalf. He was ſo; and the Effect was, God ſent an Army of Gnats and Flyes among the *Perſians*, which ſo vexed and tormented them, as that they were forced to raiſe the Seige and depart.

Sympſon's *Eccleſiaſtical Hiſt.*

Amongſt the *Waldenſes* ſometimes an inconſiderable Number have prevailed over their popiſh Adverſaryes. At one Time five hundred of theſe poor praying Saints overthrew two thouſand and five hundred of their Enemies who ſcoffed at them becauſe they would fall upon their knees and pray before they would fight.

Morland *Hiſt.* Waldenſes.

In the Land of our Father's Sepulchres, when *Oſwald* (who ſucceded his Father *Ethelfride* in the Northern Kingdom) was aſſaulted by *Cedwalla* and *Penda*, two Heathen Kings, that raiſed a great Army, deſigning the Ruin of *Oſwald* and his People, he humbly and earneſtly addreſſed himſelf to the Lord of Hoſts, the great Giver of Victory, entreating him to ſhew his own Power in ſaving and protecting his People from the Rage of heathen Adverſaryes: which, joyning battle with his Enemyes, [4] albeit their Army

See Clark's Example, *Vol.* 1, *C.* 100, [318] *Idem eodem Lib.*

[318] This Reference would ſcarcely be known at this Day. The Work referred to is—*A Mirrour or Looking-Glaſs both for Saints and Sinners, held forth in ſome Thouſands of Examples*, &c. Printed in London in 1671. Chapter C. is headed *Examples of the Power, and Preva-*

was far greater than his, he obtained a wonderful Victory, wherein *Cedwalla* himſelf was ſlain.

When *England* was invaded by the Danes under the Conduct of their King *Oſrick*, who encamped at *Aſhdon*, King *Ethelred* betook himſelf to Prayer; and marching againſt the Daniſh Army, put them to flight, and ſlew the greateſt Part of them.

Guſtavus Adolphus the King of Sweden, no ſooner landed in his Enemies Territoryes, but he addreſſed himſelf to Heaven for Victory, and encouraged his Counſellors and Commanders by ſaying *The greater the Army of Prayers is, the greater and more aſſured ſhall be our Victory.* Yea it was his Manner when the Armyes were ſet in Battle array, to lift up his Eyes to Heaven and ſay, *Lord proſper the Battle of this Day, according as thou ſeeſt my Heart doth aim at thy Glory, and the good of thy Church.* And how ſucceſsful did God make that excellent Prince to be?[319]

But what need we go far to find Examples confirming the Truth of this Aſſertion, that *Prayer is of Wonderfull Prevalency,* ſince our own Eyes have ſeen it? New England may now ſay, if the Lord (even the Prayer hearing God) had not been on

lency of Prayer. But the Author has given a wrong Reference, for there is nothing in the Chapter of Clarke's *Examples* referred to upon the Subject in the Text. See the *Brief Hiſtory*, 161, for a *Note* upon the Author of the *Examples.*

319 "His Army won the Day, "though they loſt their King; which "made one ſay,

'Vpon this Place the great Guſtavus di'd,
'Whilſt Victory lay bleeding by his Side.'

"He was ſlaine in the Battell "at Lutzen, November the 16 "Anno Chriſti 1632. and of his "Age thirty eight." Clarke's *Marrow of Eccl. Hiſt.*, Pt. II, p. 265, Edit. 1650. 4°.

our Side when Men roſe up againſt us, they had ſwallowed us up; then the proud Waters had gone over our Soul. And thus hath it been more than once or twice, eſpecially ſince the late Inſurrection and Rebellion of the Heathen Nations round about us. We cannot but acknowledge, and Poſterity muſt know, that we were in Appearance a gone and ruined People,[320] and had been ſo ere this Day, if the Lord had not been a God that heareth Prayer.

And there are eſpecially *two Conſiderations that doe evince, that New Englands Deliverance from the Rage of the Heathen is an eminent Anſwer of Prayer,* I. In that God hath graciouſly anſwered us as to the very Petitions that have bin moſtly inſiſted on, as will appear to Admiration by inſtancing in ſome Particulars.

1. Then, *How often have we prayed that the Lord would divide, infatuate and fruſtrate the Counſiles of the Heathen that ſought our Ruine.* As ſometimes David when purſued by Abſalom prayed ſaying, *O Lord divide their Tongues.* Pſal. 55. 9. Again David ſaid, *O Lord I pray thee turn the Counſell of Achitophel into fooliſhneſs.* 2. Sam. 15. 31. Thoſe Requeſts of David were heard, and therefore Abſaloms Counſellours were divided, one giving this,

[320] It is a well known Portion of New England Hiſtory, that the early Settlers were importuned by their Friends in England to abandon the Country, as not fit for Habitation. Its ſevere Winters and ſterile Soil it was argued, would forever prevent it being anything but a Deſert. Some of the Weſt India Iſlands were ſtrongly recommended to them in the Time of Cromwell's Commonwealth. Some thirty Years later many "pulled up Stakes" and went to New Jerſey, and other Points ſouth.

and another that Advice; and the ſubtle Counſell of Achitoplel (which had it been hearkened unto, David and thoſe with [5] him had periſhed) muſt not be followed. In like Manner hath the Lord done for us; we have heard how that after the Fort fight, Decemb. 19. 1675. ſome of the Indian Counſellors adviſed that they might purſue our Army when upon their Retreat;[321] which if they had ſo done, how fatal would the Conſequence have proved? But therefore God divided their Counſells, that others were of another Mind.

Moreover we have received Informations, concerning a great Conſultation amongſt the Indians, ſoon after their Miſchief done at *Sudbury* in April. 1676.[322] Had they then continued to moleſt the Engliſh, our Caſe had been ſad; but they ſuppoſed they had Time enough before them, and therefore reſolved to be quiet a Month or two, in order to Attendance upon their own Planting and Fiſhing.

We have alſo heard that the old crafty Serpents amongſt the Indians adviſed that they might ſhun all Encounter with the Engliſh Forces, and rather diſperſe themſelves into ſmall Partyes, and ſo fall upon the Engliſh Towns, burning their Houſes, deſtroying their Cattle &c. but that the young Men

321 This was reported by Captives taken ſometime after the Fight.

322 Mrs. Rowlandſon who was a Priſoner among them at the Time ſpoken of, does not mention any "great Conſultation" about following up their Victory. On the other Hand ſhe ſays they returned from that Fight "rather like Dogs which "have loſt their Ears." And, "when they went they acted as if "the Devil had told them that they "ſhould gain a Victory, and now "they acted as if the Devil had told "them they ſhould haue a Fall." *Captivity*, 49. Ed. in ***Indian Narratives.***

thought it beſt to cut off our Souldiers, and then they ſuppoſed they might do what they pleaſed with our Towns. Thus were their Tongues divided and Counſils turned into fooliſhneſs.

2. *How often have we prayed that God would do for us as in the Days of Midian, by cauſing the Heathen to deſtroy one another, and that the Egyptians might be ſet againſt the Egyptians.* The Lord hath anſwered that Requeſt alſo. For the Indians have been waſting and killing one another,[323] yea not only ſuch Indians as do pretend Friendſhip to the Enliſh, (*e. g.* the *Natick* and *Punkapaog* Indians, and the *Mohawks* and the *Moheags* under *Vncas*, albeit it is too evident that he was ſecretely conſpiring with *Philip* in his deſigned Miſchief, a little before the War brok forth, but God turned him about,[324] and made him a Friend to the Engliſh, and an Enemy to *Philip*) but alſo ſome of thoſe that were once in Hoſtility againſt us, did at laſt help to deſtroy their own Nation, Friends and Kindred, that ſo they might do Service for us. So

323 This has been pretty fully illuſtrated by Examples already given. About July 10th, 1637, Roger Williams wrote to John Winthrop—" The laſt Weeke is a " Battell fought betweene the hither " Neepmucks [thoſe on the Upper " Thames] and the further, the " Wunnaſhowatuckoogs [Naſhuas?] " &c. the Succeſſe is not yet knowne: " it will be of Conſequence, for it " ſaid they fortifie, ioyning with " ſcattered Pequts." *Maſs. Hiſt. Colls*, 36, 197. On the 15th he wrote that " the Neepmucks are " returned with three Heads of the " Wunnaſhoatuckoogs, they ſlew " ſix, wounded many, and brought " Home twenty Captives." *Ibid.* 204. But little is known of the internal Wars of the Indians.

324 Before the Reader conſents to accept Uncas into his Calendar as a Saint, he ſhould read the Letters of Roger Williams, and the Records of the Commiſſioners of the United Colonies.

have they that ſought to deſtroy us, gone into the lower Parts of the Earth, they are fallen by the Sword.

3. How often have we prayed that the Lord would take thoſe his Enemies into his own avenging Hand, pleading that though we know not how to come at them, they had ſuch Advantages in reſpects of Woods and Swamps and dark Corners of the Earth to lurk in; yet the Hand of God could reach them, and that therefore he [6] would ſcatter them by his Power and bring them down and let them wander up and down for Meat, and the deſtroying Angel amongſt them. This Prayer hath been heard; For it is known that the Indians were diſtreſſed with Famine, Multitudes of them periſhing for Want of Bread; and the Lord ſent Sickneſſes amongſt them, that Travellers have ſeen many dead Indians up and down in the Woods, that were by Famine or Sickneſs brought unto that untimely End. Yea the Indians themſelves have teſtified, that more amongſt them have been cut off by the Sword of the Lord in thoſe Reſpects, then by the Sword of the Engliſh.

4. *How often have we prayed that the Lord would remember the Cruelty, Treachery, and above all the Blaſphemy of theſe Heathen?* This Prayer hath been heard in Heaven. As for their Cruelty, God hath remembered that, many of them falling into the Hands of the *Mohawks* or other Indians, who fought in our Quarrel uſed their Enemies after their own Kind; and it hath been obſerved, that the Vengeance from the Lord did purſue them preſently

upon the Perpetration of ſome horrid Acts of barbarous Cruelty towards ſuch as fell into their murdrous Hands' And as for the Treachery, God hath retaliated that upon them; as for the perfidious *Narraganſets*, *Peter* Indian was Falſe and Perfidious to them, upon a Diſguſt received amongſt them, and directed our Army where to find them.[325] Treacherous *Philip*, one of his own Men ran away from him, and told Capt. *Church* where that grand Enemy had hid himſelf, the Iſſue of which was, another Indian ſhot a Bullet into the treacherous Heart of that Covenant-breaking Infidel. Yea many of thoſe bloudy and deceitful Indians who were taken by Capt. *Church*, would frequently deſtroy and betray their bloudy and falſe-hearted Comrades. *Matoonas* who was the firſt Indian that treacherouſly ſhed inocent Engliſh blood in *Maſſachuſets* Colony,[326] he ſome Years before pretended to ſomething of Religion, being a Profeſſor in general (though never baptized, nor of the inchurched Indians) that ſo he might the more covertly manage the helliſh Deſign of Revenge that was harboured in his diveliſh Heart; but at laſt Sagamore *John* with ſome of his Indians unexpectedly ſurpriſed him, and delivered him to Juſtice. That abominable Indian *Peter Jethro*[327]

[325] See the Author's *Brief Hiſtory*, new ed., 105, 249-51. After the War he went by the Name of Peter Freeman.

[326] At Mendon. In the *Brief Hiſtory* the Author could not forbear the undignified Torture of Language by ſaying that the Calamity fell upon that Town becauſe "we "had not *mended* our Ways!" A wretched Pun it muſt be confeſſed.

[327] For a farther Account of "that abominable Indian," ſee the *Book of the Indians*, 265-7, 274.

betrayed his own Father, and other Indians of his ſpecial Acquaintance, unto Death. Many of the *Nipmuck* Indians, who were wont to lay Snares for others, were at laſt themſelves taken by a Stratagem, and brought to deſerved Execution.

[7] And as for their Blaſphemy, God hath remembered it, the moſt notorious Blaſphemers amongſt them have been made Examples of divine revenging Juſtice, *Quanonchet*,[328] *Pomham*, *Monoco*,[329] all of them curſed Blaſphemers; the Vengeance of Heaven hath not ſuffered them to live. It is alſo reported that an Engliſh-man belonging to one of the weſtern Plantations, being mortally wounded by an Indian, the Indian upbraided him with his Prayers, ſaying to him, *You were wont to pray to Jeſus Chriſt, now pray to him, He cannot help you*, and withal added a moſt hideous Blaſphemy (not fit to be named) againſt our bleſſed Lord Jeſus Chriſt, imediately upon which a Bullet took him in the Head and daſhed out his Brains, ſending his curſed Soul in a moment amongſt the Devils, and Blaſphemers in Hell forever.[330]

5. *How often have we prayed that the Lord would take away Spirit and Courage from thoſe that have*

328 Uſually written Canonchet. A thrilling Account of his Capture and Death may be read in Hubbard's *Narrative*.

329 He was uſually known among the Engliſh as *One-eyed John*. Conſiderable Space is devoted to him in the *Book of the Indians*. He lived at or near Lancaſter, and his Depredations were quite extenſive, leading the Nipmucks at the Deſtruction of Medfield and Groton. He ſuffered on the Gallows "at the "Towns end," Boſton, September 26th, 1676.

330 I have not been able to aſcertain who the Parties were, nor any Tranſaction correſponding with it.

been in Hoſtility againſt us, and cauſe thoſe Haters of the Lord to ſubmit themſelves.. In this Thing alſo the Lord hath had Reſpect to our Requeſts. For hundreds of Indians the laſt Summer came and ſurrendered themſelves to the Engliſh, e. g. in *Plymouth* Colony the *Squaw-Sachim* of *Saconet*, with above an hundred Indians ſubmitted themſelves to Mercy,[331] June 30, 1676. Not long after that two hundred Indians more ſurrendered themſelves. And in the eaſtern Parts of this Colony (July 6.) there were ſix Sachims addreſſed themſelves to the Engliſh in order to the obtaining Peace, bringing in with them three hundred Men beſides Women and Children.[332] Likewiſe in the ſame Month *Sagamore John* ſubmitted himſelf with about one hundred and eighty Indians;[333] and hundreds of them came and ſubmitted themſelves to the Engliſh in *Connecticut* Colony. Theſe Things came not to paſs without the Finger of God, ſo manifeſt as that the Enemy himſelf could not but take Notice of it. For a ſtout Indian Captain who was afterwards executed at *Boſton*, profeſſed to ſome of our Souldiers, that they could never have ſubdued the Indians, *But* (ſaid he ſtriking upon his Breaſt) *Engliſhmans God maketh us afraid here.*

6. *How often have we prayed that God would in ſpecial look after thoſe Places, which were in moſt*

331 Theſe were Awaſhonks and her People.

332 This doubtleſs has Reference to thoſe Indians entrapped at Dover by Capts. Hathorne, Sill, Froſt, and Maj. Waldron. See *Hubbard*, 110.

333 He "came in" to Boſton July 27th, bringing Matoonas, Father and Son. See *Brief Hiſtory*, 184.

eminent Danger, as being above others expoſed to the Fury of the Enemy? And we have had the Petitions we deſired of him in that Reſpect. What a black Appearance of Death and Ruine was before the poor People at Quaboag,[334] when they were all cooped up in one unfortified Houſe, and ſurrounded by a barbarous Multitude of cruel Indians, who thirſted after their Blood? But [8] God by a ſtrange Providence ſent Major *Willard*, who with a ſmall Party of Souldiers, came a few Hours or Minutes before it was too late, by which Means the remaining Inhabitants of that Place had their Lives given them for a Prey. After that the weſtern Plantations, *North-Hampton*, *Hadley*, *Hatfield*, &c. were in the eminentſt Danger, by Reaſon of the Enemy taking up their Rendezvouze in thoſe Parts; but God preſerved and delivered them, in Anſwer unto Prayer. That memorable Providence ought not to be forgotten, how that in the Begining of March, 1676. Our Army miſſed their Way (deſigning to ſurprize the Indians about *Wachuſet* Hills) and were providentially led to North Hampton. Alſo Major *Treat* with Souldiers under his Command, did then take up his Quarters in that Town, coming thither a Day ſooner than was intended; the next Day a great Body of Indians brake in upon the Town, and in probability had laid it Waſt, had there not been ſuch a Supply of Souldiers as hath been mentioned, which the good Providence of God brought thither, in Anſwer to

[334] Brookfield. See *Brief Hiſtory*, 68.

the Prayers of his People. Moreover the whole Colony of *Plymouth* was in moſt apparent Danger of being overrun and overwhelmed with the Enemy; eſpecially in the Spring of the Year 1676. when (as we have been informed) the Indians were deſigning, with fifteen hundred Men to fall upon all the ſcattered Towns throughout that Juriſdiction. But God gave Men, yea a great *Sachim*, for the Life of his dear People in that Colony. We have heard that *Quanonchets* Surpriſal and Death, ſtruck an Amazement into the Heathen, and diverted their purpoſed Miſchief. May 8. 1676. when Bridgwater was aſſaulted, and in Danger of being laid Waſt, God ſent Thunder and Rain from Heaven, which cauſed the Indians to turn back. And when they attempted to make *Taunton* a Deſolation, July 11. how wonderfully did the Lord ſave that Town? So ordering by his Providence, as that a Captive *Negro* eſcaping from the Indians, informed of their Purpoſe to fall upon that Place, whereupon the Inhabitants ſtood upon their Guard, and Souldiers were timouſly ſent in to them for their Relief and Defence.

7. *How often have we prayed for our poor Captives, that God would preſerve them and return them?* When ſome of ours not many Years ſince, were in Captivity under *Mahomet*, what Prayer was made for them continually? Eſpecially it was ſo in reſpect to Mr. *Foſter* and his Son,[335] the Church in *Charleſtown* ſetting a Day apart to ſeek unto the

[335] What Foſters theſe were I am unable to determine. Mr. Savage does not ſeem to have ſtumbled on them; if he has he did not know it.

Lord by Faſting and Prayer, that the Perſons mentioned might be ſet at liberty, and although at that Time there was [9] no likelihood that ever it ſhould be, the infidel King under whoſe Power they were, not being willing to accept of Money for their Redemption, yet God brought it about wonderfully, and rather then his Peoples Prayers ſhould not be anſwered, that Tyrant muſt dy by a ſtrange and unexpected Providence. But I ſpeak now concerning thoſe that have been Captives amongſt the Heathen in this Land. And God hath heard us for them. Whereas upon the 9th of May, 1676. the Magiſtrates and Miniſters of this Colony, and the Deputyes of the General Court, ſought the Lord together by Faſting and Prayer, and did in ſpecial Manner beg that Captives might be returned, as a Token for Good, and Pledge of further Anſwers of Prayer, within a few Weeks after this, neer upon twenty of our Captives were ſet at Liberty. For ſome, Prayer hath been more abudantly poured forth; ſo for Mr. *Rowlandſon* his Wife and two Children, and we have ſeen the Lord returning them all again. And whereas in October 1676. Amongſt others, the Son of that Man of God, and Man of Prayer, Reverend Mr. *Cobbet* (the faithful Paſtor in Ipſwich) was ſurpriſed in a Veſſel by the Northern Indians, and led away into Captivity; doubtleſs God did it, that ſo glory might be to his holy Name, and that the World might ſee how Prayer can prevail with him. Mr. *Cobbet* no ſooner heard what was befallen his Son, but he called together about thirty of his Chriſtian Neighbors (that being as many as could on the ſudden convene) and they ſet ſome Time apart to pray for him that was now a Captive, after this his Fathers Heart was ſweetly quieted, believing that God had heard them: Some others alſo that attended that Service, were as confidently perſwaded that God would return (and that in comfortable Plight) Mr. *Cobbets* Son to him again as if he were already come; Prayer alſo was made in publick Congregations in particular for that young Man; and in December following, thoſe Prayers were fully anſwered, the Lord bringing it about in ſtrange Wayes, the Particulars and Circumſtances whereof are too large here to be inſiſted on.[336]

Let me further take Notice here, that whereas no longer then three Weeks ſince, (viz, July 25. 1677.) the Church in *Salem* ſet a Day apart to ſeek the Lord in ſpecial on Behalf of thoſe belonging to that Town lately fallen into the Hands of the Indians; whilſt they were praying, God brought Home one of the Veſſels that the Indians had ſurpriſed, and two Perſons (who were Maſters of Veſſels) that had been particularly prayed for in the Morning, returned [10] ſolemn Thanks to God in the after Part of the Day, in that he had in Anſwer of the Prayers of his People, brought them out of their Captivity.[337]

[336] The Rev. Thomas Cobbet of Ipſwich gave the Author an Account of the Capture and Liberation of his Son, in a Letter of great Length, which is publiſhed in the *N. E. Hiſt. and Gen. Regiſter*, Vol. VII, 209-19. There is alſo an Account in Mr. Hubbard's *Indian Wars*, Pt. ii, 57-8.

[337] "The Lord having allowed "the Indians to take no leſs than

8. *How often have prayed that God would cutt off the Ring-leaders, and principal bloudy Promoters of the late Troubles?* That the Lord would doe unto them as unto Sisera, as to Jabin at the Brook of Kison (which perished at Endor, they became as Dung for the Earth) and make their Nobles like Oreb and like Zeeb, yea all their Princes like Zeba and Zalmunna.

Now in these Cryes to Heaven our God hath heard us even to Admiration. *Philip* the grand Enemy and Beginner of the War, is gone to his own Place. It was observed that a little before the Destruction of that bloudy Foe, the Lord stirred up the Hearts of some of his Servants, to be instant in Prayer against that Enemy in particular, yea and caused them firmly to believe that it should be so. Nor could they cease crying to the Lord against him, untill they had prayed the Bullet into *Philips* Heart. And concerning what Prayers have been in the Closets about that Thing, we shall hear more at the Day of Judgment when the Lord Jesus will reveal it and reward it openly. Are not all the Chieftains amongst the Heathen who have been in Hostility against us cut off forever? and their Memorial is perished with them.

" thirteen Ketches of Salem and " captivate the Men (though divers " of them cleared themselves and " came Home) it struck great Con- " sternation into all People here, and " it was agreed that Lecture-day, " July 25th, 1677, should be kept " as a Fast." *Salem Ch. Records* in Felt's *Salem*, 258. Nineteen wounded Men had been sent in a little while before, and some of the Ketches arrived the same day of the Fast. *Hist. Salem, Ibid.* No Names are given.

O thou most High, Thou hast rebuked the Heathen, thou hast put out their Name for ever and ever!

We have heard of two and twenty Indian Captains slain all of them, and brought down to Hell in one Day, viz. Decemb. 19. 1675.[338] And some of the Indians have confessed that at the Fall fight, May 18. 1676.[339] they lost no less then three and thirty of their Counsellours, which put them into an absolute Confusion, that they were like Men amazed ever after.

Where are the six *Narraganset* Sachims, with all their Captains and Counsellors? Where are the *Nipmuck* Sachims, with all their Captains and Counsellours? Where is *Philip* and *Squaw-Sachim* of *Pocasset* with all their Captains and Counsellours?[340] God doe so to all the implacable Enemies of Christ and of his People in New England!

2. *If we consider the TIME when God hath appeared for us, it is manifest that our Salvation is our Answer of Prayer.* It was a fatal happy Blow

[338] The Author's Statistics of the Narraganset Swamp Fight are no doubt too large, as they are of the Destruction at the Falls.

[339] The Fight at the Falls in the Connecticut River. See *Brief History*, 148.

[340] These Questions were easier asked than answered in the Author's Time. The six Narraganset Chiefs or Sachems can be pretty easily made out: *Canonchet, Potock, Pumham, Quinnapin, Quaqualh, Chicon,* and there might be several others named. A larger Number of the Nipmucks might be reckoned up: There were several Johns— as John *Monoco, Stonewall John, Sagamore John, Old Jethro, Mautamp, Sagamore Sam* (Uskuttugun), &c. Then of the Wampanoags, *Philip, Annawan, Sam Barrow, Nimrod, Totoson, Pebe, Watuspequin, Akkompoin, Tokamona, Woospasuck, &c.,* were the most prominent; among these the Female Chief Weetamoo was regarded next to Philip on some Accounts.

which the Indians received at the Fort-fight in the *Narraganſet Country;* and a little before that, all theſe Churches [11] were ſolemnly by Faſting and Prayer ſeeking to the Lord, that the Heathen might be rebuked at that Time. When *Quanonchet* was taken and ſlain it was an amazing ſtroke to the Enemy. And but a few Dayes before that many Churches in *England* kept a Day of Faſting and Prayer for poor *New-England.* In the later End of June. 1676, (and ever after that) Succeſſes againſt the Enemy were wonderfull; eſpecially in Plymouth Colony. Now on the 22. of June, all the Churches in that Colony ſet apart a Day of ſolemn Humiliation, and renewed their Covenant. And on the 29. of that Month, was a Day of Thankſ-giving throughout this Colony, the Prayers and Praiſes of which Day were ſignally owned by the Lord, who did then ſet Ambuſhments againſt the Enemy and they were ſmitten. Alſo in this very Moneth, the Churches in *Dublin* in Ireland were ſolemnly ſeeking to the Lord on our Behalf.[341] Why ſhould not theſe Things be written and recorded for the Generation to come? Why ſhould they not be made known to our Children, that they might ſet their Hope in God, and not forget the Works of God, but keep his Commandments.

Some one perhaps will ſay, did not God in the Time of your late War ſeem to be angry with your Prayers? Had you not the ſaddeſt Tidings on your ſolemn Dayes of Humiliation?

341 Nathaniel Mather, the Author's Brother, was then Miniſter in Dublin.

Aisw. This is true, and the Thoughts of it ſhould forever humble us; yet we know, ſometimes the Lord ſeems to be diſpleaſed with the Prayers of his People only to try their Faith (as with the Woman of Canaan) when as indeed they are his delight. Moreover (alas!) it cannot be denied or doubted of, but that the Lord ſaw Formality and Hypocriſy in the Prayers of many amongſt us, which he was offended at, howbeit there are ſome living Chriſtians, that walk cloſely with God; a few Names that have not defiled their Garments with the Sins, and generally prevailing Temtations of theſe Times; unto them and to their Prayers hath the Lord had Reſpect. It muſt alſo be confeſſed, that the Prayers of the Churches in *Europe* have had no ſmall Influence into our Mercyes. I can aſſure the Reader, that the Churches in *London*, in *Suffolk*, in *Dorſet*, in *Devon*, in *Somerſet*, in *Lancaſhire*, have by Faſting and Prayer, ſought the Lord for New-England, in the Time of our late Troubles. And I doubt not but that the Lords praying People in other Countryes, where I have no Acquaintance or Correſpondence, have done the like. We are infinitely indebted to that God, who having a Purpoſe to glorify himſelf by hearing Prayers, put into their Hearts to be earneſt in our Behalf.

[12] Who knoweth but that we may be again involved in Trouble by the Remainder of the Heathen, or otherwiſe. Let us then be encouraged to take in Hand our old tried Weapons, even *preces et lacryme* the Auntient *Armes of the Church.* If Enemyes ariſe, let us pray them down again.

And that is the ſpecial Improvement which ſhould be made of what hath been diſcourſed; ſince we have ſeen what Prayer can do. *The Conſideration of theſe Things ſhould ſtir up an holy Reſolution in every one, to be ſincere, frequent, and conſtant in this ſo great and powerful a Duty.* It is reported of Joachim (the Father of the Virgin Mary) *that Prayer was his Meat and Drink.* And we know what was David's Profeſſion, Pſal. 116. 1. 2. *I love the Lord, becauſe he hath heard my Voice, and my Supplication, becauſe he hath enclined his ear to me, therefore I will call upon him as long as I ſhall live.*

Wherefore to the Particulars already mentioned, I ſhall (for how ſhould a man when writing upon ſuch a Subject, eaſily break off) add a few more. It would indeed fill a Volume, ſhould all the Inſtances this Way be produced, which ſtand upon record in approved Authors; nor have I preſent leiſure to revolve many books that treat upon this Subject; only ſuch Particulars as do preſently occur to Mind I ſhall relate, hoping it will not be unprofitable to the Reader, who poſſibly hath not had the knowledge of them. To proceed then,

There have been, whom Prayer hath brought back from the Gates of the Grave, whenas to all outward Appearance they have been otherwiſe paſt Recovery; not to inſiſt upon Scriptural Examples here neither; It is a memorable Paſſage which a great Hiſtorian hath noted concerning that learned and religious, Sir *John Cheek,* who was

Tutor to our Englifh Jofiah, King Edward 6th.[342]

Sir John being fick nigh unto Death, the King did carefully enquire after his welfare every Day; at laft the Phyfitians told him that there was no Hopes of Life; Nay (faid the King) he will not dye at this Time, for I have this Morning begged his Life of God in my Prayers, and obtained it; which accordingly came to paffe; and foon after Sir John wonderfully recovered beyond all Expectation.

Fullers *Hiftory of the Church*, p. 424.

Melancthon was taken defperately fick at *Vinaria*, as he was in a journey towards *Hagenaw*, in order to a Conference with fome of the reformed Divines in Germany about Matters of Religion, *Luther* hearing of it, haftned to vifit him, and with Tears faying Alas! how [13] precious and profitable an Inftrument of the Church, is miferably weakned, and ready to perifh! and falling upon his knees, he did moft earneftly wreftle with the Lord for his Recovery, and prevailed, fo as that *Melancthon* would afterwards confefs, that if it had not been for *Luther's* Prayers, he had died by that Sicknefs.

Melchior Adam *in vita Melancthonis*.

Idem in vita Myconii.

At another Time, *Myconius* being fallen into a deep Confumption, Luther was earneft in Prayer to God for his Recovery; and he wrote a Letter

342 Whofe Reign was from 1547 to 1553. How much of a Jofiah that puny Boy at nine Years of Age could have been is left for the judgment of thofe whofe Imaginations fet down Kings as a fort of Divinities. Edward was only fifteen Years old when he died. Old Fuller was a blind Believer in the Saintfhip of Kings.

to him, wherein he thus expreſſeth himſelf, 'I pray Chriſt our Lord, our Salvation, our Health, 'that I may not live to ſee thee, and ſome others 'of our Colleagues to dye, and go to Heaven, and 'to leave me here amongſt the Divels alone. Fare-'well and God forbid that I ſhould hear of thy 'Death whilſt I live, *ſed te ſuperſtitem faciat mihi 'Deus, hoc peto et volo, et fiat voluntas mea, Amen! 'quia hæc voluntas gloriam mominis Dei, certe non 'meam voluptatem, nec copiam quærit.*' A while after *Myconius* recovered, and outlived *Luther*, ever acknowledging that he was beholding to God for putting it into the Heart of *Luther*; ſo to pray for him, and inſtrumentally to lengthen out his Life ſeven Years beyond his own, and Friends expecta-tion.

Yea more, Divels and Powers of Darkneſs had fallen before the Power of Prayer. A deſ-perate young Man in *Germany*, who in a helliſh Pang of Temptation had ſold himſelf to, and made an explicite Covenant with the Divil; having revealed his miſerable Condition to *Luther*, he called the Church together, they faſted and prayed, ſo that the Divil threw the Writing, which he had received of the young Man in at the Window, and a forlorn Soal was reſcued out of the Hands of that devouring Lion.[343] How often have

Idem in vita Lutheri.

[343] This was quite up to the Spirit-writings of the preſent Day. An Acquaintance of ours ſome few Years ago went about exhibiting what many believed to be the Devil's Autograph, obtained by a Medium. Doubtleſs Mediums were common in thoſe Days as well as at the pre-ſent Time, but it may be queſtioned whether thoſe of that Day were more under his Satanic Majeſty's Government than thoſe of this Age.

poore Creatures under bodily Poſſeſſions been delivered from that thraldom by earneſt Prayer? *Auſtin* by his Prayers caſt out Divils. The Hiſtory of thoſe ſeven poſſeſſed in *Lancaſhire*, in whoſe Diſpoſſeſſion Mr. *Darrel* and others were by Faſting and Prayer inſtrumental, is well known.[344]

Refertur in vita Auguſtini.

There was a Man that lived not far from *Nottingham*, whoſe Name was *John Fox*. This Man was poſſeſſed by the Divel, who would violently throw him down, and take away the Uſe of every Member of his Body, and was ſometimes heard ſpeaking when his Lips moved not at all; yea (albeit the Man could ſpeak no other Language beſides his Mother Tongue) the evil Spirit in him would frequently quote Scriptures out of the Originals, Hebrew and Greek, and play the Critick, and back his Allegations with Sayings out of the Fathers and [14] Poets. Among others that came to pray with this poor miſerable Man, Mr. *Rothwel* (a Minſter that was famous in thoſe Parts in thoſe Days) was one. As he was coming, the Divel told them in the Houſe with the poſſeſſed Man, yonder is *Rothwel* a coming; and upon his entering into the Houſe, raged and blaſphemed, ſaying alſo wilt thou go to Prayer, I'le make ſuch a Noiſe as ſhall diſtract thee, and doſt thou think that God will hear diſtracted Prayers? Mr. *Rothwel* replied, God heareth the Prayers of

Read Mr. Rothwells life written by Mr. Gower.

344 If the Reader is inclined to learn ſomething more of Mr. John Darrel he may find it in Hutchinſon's *Hiſtorical Eſſay concerning Witchcraft*, Ed. London: 1720, 242, 262.

the Upright, and hath promiſed to give his Spirit to help Infirmityes in Prayer, therefore in Confidence of his Promiſe, & powerfull Aſſiſtance of his Spirit, and in the Name of his Son Jeſus Chriſt, we will go to Prayer. So he did. The Divel for above a Quarter of an Hour made an horid Noiſe, and roared at Mr. *Rothwells* Face, but at laſt was forced to be ſilent, and departed out of the Man, who before the Prayer was ended, did to the Amazement and Joy of all the Auditors preſent ſay Amen to the Petitions that were preſented before the Lord on his Behalf. After Mr. Rothwel left him, he was ſtricken dumb for three Years together; at length by Prayer alſo, God opened his Mouth, and reſtored his Speech to him; One uſing this Petition, Lord open his Mouth, and his Lips ſhall ſhew forth thy Praiſe; he anſwered in the Congregation, *Amen*, and ſo continued to ſpeak and ſpake graciouſly to his dying Day.[345]

I remember I have met with another Example not unlike unto this but now mentioned. In the Town of *Barwick* upon *Tweed*, there was a Man (Steward to the Lord of *Granſon*) reputed Godly, who was very much afflicted in his Mind. Mr.

[345] The Author may not intentionally intended to have evaded Purſuit by referring to a Work not publiſhed except in Mr. Clarke's *Martyrology*. The Reader will there find "Maſter Richard Rothwell" among the "Army of Martyrs," And at the End Mr. Clarke tells us "This Life was drawn up by my "reverend Friend Maſter Stanly "Gower of Dorcheſter." But in his *Looking-Glaſs for Saints and Sinners*, ii, 166, the ridiculous Devil Story is told alſo, a brief Abſtract of which is in the Text. Brook, in his *Lives of the Puritans*, gives that of Rothwell, but avoids the Devil Story, though he copies from the *Martyrology*. Clarke's Works are but little known at this Day.

Balſom (an eminent Preacher by whoſe Miniſtry in that one Town, ſixty Perſons were (as was judged) ſavingly wrought upon, did ſeveral Times viſit him, and ſought to apply Words of Comfort to him, but nothing of that Nature taking place, he whiſpered the Steward in the Ear to this Purpoſe, *I doubt there is ſomething within which you would do well to diſcover;* whereupon immediately the mans Tongue ſwelled out of his Mouth that he was not able to ſpeak, and to the Aſtoniſhment of thoſe in the Room, a ſhrill Voice was heard, as it were ſpeaking out of his Throat, ſaying, what doſt thou talking to him of free Grace and Promiſes? he is mine. Mr. *Balſom* perceiving that it was the Devil that ſpoke, told him, he did not know that Men were his as long as they were alive in this World. To whom the Devil replyed, If God would let me looſe, I would find enough in the beſt of you all to make you mine, and as for this Man he hath given himſelf[15] to me. I will not (ſaid Mr. *Balſom*) believe the *Father of Lyes*, but I will goe home and pray for this poor Man, and get all the Force in the Town I can to join with me, and I do believe that thou Satan ſhalt looſe thy hold before tomorrow Morning. Mr. *Balſom* upon his return Home that Night, found divers Chriſtians in his Houſe, who waited to ſpeak with him, unto whom he declared that he could not but admiringly take Notice of the Providence of God in bringing them to his Houſe, whom otherwiſe he had purpoſed to ſend for; and deſired them to ſpend Part of the Night

See Mr. Balſom, his life by Clark.

with him, in ſeeking to the Lord in the Behalf of ſuch a diſtreſſed poſſeſſed Man: which they did, and the next Morning Satan had loſt his Poſſeſſion: and when Mr. *Balſom* enquired of the poor Man how it was with him, He anſwered; through the goodneſs of God, I have overcome, and am now as full of Comfort, as before I was full of Trouble.[346]

I have alſo heard a worthy Divine in *Dublin*, ſpeak of a Man, that being under bodily Poſſeſſion by an evil Spirit, a Company of praying Chriſtians met together, to ſeek the Lord in his Behalf; amongſt them there was a precious holy Woman, who kneeled behind the Door in the Room where they were praying together, and there were ſtrong Actings of Faith in her Soul; at laſt the Devil was forced to depart: only as he was going out of the poſſeſſed Party, he cryed out. *O the Woman, the Woman behind the Door!*[347]

Dr. *Winter.*

Some very learned and judicious Writers concieve, that *Epileptick* and *Lunatick* Perſons are thoſe *Domoniacks* whom we read ſo much of in the New Teſtament. There is a *Deliration* that proceeds *ex vi morbi*, being from or with a Fever, and another Kind of Delira-

Mr. Mede's *works in Folio, Book* 1. *Diſcour.* 6.

[346] This Story of "Maſter Robert "Balſom" is alſo told in the *Martyrology* of Mr. Clarke, ii, 179, &c. His Converſation with the Devil in the poſſeſſed Man is exceedingly amuſing. In the Courſe of the Debate the Devil ſaid to Mr. Balſom: "If God would let me looſe "upon you, I ſhould find enough "in the beſt of you to make you all "mine." This certainly is pretty well for the old "Father of Lies," and ſhows that he could ſometimes tell the Truth.

[347] Here we loſe much intended for us by not being informed of the Names of the Parties. The Name of "the Woman behind the Door," capable of doing what many thou-

tion which is *ſine Febre*, when a Man having no other Diſeaſe is crazed or diſtracted. Not they that are ſubjected to the former, but to this latter have been accounted Ενεργούμενοι poſſeſſed Perſons. The Jews of old had ſuch an Opinion concerning mad Men. Joh. 10. 20. Conſider alſo Math. 17. 14, 15,—18. with Luk. 9. 39. Whatever of Solidity may be in that Notion, is not a Place here to diſpute; but this is certain, that diſtracted Perſons have been reſtored to the uſe of their underſtanding again by Faſting and Prayer. That Moſes of his Time, Mr. *Dod*[348] (concerning whom Mr. *Burroughs*[349] giveth this Teſtimony, that he was the meekeſt Man upon the Face of the Earth) had a godly Son, whom it pleaſed the Moſt High to leave unto ſore Deſtraction in his Mind, whereupon Mr. Dod called ſome of his godly praying Friends together, who ſet a Day apart ſolemnly to ſeek [16] the Lord about that Matter, and whilſt they were yet ſpeaking in Prayer, God heard them, ſo as that the diſtracted Perſon was not only reſtored to his right

Beza *in Mat.* 8. 16. & 17. 15.

Mr. Burroughs *on Math.* 11. 28. 2*d pt. p.* 358.

ſands of Men have failed to do, ſhould be handed down to Poſterity. An Author guilty of withholding the Name of ſuch a Perſon deſerves the hearty Reprehenſion of all his Readers.

348 "Maſter John Dod" is probably referred to. He was a famous Puritan, and the Author of ſeveral Works in much Repute formerly. He was of a Cheſter Family and the youngeſt of ſeventeen Children. He lived to the great Age of 96, dying in 1645, according to Clarke's *Martyrology*, ii, 168, &c.

249 Jeremiah Burroughs, another noted Divine, who will be found duly noticed in Brook's *Lives*, iii, 1-6. He was at one Time Colleague with the Rev. Dr. Edmund Calamy at Bury St. Edmunds.

Mind again, but did himſelf conclude that Day of Prayer with ſolemn Thankſgiving unto God. This Information I received from a Reverend Miniſter, who was preſent in Mr. Dods Houſe, when that Day of Faſting and Prayer was there obſerved, upon the Occaſion mentioned.

See Mr. Lewiſton of fulfilling the Scriptures. p. 431.

It is reported concerning that excelent Man and famous Miniſter in *Edinborough*, Mr. *Bruce*[350] (concerning whom the Learned *Didoclavius* hath given a moſt honorable Teſtimony) that divers Perſons that were diſtracted, and ſome who were Epileptick, paſt Hopes of Recovery, were nevertheleſs reſtored to perfect Health in Anſwer to Mr. *Bruces* Prayers.

Fulfilling of the Scriptures. p. 437.

But I have not met with any Inſtance to this Purpoſe more affecting than that which is (by an Author worthy of Credit) publiſhed concerning Mr. *Patrick Simpſon* a learned and very holy Miniſter, ſometimes of Sterling in Scotland. The Story in brief is this.

Mr. *Simpſons* Wife (a gracious Woman) falling ſick, was ſorely aſſaulted by Satan, who told her that ſhe ſhould be given over into his Hand. The Temptation and Affrightment prevailed ſo far as to reſolve in a viſible Diſtraction, that the good Woman, moſt unlike her former Way whilſt ſhe was herſelf, would break forth ſometimes with dreadfull and horrid Expreſſions; This was (and could not be otherwiſe) a moſt bitter Affliction to

[350] I do not find the Chriſtian Name of this Divine among the Puritan Biographers. Calamy mentions a "Mr. Bruce" among the Ejected. The ſame probably mentioned by Wilſon, iv, 62.

her precious hufband, who told thofe about her that he was affured that Satans Malice fhould at laft receive a fhameful Foyle; wherefore he retired himfelf into his Garden, and fhutting the Door, betook himfelf to Fafting and Prayer. One *Helen Garner* (a godly Woman) being follicitous for Mr. *Simpfon*, as fearing that his Labours, Grief, Fafting might be too hard for him, ufed fome Means to get over into the Garden, where Mr. *Simpfon* was alone wreftling with God; being come near the Place where he was, fhe was terrified with an extraordinary Noife which caufed her to fall upon the Ground; It was like the Noife of a great rufhing of Multitudes together, and therwithal fuch a melodious Sound as did make her know it was fomething more than humane; fo that fhe fel to Prayer, entreating the Lord to pardon her Rafhnefs in fo coming thither, confidering it was Refpect to his Servant, who had been an Inftrument of Good to her Soul, that did induce her. After going forward, fhe found Mr. *Simpfon* lying upon the ground; nor would he reveal what he had met with, until [17] Promife was made not to fpeak of it whilft he was alive in this World. Upon this he faid, *O what am I being Duft and Afhes, that the holy miniftring Spirits fhould be fent by the Lord to deliver a Meffage to me*, and fhewed that Angels from Heaven had by an audible Voice given him Anfwer concerning that which he had been praying about. [This was a Thing extraordinary, and in no wife to be expected by Chriftians ordinarily][351] and returning into his Houſe, he bid thoſe that were in the Room with his Wife, be of good Comfort; for he was aſſured that within ten Hours ſhe ſhould be delivered from that Diſtraction. After this he went to Prayer by the Bedſide, and as he was in Prayer, mentioning Jacobs wreſtling with God, his Wife ſate up in the Bed, and caſting aſide the Curtain ſaid, *Thou art this Day Jacob, thou haſt wreſtled, and haſt prevailed, and now God hath made good his Word which he ſpake to you this Morning, for I am plucked out of the Hands of Satan, and he ſhall no more have Power over me.* This Interruption made him ſilent for a while, but after in great Meltings of Heart he proceeded in Prayer, magnifying the Riches of divine Grace and Love, and from that Hour his Wife continued to diſcourſe Chriſtianly and comfortably even to her dying Hour.

As for thoſe ſpiritual (which are worſe then bodily Poſſeſſions) that Satan holds in the Souls of Men, how often hath Prayer been a Means to out him, and cauſe him (full ſore againſt his will) to quit his ſtrong Hold for ever. Prayer hath (i. e. inſtrumentally) converted many a Soul. *Peter Martyr* was wont to pray much for the Converſion[352] of *Bernard Gilpin*, and the Lord an-

Clark, *ubi ſupra.*

[351] The Author can hardly be ſaid to have improved his Account by throwing in this bracketed Caveat. He probably had not had Experience with diſordered or diſeaſed Imaginations in 1677, but ſixteen Years later in Life he witneſſed ſimilar Deluſions, yet with no more Light on his Mind, apparently.

[352] Peter Martyr was a Florentine, born at the City of Florence in 1500. Clarke has given his Life and Portrait in his *Marrow of Eccl. Hiſt.*,

ſwered his Prayers, and that *Gilpin* proved an eminent Inſtrument of Gods Glory and of Good unto his Church.

I have read of one who having a Brother that ſpent his Time in Hawking, Drinking and other profane Vanityes, upon a Saturday, when his ungodly Brother was gone upon an hawking Match, he ſet that very Day apart by Faſting and Prayer to beg of God that his Brother might be converted. And the Lord anſwered his Prayers wonderfully; For within a Week after his Brother was ſtrangely changed, and did himſelf (inſtead of ſpending his Time in Hawking and Drinking) obſerve many Days of ſecret Humiliation between the Lord and his own Soul, on the Account of the Sins he had been guilty of, in the Days of Vanity, and made a very godly End at laſt.

Mr. White, *his Relation.*

That precious and famous Miniſter of Chriſt, Mr. *Welch*,[353] being in a Journey, his Entertainment came to more than he expected, ſo that the next Morning he had not wherewith to pay for his Horſe meat: the Hoſtler ſware and railed exceedingly for his Money: Mr. *Welch* [18] ſhut his chamber Door and went to Prayer and the Hoſtler

201-13. He was obliged to fly from his own Country to avoid Perſecution, and reſided for a Period in Devonſhire, England. The Biographical Dictionaries are ample upon him. He has ſometimes been confounded with another Peter Martyr, who wrote the *Decades of the New World*, publiſhed by Richard Hakluyt. He was celebrated for his varied Learning.

353 Perhaps Mr. Henry Welſh, of whom Dr. Calamy gives ſome Account. See *Nonconformiſts Memorial*, ii, 88.

ſtanding at the Door overheard him, and was converted by that Prayer; ever after that Time highly reſpecting Mr. *Welch*, and refuſing to accept of anything for his Entertainment, either then or at any other Times afterwards, when Occaſion was offered.

I knew one, the Son of an holy and eminently faithful Miniſter, who in ſome of the Dayes of his Youth had been wild and vain, but was (through the Grace of Chriſt) converted in his young Years, and after his Fathers death, peruſing his private Papers, he perceived, that not many Days before he was in the Pangs of the new Birth, his Father had been by ſecret Faſting and Prayer ſeeking unto the Lord that converting ſanctifying Grace might be beſtowed upon that Son of his.

That notable Iſraelite, Mr. *Hugh Kennedy*, Provoſt of Air in Scotland, one Day being long alone in Prayer, while ſome of his intimate Friends ſtayed a great while to ſpeak with him, upon their enquiry into the Reaſon why he made them wait ſo long; he told them it was no wonder, *for* (ſaid he) *I have this Day obtained Mercy for me and all mine.* And ſo indeed it came to paſs; for not ſo much as one of his Children, but evident Signs of Converſion and true Godlineſs were obſerved in them. This was that *Kennedy*, who when he was dying could ſay, *If the Wals of this Houſe could ſpeak, they could tell how many ſweet Dayes I have had in ſecret Fellowſhip with God, and how familiar he hath been with my Soul.* This is he concerning whom Mr. *Welch*

MR. LEVISTON *in lib. ſupra citat p.* 441. 442.

once ſaid, ‘ Happy is that City, yea, happy is that ‘ Nation that hath an *Hugh Kennedy* in it. I ‘ myſelf have certainly found the Anſwers of his ‘ Prayers to the Lord on my behalf.’ There is one Paſſage recorded concerning him which is exceeding ſtrange. It is this.

One of his Sons being abſent at Sea, on a certain Night he roſe early, before break of Day, and came to his familiar Friend *John Steward*, and deſired him to riſe, and go with him into a room to pray, for (ſaid he) my Son with the reſt of our Chriſtian Friends now at Sea, are at the very nick of periſhing. After he had ſpent ſome Time in pouring out his Soul before the Lord, he roſe up cheerfully, ſaying, *now are they ſafe*, John Steward being amazed thereat, writ this down, with the Day and Hour, and at the Return of the Ship made Enquiry, and found that in that very Hour of that Night, they then were in a moſt Dangerous Place, ſo that all Hope, that they ſhould be ſaved was taken away, only they were by an extraordinary unexpected Providence then delivered.

[19] To draw to a Concluſion, let the World beware, of doing any Wrong to a praying People. Such blaſting Strokes from God were upon thoſe that ſet themſelves againſt the reformed Churches and Profeſſors (who were called *Piccardines*) in *Bohemia* of old that it became a proverbial Speech, *If any Man be weary of his Life, let him become an Enemy to the Piccardines.* So I ſay, *If any Man be weary of his Life, let him become an Enemy*

to a praying People, ſuch as (through Grace) many in *New England* have been, and are to this Day. And wo to that Man, whoever he be, upon whom the Prayers of *New England* ſhall fall. It were better for that Man that a Mill-ſtone were hanged about his Neck, and he thrown therewith into the midſt of the Sea. It is ſaid concerning the Witneſſes, Rev. 11. 5. "if any Man hurt them, fire pro-" ceedeth out of their Mouth, and devoureth their " Enemies, and if any Man will hurt them, he muſt in this Manner be killed." Is not the Spirit of Prayer that Fire? That Scottiſh Queen once profeſſed, that ſhe was more afraid of Mr. Knox his Prayers, then of an Army of ten thouſand Men.

And it is noted concerning *Leolin* Prince of Wales, that being perſwaded by ſome to take up Arms againſt a Prince that was famous for Religion; he replyed that he was afraid of that Mans Prayers more then of Armyes.

Refer t[o] *Dr. Powell.*

Wherefore I ſhall finiſh this Diſcourſe with the ſolemn Expreſſion of one (whom I have peculiar Reaſon to love) that was well known in this Place ſeven and twenty Years agoe.[354] *I had rather* (*ſaith he*) *be environed with Armyes of armed Men, and compaſſed round with drawn Swords and Inſtruments of Death, then that the leaſt praying Saint ſhould bend the Edge of his Prayers againſt me; for there*

My bleſſed Brother and Predeceſſor in this place in his Sermons on 2. Kings 18. 4. *p.* 7.

[354] The Author refers to his Pedigree in the *Brief Hiſtory*. See Brother Samuel. See the Family alſo *Hiſt. and Antiqs. Boſton*, 310.

is no ſtanding before the Prayers of Saints, eſpecially if they unite their Forces, and join together in the ſame Requeſts. Riſe up, O Lord, and let thine Enemyes be ſcattered, and let them that hate thee, flee before thee.

שמע תפלה עדיך כל-בשו יבאך

APPENDIX.

A.

Capt. Iſrael Stoughton to John Winthrop.

[Not dated, but endorſed, "Recd 5, 6." 1637]

HONORED Sr

By ye Pinnace, being Giggles,[355] you ſhall Receive 48 or 50 women & Children vnleſſe there ſtay any here to be helpfull &th, concerning which there is one I formerly[356] mentioned yt is ye faireſt & largeſt yt I ſaw amongſt them, to whome I haue given a coate to Cloath her: It is my deſire to haue her for a Servant if it may ſtand wth yor good liking: ells not. There is a little Squa yt Steward Calacot deſireth, to whom he hath Given a coate Lifetenant Damport [Davenport] alſo deſireth one, to witt, a tall one, yt hath three ſtroakes vpon her ſtumach, thus. —lll +: he deſireth her if it will ſtand with yor good likeing: Soſomon[357] ye jndian deſireth a young little ſqua wch I know not. But I leave all to your diſpoſe: He had one here for one of his men.

At preſent Mr. Noyes, Mr. Ludlo, Captayne Maſon & 30 men are wth vs in Pequid Riuer, & we ſhall ye next weeke joyne in ſeeing wt we can do agst Saſacos, & an other great Sagamor: Momowattuck: Here is yet tuff worke to be done. And how deere it will coſt is unknowne: Saſaos is reſolued to ſell his life & ſo ye other with their Company as deere as they cann: but we doubt not but god will giue him to vs; we are in a faire way. One of ye former yt we tooke (or yt was taken to or hands in a great meaſure) is a great Sachem, ye third of ye pequids: whome we reſerue for a help,[358] & find Gods prvidence derected it well, for we are all cleere he is like to do vs good: yet we are farr from giuing him aſſur-

[355] Roger Williams wrote his Name *Jiglies*. There was a *Thomas Jiggles* of Boſton; doubtleſs the ſame Perſon. Mr. Savage does not ſeem to have heard of him. See our *Note*, 149.

[356] There is a long Letter from Capt. Stoughton dated after this, printed in the Appendix to Winthrop's Journal, i, 398, &c. That referred to in the Text is not known to exiſt.

[357] Perhaps the ſame killed by Philip's Men juſt before the War of 1675, as detailed in this Work.

[358] This is probably a Reference to Wequaſh.

ance of life. We fee fo much worke behind y[t] we dare not difmife more men yet:

We hope to find a way to bring them in plentifully, and to get y[e] murderers too: & to make their affofiates tributary if they ftill adhere to them: for we heare of a great Number vp y[e] Country among y[e] Neepenetts: but we fhall not deale with them with out yo[r] advice, vnlefs more remotely.

We have fettled on a place for our randavooze: not full to o[r] Content but y[e] beft we could for y[e] prefent: vpon y[e] mouth of Pequid Riuer; on y[e] Naanticot fide, where we haue 100 acres corne, if not 2 or 300 neere at hand. & a Curio[s] fpring of water within o[r] Pallazado, & may by great Gunns Command y[e] Riuer.

So y[e] Charg of keeping y[e] fort need not be great, feeing Corne, water & wood are fo neare at hand: & fifhing &[th].

I pray let not p[r]vifions be neglected with y[e] firft, fuch as y[e] Country affordeth fhall content vs: only w[n] we haue frends, as now, we could beteeme them a peece of Beef ets: if we had it. y[e] Rudlet of Sack we haue is fome comfort & credit: but many hands make light worke: and in cafes of fayntings, ficknes &ts among a many, it cannot be but occafions will happen of fome expence of fuch things as are a little better then ordinary.

Thus wth my deereft Refpects remembred to yo[r] felf with y[e] Councell &[ts] I take leaue Refting Yor[s] as in duty I am bound.

(. Israel Stoughton.)[359]

B.

Edward Winflow to John Winthrop.

[Endorfed "Mr. Winflow about the Pequots."]

WORTHY S[r].

Yo[r] L[r] by my wiues fonne I re[d] the 6th day of the laft weeke being very forry mine came fo unfeafonable to yo[r] hands. ffor anfwere to yo[rs] Our Cowncell having weighty occafions this day to meete & confer about divers bufineffes w[ch] much concerne us I impted yo[r] L[r] to the Gov[r] and them, who feeing it impoffible for the Gov[r] or myfelfe to bee at yo[r] Court to morrow requefted me to write by the bearer & thereby falute yo[r] Gov[r] yo[r] felfe & affiftants. Concerning yo[r] prent bufnies we conceiue it will be fimply neceffary for you to pceed in the war begun wth the Pequots, otherwife the natiues we feare will grow into a ftronger confederacy to the further prejudice of the whole Englifh. We are very glad to heare that the Munheges are fallen from the Pequots & brought to a pfeffed war wth them knowing their inueterate hatred & defire it may be nourifhed by all good meanes, who are foldiers as well as the

[359] A Fac-fimile of Capt. Stoughton's Autograph is in the *Hift. Antiqs. Bofton*, 214.

others. Thefe beft know the Pequots holds & holes & the fitteft inftruments can be employed & fuch a people as will alfo well accord wth the Narrohigganfets. But there is one thing of ill confequence w[h] we heare from Conectncut viz[t]. that there are fome Englifh there that furnifh the enemy by way of trade having made a league wth them, If you enquire of Mr. Jefop who came in the barke with Mr. Harding you may receiue pticular informacon thereabout. That this will be ill taken I dowbt not, yet durft not doe no other then informe you, yet let me comend one thing to yo[r] confideracon how dangerous a thing it may proue if the Dutch (who feeke it) & they fhould clofe by reafon of the Pequots neceffity: I fpeake not this as defiring the benefit of their trade, for we are waary of the worke as we are dealt w[th]all. Concerning things Eftward, Capt. Standifh is returned who reporteth of the Royall entertainem[t] Shurt hath given Dony[360] at Pemaquid. He faith (being commander Generall) that if he receiue a Comiffion he muft take him, onely fix weekes before he will giue him notice, and in lue thereof tis [—] Mr. Shurt hath promifed him to informe him of whatever prepacon fhall be made or intended againft them. He further faith that if his commiffion be to take the Grand Bay (yo[r]felues) he will attempt it though he fhould haue no other veffell then a Canoe. But the Englifh are all his ffriends except Plimoth: nor is he enemies to any other. Shurt hath undertaken to furnifh him w[th] powder fhot yea all manner of provifions, And to that end under a colour of gathering vp fome debts is come to make provifions for them till his owne fhip come. Tis alfo reported that S[r] fferdinando Gorges hath written to Saco that the ffrench here are not fett out nor allowed by the King of ffr. but a bafe people w[ch] their ftate difclaime, & therefore ftirreth them up to informe both you & us that we might joyne together to expell them. One thing more w[ch] I had almoft forgotten they have loft their Gally & a pinnafe at Ile Sable & brought away their people who are at Penobfcot where they haue built a pinnafe of threefcore tunne. I report thefe things fro Capt. Standifh but as the reports y[t] are familiar in the Eftern pts, y[t] you may likewife make yo[r] ufe of them. The laft news is this whereat I am moft grieved That all the late differencs betw. m[r] Wheelwright & yo[r] felues in Church & Court are in writing at Richmunds Ile where Turlany[361] fhewed him fix fheets of pap full written about them. The Lord in mercy look upon us and leaue us not to the malice of Satan & wicked men his inftruments, but fo direct us, by his fpirit as the end may redownd to his glory & our mutuall good.

S[r] howeuer I could not come at this fudden warning by reafon of our publick occafions & the fowlenes of the latter pt of the weeke paft yet neverthelefse if you conceiue my coming may be any furtherance in any

[360] D'Aulney. It was within his Territory. See *Hutchinfon*, i, 128; *Davis Morton*, 180-1, 232.

[361] No doubt Robert Trelawny, who owned the Ifland. He died before 10th Oct., 1648. See Willis's *Portland*, 227.

good accou God giving health & ability mine owne occaſions ſhall giue place, & I ſhall be ready to doe any ſervice God ſhall inable me In the meane time & whileſt I haue being my prs I hope ſhall be to the Throne of grace for you & yors whom I ſalute in the Lord & reſt.

Yors aſſured

Plym: the 17th of the 2d mo. 1637.

Edw. Winslow.

If now after your Court you have any deſire to ſpeake wth me at goodman Stows of Roxbury you ſhall heare of one that is to come foorthwth hither.

C.

John Humfrey to John Winthrop.

[Dated June 7th, 1637.]

MUCH honoured

Hitherto the lord hath beene wth us, bleſſed for ever be his ever bleſſed name. Or nation, the goſpel, the blood of thoſe murthered perſons of ors ſeems to triump in the prſent ſucceſſe; now I onely deſire to ſuggeſt it to yor wiſe & deeper conſiderations whether it be not prbable the confederates of the Pequots will not be glad to purchaſe a ſecure & fearleſs condition to themſelves, by delivering up thoſe men or their heads, who have wrought & brought ſo much miſerie upon themſelves & theirs. Or if not ſo, whither (if they give good aſſurance by hoſtages &c.) the blood ſhed by them may not ſeeme to be ſufficiently expiated by ſo great an inequalitie on their ſides. Hitherto the honor & terror of or peeple to all the natives is abundantly vendicated & made good. If prvidence for or humbling (as in regard of myſelfe I much feare) ſhould fleſh them [word worn off] by ſome new cruelties upon anie of ors, how low wee may be laide both in their, & the eyes of or confederate Indians, & to how great daunger to us, yea poſſiblie or poſterities, I leave to yor graver thoughts, if it be worth the conſideration. Onely to my ſhallownes it ſeemes conſiderable whither it were not ſafe pawſing to ſee what effect this will or may work upon ſuch a demaund,[362] 2dly whither not beſt to reſt in certaine victorie & honor acquired, upon ſo ſmall a loſſe. 3dly whither, (if wee carrie away the greateſt glory of theſe poore barbarous people in or triumphs over them,) the loſſe of three men more (if we ſhould not exceede) may not be paraleld wth ſo manie hundreds more of theirs. 4thly whither we muſt not be forced at laſt (& it may be in worſe cir-

[362] This has Reference to the Capture of the Fort at Miſtick, which was done only eleven Days before this Letter was written. See Page .

cumstances) to take this course unlesse divine iustice will miraculously shew it selfe in bringing them all into o[r] net, w[ch] according to reason is not likely. 5[thly], whether the dreadfulnes of o[r] maine Battallio (as it were) be better to be measured by their feares raised on this last, then to see, say or thinke, that o[r] former victorie was not so much of valo[r] as accident w[ch] we o[r]selves do acknowledge p[r]vidence. 6[thly], if we refuse to give or take such conditions now, they may not be likely to hold us to worse, or necessitate us to a perpetual war if for o[r] owne ease wee after seeke them, & when they see us (as they may) afraide in like manner.

Much more, & to as little purpose might be saide. But if you continue yo[r] resolutions to p[r]ceede according to former intentions you may please to consider whither these bottles to be used granado wise, may not be of some use; and whither (if the fort[363] be so difficile as it is reported) into which they shall for their last refuge retire) it were not operæ preciu to p[r]pare a petar or two to command entrance. Thus laying my low thoughts and myself at yo[r] feete to be kicked out or admitted as you see good, being glad to hope of the continuance of yo[r] purpose to see us in yo[r] way to Ipswich, W[th] my service to you & yo[rs] I rest yet and ever yo[rs] (anie thing) to serve you.

Jo: Humphrey.[364]

D.

Yarmouth Port [Mass.], March 9, 1863.

Samuel G. Drake, Esq.

Dear Sir: I have delayed answering your letter of Feb. 12, in order that I might thoroughly investigate the tradition in the Davis family, that their ancestor Robert bought of Iyannough a tract of land at the north east corner of Barnstable for a brass Kettle.[365] Robert Davis bought lands of the Indians; but it unfortunately happens, that the purchase was made after the year 1650, and was a part of the Indian reservation.

It will not be justifiable to depart from the authority of Winslow, without we can substitute a better. I think no such authority can be substituted, and I shall not therefore occupy space by quoting accounts more familiar to you than to me. The description of the localities so far as given by

[363] It was not then known that the strongest Fort of the Pequots had been abandoned, which some feared was impregnable, and would never be exposed as the other was, to be surprised.

[364] A Fac-simile of Mr. Humfrey's Autograph may be seen in the *History and Antiquities of Boston*, p. 52. This Letter has never been published before, entire.

[365] Mr. Otis wrote in a previous Letter, that there was a Tradition in the Davis Family, that their Ancestor, "Robert "Davis, bought his Farm of Hyanna for "a brass Kettle."

the early writers is accurate, and I ſet it down as a hiſtorical fact that Iyannough periſhed in a ſwamp, as repreſented, and that the ſwamp in which he died is probably the one about half a mile eaſt of his town. There is an iſland in the ſwamp where tents could have been built. The "Dead Swamp," not far diſtant, is almoſt impenetrable to this day. It is wet and muddy; and I do not think even an Indian would have attempted to reſide in it.

Firſt we will examine the queſtion genealogically. In 1620 Iyannough is repreſented as being only 25 years of age; if ſo he could not have had a ſon of ſufficient age in 1626, to ſucceed him as Sachem. In 1639, the territory of Iyannough was owned, the northerly portion by Nepogtano (who had by deed of gift conveyed one half to Tuacommicus), and the ſoutherly portion (that portion of Barnſtable now called Hyannis and all the ſouth part of Yarmouth) by an Indian Sachem whom Antony Thacher calls Hyanna, and whoſe name in the reecords is written H y an a, Hyanus, Yana, Ianna. Sampſon, ſon of Maſhantampanu and his ſiſter claimed a right in thoſe lands; but it was afterwards proved that they had no right, and Nepoitan and Tuacomicus conveyed their lands to the proprietors, reſerving about 60 acres 'at 'Mattakees Swamp or Iyannough's town. Hianna and his ſon John Hianna, ſold that portion of their territory within the preſent bounds of Barnſtable to the proprietors, reſerving certain lands and a tract which John ſays was given by his father Yano to Nicholas Davis. Hiano ſold to the proprietors of Yarmouth all the lands on the ſouth ſide of the town of Yarmouth, reſerving certain lands in the vicinity of Baſs River for the uſe of the Indians.

The deed of Nepoyetam to Barnſtable is dated in 1641. He was then of age, and could hardly have been a ſon of Iyannough, if the latter's age is reported rightly. Yanno's deed is dated 19th July, 1664, in which he makes the reſervation to the Indians and Nicholas Davis. John Yanno's deed is dated 7 Sep. 1680, and in it he names his father and Nicholas Davis, both deceaſed. Nepaiton and Yanno may have been ſons of Iyannough, but if ſo I think he was an older man than he was repreſented to be, and in fact his teeth ſhow that he was probably older. There is much preſerved ſhowing the relationſhip of the ſeveral Indian Sachems who lived in this vicinity between 1639 and 1680, and their individual hiſtory can be quite ſatisfactorily traced. I am entirely ſatisfied that the ancient Indian grave recently diſcovered, was not that of Tuacomicus, Napoyetan (or his ſucceſſor Keencomſet) of Paupmunmeeke, Sachem of Barnſtable and Marſhpee, of Yanno (or his ſon John), of Maſantampaine (Sachem of Nobſcuſſet), of Sachemus (Sachem of South Dennis and part of Harwich) or of Mattaquaſon, Sachem of Monamoiet (though his ſon John Quaſon claimed to be an heir of Nepogetain. It is a more ancient grave, and after a very careful examination of all the facts, which I have not time to recapitulate, I am entirely ſatisfied that the Indian grave diſcovered in Barnſtable on the 18th of May, 1861, is the grave of that Indian Chief whom the Pilgrim Fathers called Iyanough.

The following are the facts in relation to the finding of the grave:

On Saturday, May 18, 1861, Patrick Hughes an Irishman, a hired man of Mr. Enoch T. Cobb, and David Davis, a son of Benjamin Davis of Barnstable, aged 16, were ploughing in a field on the south of the Great Swamp, which is situate about half a mile east of Mattakeese pond or swamp, now called the "Perch Pond" (on the borders of which in 1620 Iyanough's town was situate). While ploughing the plough struck against something that looked like metal. On examination they found it to be a brass kettle, lying bottom upwards, about seven inches below the surface of the ground. They procured a pick-axe and dug around it, and taking it up found it much rusted and decayed. Under the kettle they found a skull, and other bones. It was so left for the night. Sunday morning following David Davis and his brothers, Adolphus and Robinson, and their father, and Mr. Nathaniel Gorham, being provided with tools, continued the excavation, and found the skeleton of a man who had been buried in a sitting posture, an Indian pestle, an iron hatchet, a bowl, some white and black wampum, several iron nails and one spike. In making the excavation traces in the earth were noticed in the form of a bow and arrows.

The body was buried in a sitting posture, the kettle placed over the head, the pestle on his right arm, the hatchet and bowl at his feet; dark lines in the earth indicated that his bow and arrows had been placed across his breast.

These facts respecting the exhuming of the remains, I obtained by a personal and separate examination of the parties who were present. All the remains I had packed in a box and sent to the Pilgrim Society at Plymouth, and the late James Davis, Esq., on whose land the grave was found, provided a suitable case, and they are now deposited in the Hall of that Society.

I believe I have now given you all the facts you will want in preparing your article on Iyanough. I have named his contemporaries and their successors. Nepogetam, Tuacommicus and Keencomset, who resided at the Indian village (Iyannough's town) were Christianized Indians, and would not have been buried in that posture. In fact their burial place is known, it was farther west, and the Indian graves are named in ancient deeds, and the lands reserved in the sale. Yanno or Hianna resided at Hyannis, where there is an ancient Indian burial ground containing one acre, reserved when the lands were originally laid out, and if he was brought (after 1664) to the north side of the town to be buried, it is probable that he would have been entombed on the land set apart for that purpose.

Masantampaine lived to be very aged and is buried at Nobscusset. Paupnummucke was probably buried at Massapee (Marshpee) of which tribe he was Sachem.

There is another confideration ; none excepting the chiefs had brafs kettles and hatchets at that time, and if they had, they were too fcarce and too valuable to be buried with a common man.

The remains indicate great antiquity, and the articles found indicate with fome precifion the time of the burial. It was after the time that Capt. John Smith and Hunt vifited Barnftable harbor, and before the time that the Indians had laid afide the ufe of the bow and arrow, in their wars and in hunting. It was before wampum had ceafed to pafs for money, and before iron nails had become common, and ceafed to be regarded as articles of high value. Perhaps the latter fact is the moft important in fixing the time of the fepulchre. Taking this as the rule a later period than 1625, can not be fafely named as the time of the burial. Very foon after the fettlement of Plymouth, nails ceafed to be an article of value or curiofity to the Indians. They wanted hatchets, knives or other articles of ufe.

In regard to an event which happened more than two centuries ago, and of which no record was made at the time, it is unreafonable to expect that the proof will be as ftrong as a mathematical demonftration.

I have drawn out this letter to an unreafonable length ; but I will repeat that I have no reafonable ground to doubt that the grave of Iyannough has been difcovered, and that fome of his remains are now in Pilgrim Hall, Plymouth.

Refpectfully yours,

Amos Otis.

INDEX.

SUBSCRIBERS FOR THE WORK.

[*When not otherwiſe mentioned, copies are iſſued in ſmall 4to.*]

Adams, Charles, Jr. ;	North Brookfield, Ms.
Alofsen, Salomon ;	Jerſey City, N. J.
Ames, Ellis ;	Canton, Maſs.
Appleton, Wm. Sumner ;	Boſton, Maſs.
Arnold, Samuel G. ;	Providence, R. I.
Balcom, George L. ;	Claremont, N. H.
Bancroft, George ;	New York, N. Y.
Barlow, S. L. M. ;	New York, N. Y.
Barstow, John ;	Providence, R. I.
Bartlett, John R. ;	Providence, R. I.
Boston Athenæum ;	Boſton, Maſs.
Bourne, E. E. ;	Kennebunk, Me.
Bouton, J. W. ;	New York, N. Y.
Brackett, Jeffrey R. ;	Quincy, Maſs.
Brevoort, J. Carson ;	Brooklyn, N. Y.
Brevoort, J. Carson *(Large Paper)*;	Brooklyn, N. Y.
Brinley, George ;	Hartford, Ct.
Bronson, Henry ;	New Haven, Ct.
Brooks, H. M. ;	Salem, Maſs.
Brotherhead, William ;	Philadelphia, Pa.
Brown, Andrew ;	Middletown, N. J.
Brown, John Carter *(Large Paper)*;	Providence, R. I.
Brown, John Marshall ;	Portland, Me.
Brown, Philip Henry ;	Portland, Me.
Bryant, Hubbard W. ;	Portland, Me.
Buck, Jas. Smith ;	Milwaukee, Wis.
Buckley, J E. ;	New York, N. Y.

Bushnell, Charles I.;	New York, N. Y.
Case, L. B.;	Richmond, Ind.
Caulkins, Mrs. F. M.;	New London, Ct.
Chaldecott, Mrs. Elizabeth;	London, Eng.
Chapin, E. H.:	New York, N. Y.
Clapp, Ebenezer, Jr.;	Dorcheſter, Maſs.
Clark, George F.;	Stow, Maſs.
Clark, Wm. Henry *(Large Paper)*;	New York, N. Y.
Colesworthy, Daniel C.;	Boſton, Maſs.
Colman, Samuel;	New York, N. Y.
Concord Town Library;	Concord, Maſs.
Cothren, William;	Woodbury, Ct.
Crowell, Geo. E. (F. P. C.);	Hopkinton, N. H.
Curtis, Geo. William;	Staten Iſland, N. Y.
Cutter, Abram E.;	Charleſtown, Maſs.
Cushman, Charles;	Boſton, Maſs.
Cushman, Henry W.;	Bernardſtown, Maſs.
Davis, Samuel S.;	London, Eng.
Davis, William J.;	New York, N. Y.
Deane, Charles *(Large Paper)*;	Cambridge, Maſs.
Dean, John Ward;	Boſton, Maſs.
Dewing, G. B.;	North Brookfield, Maſs.
Dexter, Henry M.;	Boſton, Maſs.
Everett, Edward;	Boſton, Maſs.
Farwell, O. A.;	Boſton, Maſs.
Fellows, Charles S.;	Bangor, Me.
Fogg, John S. H. *(Large Paper)*;	S. Boſton, Maſs.
Fowle, Wm. Fisk *(Large Paper)*;	Boſton, Maſs.
Fowler, M. Field;	Boſton, Maſs.
Fowler, Samuel P.;	Danvers Port, Maſs.
Fowler, Wm. C.;	Durham Centre, Ct.
Goodell, A. C., Jr.;	Salem, Maſs.
Gray, George H.;	Boſton, Maſs.
Green, Joshua;	Groton, Maſs.

GREENWOOD, ISAAC J.;	New York, N. Y.
HADDOCK, LORENZO K.;	Buffalo, N. Y.
HORN, WILLIAM T.;	New York, N. Y.
HOFFMAN, FRANCIS S.;	New York, N. Y.
HOSMER, JAMES B.;	Hartford, Ct.
HOYT, D. W.,	Boston, Mass.
HUMPHREY, HENRY B. *(Large Paper)*;	Thomaston, Me.
HURLBUT, HENRY H.;	Racine, Wis.
IRWIN, THEODORE *(Large Paper)*;	Oswego, N. Y.
JORDAN, JOHN, Jr.;	Philadelphia, Pa.
KETCHUM, SILAS (F. P. C.);	Hopkinton, N. H.
KING, DAVID;	Newport, R. I.
LAWRENCE, AMOS A.;	Boston, Mass.
LAWRENCE, JOHN S.;	New York, N. Y.
LENOX, JAMES *(Large Paper)*;	New York, N. Y.
LEWIS, WINSLOW;	Boston, Mass.
LINCOLN, SOLOMON;	Hingham, Mass.
LONG ISLAND HISTORICAL SOCIETY;	Brooklyn, N. Y.
LORD, RUSSELL S.;	Boston, Mass.
LOSSING, BENSON J.;	Poughkeepsie, N. Y.
McCAGG, E. B.;	Chicago, Ill.
MAINE HISTORICAL SOCIETY;	Brunswick, Me.
MASSACHUSETTS STATE LIBRARY;	Boston, Mass.
MATHER, HENRY B.;	Boston, Mass.
MATHER, SAMUEL L.;	Cleveland, O.
MEDLICOTT, WILLIAM G.;	Longmeadow, Mass.
MENZIES, WILLIAM;	New York, N. Y.
MOUNTFORT, GEORGE;	Boston, Mass;
MOREAU, CHARLES C.;	New York, N. Y.
MOREAU, JOHN B.;	New York, N. Y
MORSE, ABNER;	Boston, Mass.
NASON, ELIAS;	Exeter, N. H.
NEW YORK MERCANTILE LIBRARY;	New York, N. Y.
OHIO STATE LIBRARY;	Columbus O.

Otis, Amos ;	Yarmouth Port, Mass.
Otis, Horatio N.;	New York, N. Y.
Palmer, Ezra,	Boston, Mass.
Parker, James ;	Springfield, Mass.
Parsons, Samuel H.;	Middletown, Ct.
Patterson, D. Williams ;	W. Winsted, Ct.
Pearson, Jonathan ;	Schenectady, N. Y.
Perkins, Augustus T.;	Boston, Mass.
Polock, M.;	Philadelphia, Pa.
Pruyn, John V. L.;	Albany, N. Y.
Pulsifer, David ;	Boston, Mass.
Purple, S. S.;	New York, N. Y.
Redwood Library ;	Newport, R. I.
Reed, Jacob Whittemore ;	S. Groveland, Mass.
Richardson, C. B.;	New York, N. Y.
Robinson, Henry F.;	Boston, Mass.
Russell, John A.;	New York, N. Y.
Scott, Martin B.;	Cleveland, O.
Sears, David ;	Boston, Mass.
Sewall, Samuel ;	Burlington, Mass.
Somerby, Gustavus A.;	Boston, Mass.
Smith, Henry A.;	Cleveland, O.
Spooner, Thomas ;	Cincinnati, O.
Staples, William R.;	Providence, R. I.
Sternbergh, Jacob ;	Albany, N. Y.
Swett, Samuel ;	Boston, Mass.
Trask, William B.;	Dorchester, Mass.
Trumbull, J. Hammond,	Hartford, Ct.
Tuck, Joseph H.;	London, Eng.
Tuthill, William H.;	Tipton, Iowa.
Wales, George W. *(Large Paper)*;	Boston, Mass.
Wardwell, W. H.;	Boston, Mass.
Waterman, Thomas ;	Boston, Mass.
Wentworth, John ;	Chicago, Ill.

Wetmore, Samuel ;	New York, N. Y.
Wheeler, Richard A.;	Stonington, Ct.
Whitmore, W. H.;	Boston, Mass.
Whitney, Henry A.;	Boston, Mass.
Wiggin, John K.;	Boston, Mass.
Wiggin, John K. *(Large Paper) ;*	Boston, Mass.
Wiggin Charles P.;	Boston, Mass.
Wilkinson, Ezra ;	Dedham, Mass.
Willis, William ;	Portland, Me.
Winslow, John F.;	Troy, N. Y.
Winsor, Justin ;	Boston, Mass.

www.ingramcontent.com/pod-product-compliance
Lightning Source LLC
Chambersburg PA
CBHW031400270326
41929CB00010BA/1257
9783744661577